Bibliographic information published by the German National Library:

The German National Library lists this publication in the National Bibliography; detailed bibliographic data are available on the Internet at http://dnb.dnb.de .

Imprint:

Copyright © 2018 GRIN Verlag
Print and binding: Books on Demand GmbH, Norderstedt Germany
ISBN: 9783668794207

This book at GRIN:

https://www.grin.com/document/435400

Palaniappan Sellappan

Learn C#

The Easy Way. Through Examples

GRIN Verlag

GRIN - Your knowledge has value

Since its foundation in 1998, GRIN has specialized in publishing academic texts by students, college teachers and other academics as e-book and printed book. The website www.grin.com is an ideal platform for presenting term papers, final papers, scientific essays, dissertations and specialist books.

LEARN C#

THE EASY WAY - THROUGH EXAMPLES

PROF. DR. P. SELLAPPAN

MALAYSIA UNIVERSITY
of Science and Technology

Preface

Visual C# 2015, one of the components of Visual Studio 2015, is one of the most powerful, versatile and modern object-oriented programming languages available today. Developed by Microsoft, it combines all the best features available in programming languages.

C# provides a rich repertoire of library/built-in functions that allow programmers to develop all kinds of applications with relative ease - be it Console, Windows/Forms, Web or Mobile Applications.

This book is intended for beginners as well as those with some programming knowledge. It is suitable for those students who are pursuing a course in Computer Science, Software Engineering, Information Technology, Management Information Systems, Engineering and Mathematics. It starts with the basics, and gradually progresses to more advanced topics such as arrays, structures, classes, text files and databases. So whether you are a beginner or intermediate programmer, this book will help you master the essentials of C# very quickly. The book is written in a simple, easy-to-read style and contains numerous examples to illustrate the concepts presented. It also contains exercises at the end of each chapter to test your grasp of the subject matter.

Acknowledgements

I would like to gratefully acknowledge the contributions of several people who have in one or another assisted me in the preparation of this book. I would like to thank all my IT students and colleagues for their valuable input and feedback in the preparation of this manuscript.

My grateful thanks also go to Professor Dr. Premkumar Rajagopal, President of the Malaysia University of Science and Technology for giving me the opportunity, freedom, encouragement and support that I needed in the preparation of this manuscript. I would like to especially thank him for creating and nurturing an environment that actively promotes learning, research, teamwork and personal development. His dynamic leadership is greatly appreciated.

Last but first I would like to thank God for giving me the desire, motivation, interest, passion, strength and guidance to successfully complete this manuscript.

Dr. P. Sellappan
Professor of Information Technology
Dean of School of Science and Engineering
Provost of Malaysia University of Science and Technology

About the Author

Dr. P. Sellappan is currently Professor of Information Technology, Dean of School of Science and Engineering, and Provost of the Malaysia University of Science and Technology. Prior to joining Malaysia University of Science and Technology, he held a similar academic position in the Faculty of Computer Science and Information Technology, University of Malaya, Malaysia.

He holds a Bachelor in Economics degree with a Statistics major from the University of Malaya, a Master in Computer Science from the University of London (UK), and a PhD in Interdisciplinary Information Science from the University of Pittsburgh (USA).

Working in the academia for more than 30 years, he has taught a wide range of courses both at undergraduate and postgraduate levels: Principles of Programming, Advanced Programming, Programming Languages, Data Structures and Algorithms, System Analysis and Design, Software Engineering, Human Computer Interaction, Database Systems, Data Mining, Health Informatics, Web Applications, E-Commerce, Operating Systems, Management Information Systems, Research Methods, Mathematics and Statistics.

Professor Sellappan is an active researcher. He has received several national research grants from the Ministry of Science and Technology and Innovation under E-Science and FRGS to undertake IT-related research projects. Arising from these projects, he has published numerous research papers in reputable international journals and conference proceedings. Besides, he has also authored over a dozen college- and university-level IT text books.

As a thesis supervisor, he has supervised more than 70 Master and PhD theses. He also serves in editorial/review boards of several international journals and conferences. He is also chief editor of the Journal of Advanced Applied Sciences and the Plain Truth magazine. He is a certified trainer, external examiner, moderator and program assessor for IT programs for several local and international universities.

Together with other international experts, he has also served as an IT Consultant for several local and international agencies such as the Asian Development Bank, the United Nations Development Program, the World Bank, and the Government of Malaysia. His professional affiliation includes membership in the Chartered Engineering Council (UK), the British Computer Society (UK), the Institute of Statisticians (UK), and the Malaysian National Computer Confederation (MNCC).

Contents

Chapter 1

Introducing C#

Learning Outcomes:

After completing this chapter, the student will be able to

- *Describe the Visual Studio 2015 Integrated Development Environment.*
- *Differentiate between Console and Windows Applications.*
- *Explain the different parts of a C# program.*
- *Edit, compile and run C# programs.*

1.1 Visual C#.Net

Microsoft's Visual C# 2015 is one of the most popular general-purpose object-oriented programming languages. It's powerful, versatile and relatively easy to use. You can use it to develop a wide range of applications that run on the .NET Framework. It comes with a rich repertoire of built-in functions/methods which programmers can use to develop Console, Windows/Forms, Web and Mobile Applications, distributed components, client-server applications, and more. It comes with an advanced code editor, interface designer, integrated debugger and other tools for easy coding and testing.

Using C# has many benefits:

- It is relatively easy to use. Editing, compiling, running and debugging C# programs using the Integrated Development Environment (IDE) is easy.

- It is powerful and versatile.

- It can be used to develop Console, Widows/Forms, Web and Mobile Applications.

- It is object-oriented. Programmers have all the benefits of the object-oriented paradigm such as modularity, inheritance, polymorphism and software reuse.

- It is robust, meaning, it can handle all types of situations - both expected and unexpected. This helps us to minimize errors in programs.

- Modules are linked dynamically (at run-time). Only modules that are needed are linked. This reduces program size, saves memory, and executes faster.

- It uses the Language-Integrated Query (LINQ) to provide built-in query capabilities across a variety of data sources.

- It provides a rich repertoire of built-in/library functions that helps programmers to simplify programming and speed up the software development process.

1

1.2 Visual Studio.NET

Visual Studio.NET 2015 provides an Integrated Development Environment (IDE) for creating impressive applications for Console, Windows/Forms and Web and Mobile Applications, and Cloud services. It provides rich tools and services to candle projects of any size and complexity. (It comes with Visual C#, Visual Basic, C++, F#, Python, HTML/JavaScript, Node.js etc.)

1.3 The .NET Framework

The .NET Framework is Microsoft's computing platform created to simplify application development, especially for the Internet. It is a general-purpose development platform for developing any kind of application. It provides key capabilities for building high quality applications including automatic memory management and support for modern programming languages. With it, you can develop any application for the Microsoft platform. It comes with reusable libraries for building all types of applications. It also supports multiple programming languages.

The .NET Framework includes the following components:

Class Libraries
The .NET Framework comes with many predefined classes organized into different categories called namespaces. A namespace logically/semantically groups related functions. For example, one namespace may provide building blocks for developing Windows Applications; another, for Web Applications. Some of these may be further divided into more specific namespaces. For example, Web Development namespace may contain a namespace for developing Web Services.

The Runtime
The .NET Framework provides Runtime components including the following:

Common Language Specification (CLS): This component ensures that code written in different languages all behave in a uniform way such as when an object is instantiated or when a method is invoked with a value or reference parameter. This is important in the .NET environment as code written in different languages (e.g., C#, C++, VB, JScript) may behave differently.

Common Type System (CTS): This component defines the basic data types such as Integer, Double and String. It facilitates interoperability between languages that use the .NET Framework. It makes cross-language compatibility possible. (In the .NET Framework, you can use multiple programming languages to develop an application.)

Common Language Runtime (CLR): This component manages the execution of all applications developed using the .NET library.

Figure 1.1 illustrates the cross-language operability via the Common Type System and the Common Language Runtime.

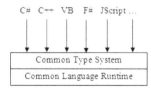

Figure 1.1 Cross-language operability

Garbage Collector (GC) is a memory manager whose job is to reclaim memory allocated to objects that are no longer needed such as when an object is deleted.

Just-in-Time (JIT) Compiler compiles the intermediate language (IL) to native code specific to the target machine and operating system. The IL code is compiled only when needed.

The compilation of a C# program from source code to intermediate code and to native machine code is shown in Figure 1.2.

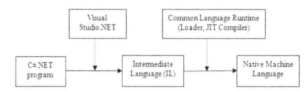

Figure 1.2: Stages of compilation of a C# program

1.4 System Requirements

The recommended system requirements for running C# programs are:

- 1.6 GHz or faster processor
- 1.5 GB of RAM
- 10 GB of available hard disk space
- 5400 RPM hard disk drive
- DirectX 9-capable video card that runs at 1024 x 768 or higher display resolution
- CD-ROM drive
- Windows XP/Vista/7/8

1.5 Visual Studio.NET IDE

When you launch Microsoft Visual Studio 2015, you will see the **Integrated Development Environment (IDE)** shown in Figure 1.3.

The IDE has several parts:

Title bar with the title Start Page - Microsoft Visual Studio

Menu bar with several menu items such as File, Edit, View, Debug, Team, Tools, Test, Analyze, Windows, and Help. When you click on a menu item, you will see a pull-down menu giving several options. The pull-down menus for some of the menu items are shown in Figure 1.4. Some of the options in the pull-down menu have Shortcut keys. For example, the Shortcut key for New File (in File menu) is Ctrl+N and the Shortcut key for Properties Window (in View menu) is F4. You can use the Shortcut keys from anywhere on the screen without selecting a menu item.

Main Window displays the introductory "Start Page" when the Visual Studio is launched. This window is tabbed such that you can switch between several files with ease by clicking on their filenames.

Server Explorer and **Toolbox** controls appear whenever they are clicked and provide various additional capabilities such as access to user interface building blocks for Windows and Mobile applications.

Solution Explorer Window displays information about the current project.

Properties Window gives you a detailed view of the contents of the current project and allows you to perform additional configuration of individual elements.

Start Options provide you options such as New Project, Open Project, Open from Source Control, and a list of recently opened projects to start or load.

Output Window displays the output when a project is compiled or executed.

The Standard Tool bar located just below the Menu bar has several icons. These icons represent some of the commonly used functions such as opening a new or existing file, saving the current file, navigating backward or forward, undo and redo previous operation. These icons represent only a subset of the functions. To use other functions not available on the Standard Toolbar, you must click the appropriate menu item and select the desired function.

The Minimize, Maximize and Close buttons perform the same functions as in other Windows based applications. Clicking the Minimize button puts the application on the Taskbar. To activate, click the icon on the Taskbar. Clicking the Maximize button causes the application to fill the entire screen and clicking it again will cause it to revert to its original size. Clicking the Close button closes the application.

Note that some of the options in the pull-down menus in Figure 1.4 are grayed out. That means they are not available/applicable for use in the current context. Thus it minimizes inadvertent errors.

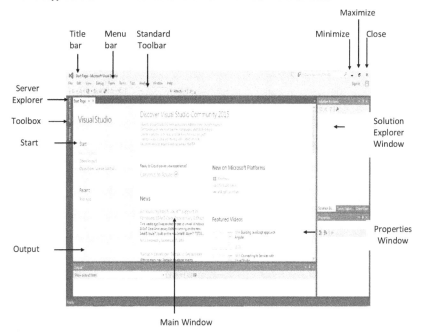

Figure 1.3: Visual Studio 2015 IDE

4

Figure 1.4: C# Menus

1.6 Console Application

To create and run a C# Console application, use the following steps:

1. Start Visual Studio, on the menu bar, Select File > New > Project

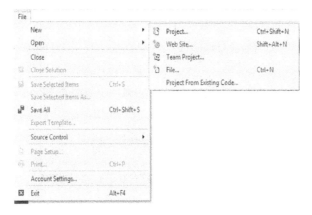

2. Expand **Installed**, expand **Templates**, expand **Visual C#,** then select **Console Application**.

5

3. In the **Name** box, give a name for your project, then click the OK button.

4. Once the project is initialized, you will see the below code in the Code window. We have added the highlightedtwo lines of code to make the program display "Hello World!"

```csharp
using System;
usingSystem.Collections.Generic;

namespace ConsoleApplication1
{
    classprogram
    {
        staticvoid Main(string[] args)
        {
            .WriteLine("Hello World!");
            .ReadLine();
        }
    }
}
```

5. Select the F5 key or click ▶ Start ▾ button to run the project. A Command Prompt window will appear with the message `Hello World!` like the one shown below.

6. Press any key to exit from the application.

6

1.7 Windows/Forms Application

To create and run a C# Windows application to display "Hello World!" message, use the following steps:

1. Start Visual Studio, on the menu bar, Select File > New > Project

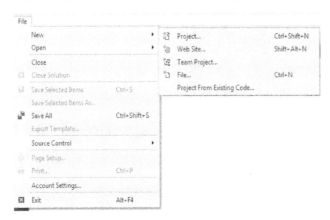

2. Expand **Installed**, expand **Templates**, expand **Visual C#**, then select **Windows Forms Application**.

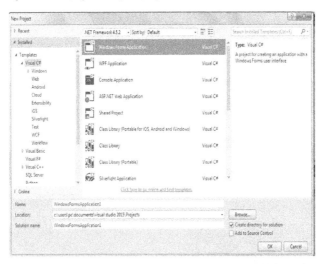

3. In the **Name** box, specify a name for your project, then click the OK button.

4. Once the project is initialized, move the mouse pointer to the Toolbox bar on the left of the screen. Select All Windows Forms and double click on the Button, Label, and TextBox icons to add them to the

7

main form of the application. Select the Form and change the text accordingly under the Properties window. Do the same for Label, and Button controls.

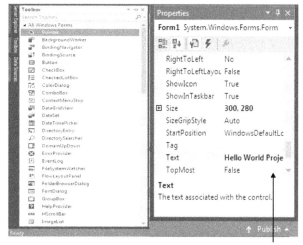

Rename the form here

5. To add code for the button, double click on the button that you just added to the form.

6. You will see some lines of code. Go to the button1_Click method and add the highlighted code shown below.

```
privatevoid button1_Click(object sender, EventArgs e)
{
        .Show(textBox1.Text);
}
```

7. Select the F5 key or click ▶ Start ▾ button to run the project. Enter "Hello World!" inside the Textbox.

8

8. Click on Display button and the program will output "Hello World!" in a message box as shown below.

1.8 Editing, Compiling& Running C# Programs

Let's illustrate these steps for compiling and executing a simple C# Console application to display a greeting message.

1. Start Visual Studio. On the menu bar, select

```
File > New > Project >Expand Installed>Expand
Templates > Expand Visual C#>Console Application
```

2. Type the highlighted code (without the line numbers) in the Code window.

```
/* This is a multi-line comment statement; the program      [1]
asks the user to enter his/her name and displays the        [2]
message Good day with the user's name   */                  [3]

// these are built-in namespaces                            [4]
using System;                                               [5]
using System.Collections.Generic;                           [6]
using System.Text;                                          [7]

// this is a programmer-defined namespace                   [8]
namespace ConsoleApplication1                               [9]
{                                                           [10]
    // class starts here                                   [11]
    classMyClass                                           [12]
    {                                                      [13]
        // Main method starts here                         [14]
        staticvoidMain(string[] args)                      [15]
        {                                                  [16]
```

```
    string name;  // variable declaration              [17]
    Console.Write("Enter you name: ");  // a prompt     [18]
    name = Console.ReadLine();  // input statement       [19]
    // the line below is an output statement            [20]
    Console.WriteLine("Good day, " + name);             [21]
    Console.ReadLine();                                 [22]
    }                                                   [23]
  }                                                     [24]
}                                                       [25]
```

3. Select the F5 key or click  button to run the program. A Command Prompt window will appear that looks like the one shown below.

Note that the program is compiled automatically when you run it. So you don't have to explicitly compile the program.

1.9 Parts of a C# Program

Let's briefly explain the various parts of a C# program.

Comments
Comments are inserted into a program to make it more readable. Comments can appear anywhere in the program. Comments are not executable statements; the compiler simply ignores them.

Comments can span several lines (lines 1 to 3 in the code) or a single line (line 4). A multi-line comment start with the characters /* and ends with the characters */. The pair of characters (/* and */) must appear together (with no space) as C# treats them as a single symbol.

A single line comment starts with two forward slashes (//). Everything on that line after the slashes is treated as a comment. It can appear on a single line (line 20) or after a statement (line 17).

Line spacing
Blank lines can be inserted in a program between statements to make it more readable. For example, we have inserted a blank line between lines 3 and 4. Blank lines are useful for separating methods, to begin a separate task, or to begin and end a lengthy loop.

Namespace
A namespace is a collection of related classes. C# provides many namespaces to simplify programming. The basic namespaces that C# programs require are System, System.Collections.Generic and System.Text. To use them, you must prefix them with the keyword **using** (lines 5-7). Note that there is a semicolon (;) at the end of each namespace directive. The semicolon terminates the statement. This is the basic rule for all executable statements unless they appear in a block enclosed between a pair of curly braces ({}).

The above namespaces provide the basic classes that all C# programs require. For example, the `System` namespace provides the class `Console` for reading input data from the Keyboard and for displaying output on the Screen. This class contains methods such as `ReadLine()` (lines 19 and 22), `Write()` (line 18), and `WriteLine()` (line 21).

Keywords
Keywords (also called reserved words) have special meaning in C#. So they must only be used for their intended purpose. You cannot use them for any other purpose. For example, in the above code, `using` and `System` (line 5) are keywords.

Case sensitivity
C# syntax is case-sensitive. C# treats uppercase and lowercase letters as different characters. So you must be careful when naming namespaces, functions and variables. For example, if you had typed the word `system` instead of `System` in line 5, the compiler will give you an error message. Similarly, the variables `name`, `Name` and `NAME` are all different.

Class
C# is an object-oriented language. Every C# program must have at least one class. The above program has one class: `MyClass` (line 12). It is prefixed with the keyword `class`. You can give your own class name - one that is meaningful. The body of a class is enclosed between a pair of braces ({ }) (lines 13 to 24).

Main() method
A C# program must have the `Main()` method (line 15). Besides this, it can also have other methods. The body of each method must be enclosed between a pair of curly braces ({ }) (lines 16 to 23).

Program execution will always start and end at `Main()`. The keywords `public`, `static` and `void` before `Main()` have certain meanings:

public	–	Specifies that `Main()` can be accessed from anywhere such as from another class another class or another project.
static	–	Specifies that `Main()` is attached to the class (`MyClass` in this case) and not to an instance of that class.
void	–	Specifies that `Main()` does not return any value to the calling program (operating system in this case).

You will need the above keywords when writing the `Main()` method. (There are also other keywords which you will learn later in other chapters.)

Parameters
The curved brackets () following `Main` is used to specify the parameter(s) that it needs. The above program doesn't require any parameters, so there are no parameters enclosed in the brackets. But the brackets are still required even if a method has no parameters.

Variable declaration
Line 17 declares a variable called `name` of type `string`. The `string` is a keyword used to declare string variables. A string variable consists of a set of alphanumeric characters (letters, digits and underscores).

A variable is used to reference a memory location where you can store a data item such as the name of a person. A variable must begin with a letter and may be followed by one or more letters, digits and/or underscores (_). Special characters such as @, %, *, &, $ are not allowed in a variable. Blanks are also not allowed. A variable may be of any length from 1 to 255 characters. However, in practice, a variable seldom exceeds 25 characters. You must give meaningful names for your variables to make your program readable.

Input statement
Input statements allow you to read data from the Console (Keyboard). In the above program, the statement (line 19)

```
name = Console.ReadLine();
```

reads data from the Keyboard, then assigns it to the variable name. The ReadLine() method on the right-hand side of the assignment operator = is part of the Console class.

Assignment statement
An assignment statement has a variable on the left-hand side, the assignment operator =, and an expression on the right-hand side. In an assignment statement, the value of the expression on the right-hand side of the assignment operator is evaluated and the result is stored in the variable on the left-hand side. The expression can be a number, a literal, a variable, an algebraic expression or a method call that returns a value. In this case, the method reads a line of text entered from the keyboard.

Output statement
Output statements are used to send output to the Console (Monitor/Screen). The above program has two output statements (lines 18 and 21). The statement

```
Console.Write("Enter you name: ");
```

displays a message/prompt on the screen asking the user to enter a name. The Write method (which is part of the Console class) displays the message enclosed between the pair of double quotes ("). After the statement is executed, the cursor will appear on the same line immediately after the prompt.

The statement (line 21)

```
Console.WriteLine("Good day, " + name);
```

is similar to the previous one but it will move the cursor to the next line after displaying the message Good day, followed by the name. The + operator acts as a concatenation (join) operator. It joins the message and the name. For example, if the name entered is Sellappan, the program will display

```
Good day, Sellappan
```

Note: Don't worry if you haven't fully grasped the material presented in this chapter. The purpose in this chapter is to introduce you to the C# programming language. The sample code is intended to give you an idea how a C# program looks like. As you progress to the next few chapters you will be able to write simple C# programs.

Exercise

1. Explore Visual Studio 2015'sIntegrated Development Environment to view some of its main features.

2. Click on each menu item on the Menu bar and explore the functions available.

3. Write a simple Console application using the steps given in the chapter.

4. Write a simple Windows/Forms application using the steps given in the chapter.

5. Explore C# debugging facilities.

Chapter 2

Object-Oriented Concepts

Learning Outcomes:

After completing this chapter, the student will be able to

- *Explain classes and objects.*
- *Explain class hierarchy and inheritance.*
- *State the purpose of abstract classes and interfaces.*
- *Discuss the scope and access levels of class members.*
- *Discuss constructors and destructors.*
- *Explain polymorphism, method overloading and method overriding.*
- *Discuss object interaction.*

2.1 Classes & Objects

As C# is an object-oriented language, you need to be familiar with object-oriented concepts before you can write C# programs. These concepts include classes and objects, encapsulation, class hierarchy and inheritance, abstract classes and interfaces, constructors and destructors, polymorphism, method overloading and method overriding, object interaction and message passing.

A **class** is a template for creating objects. All objects from the class have the same attributes (variables) and methods (functions). The methods manipulate the variables. For example, all objects created from the `Employee` class will have attributes like `employee number`, `name` and `salary`, and functions like calculate `salary()`.

A class **encapsulates** (packages) both variables and methods. It is self-contained – the methods manipulate the data. The variables store the object's data while the methods manipulate its data. The variables and methods are called *class members*.

An **object** is an *instance* of a class. You can create as many instances as you want for a class. For example, you can create objects like `Miriam`, `Wong`, `Kamala` and `Susan` for the `Employee` class as shown in Figure 2.1.

Figure 2.1: Class and its objects

A class is represented using a box diagram with three partitions. The top partition shows the class name; the middle, its variables; the bottom, its methods. Figure 2.2 shows the class `Employee` with its attributes and operations.

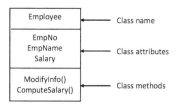

Figure 2.2: Class attributes and methods

Objects have **states**. The state of an object is determined by the values of its variables. Changing the values of variables changes the state of the object. The methods in the class change the values of these variables.

Static & Instance Class Members

Ordinary variables of type int, double, string, etc. are allocated memory at *compile time*. The C# compiler knows exactly how much memory (in bytes) these variables require. These variables are allocated memory on the **stack** maintained by the C# system.

Object variables like Employee, Student, etc. are allocated memory at *run-time*. The compiler doesn't know in advance how much memory these variables require. The memory requirements for these variables depend on the program logic. C# allocates memory dynamically for these variables when they are created and frees the memory when they are deleted or no longer needed. Object variables are allocated memory on the **heap** (maintained by the C# system). Knowing the difference between stack and heap variables can help us write more efficient code – code that executes faster and uses less memory.

Variables in a class can be static or dynamic. The static variables are called *class variables*; they are attached to the class. Only *one* copy is maintained for *all* objects. The dynamic variables are called *instance variables*; they are attached to *each* instance.

Let's illustrate: Assume company XYZ has 1000 employees. As all employees have the same company name (co_name), you need to store only one copy as shown in Figure 2.3.

Figure 2.3: All class instances share the static variable

2.2 Class Hierarchy & Inheritance

Related classes can be organized hierarchically. For example, the classes Person, Student and Employee can be arranged hierarchically as shown in Figure 2.4. Here, Person is called the **base, super** or **parent class** and Student and Employee are called **derived, sub** or **child classes**. This is an example of a two-level hierarchy.

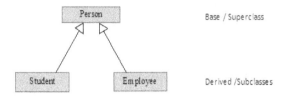

Figure 2.4: A two-level class hierarchy

Inheritance refers to a derived (sub) class inheriting the variables and methods of its base (super) class. The derived classes automatically inherit all the variables and methods of the base class. That means variables and methods declared/defined in the base class need not be declared/defined again in the derived classes.

Let's illustrate: Assume classes Person, Student and Employee in Figure 2.4 have the following variables and methods.

Classes	Variables	Methods
Person	Name, Age, Sex	Initialize(), Add(), Modify()
Student	StudNo, Course	ChangeInfo()
Employee	EmpNo, Pay	ComputePay()

Figure 2.5 shows the inherited members in the subclasses Student and Employee. Thus Student inherits the variables Name, Age and Sex and the methods Initialize(), Add() and Modify() from the base class Person. In addition, it also has its own variables StudNo and Course and its own method ChangeInfo().

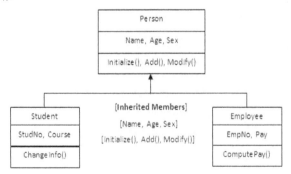

Figure 2.5: Inherited members from base class

A class hierarchy can have many levels. Figure 2.6 shows a three-level class hierarchy. Here, Local employee inherits all the members (variables and methods) of its base class Employee, as well as indirectly, all the members of the Person class.

15

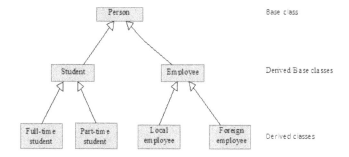

Figure 2.6: A three-level class hierarchy

Abstract Classes

Abstract classes *cannot* be instantiated, meaning, you cannot create instances of an abstract class. Abstract classes are used to specify variables and methods at a higher level. The classes that inherit the abstract class must implement these methods using the specified variables and methods.

Figure 2.7 illustrates abstract classes. The base class `Patient` declares the variable `PatientId` and the method `Delete()`. The derived classes `OutPatient` and `InPatient` then implement the `Delete()` method using the variable `PatientId`. The `Delete()` method in `InPatient` and `OutPatient` *overrides* the `Delete()` method in `Patient`.

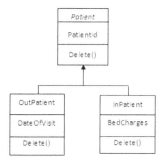

Figure 2.7: Abstract classes

2.3 Accessibility of Class Members

Accessibility refers to the scope/visibility of class members (variables or methods). Access specifiers are used for this purpose. Access specifiers can be *private, public, internal* or *protected*. If the scope is `private`, the members can only be accessed from within that class; if the scope is `public`, they can be accessed from any class (including classes from other projects); if it is `internal`, it can only be accessed

16

by any class in the current project; if it is `protected`, it can only be accessed by classes within the class hierarchy.

What this means is: If you do not want another class to access members of a class, you declare them as `private`. If you want another class (including from other projects) to access its members, you declare them as `public`. If you want other classes in the current project to access its members, you declare them as `internal`. If you only want classes in a hierarchy to access its members, you declare them as `protected`.

By default, all members of a class are `private`. In that case, the keyword `private` can be dropped altogether. In general, the scope of most variables would be `private` while the scope of most methods would be `public`. Public members are exposed to other classes; private members are not.

2.4 Constructors & Destructors

A **constructor** is a special method that is invoked *automatically* when an object is *created*. It has the *same* name as the class. It is typically used for allocating memory when an object is created and/or for initializing variables. C# automatically provides a constructor for each class. You can also provide your own constructor(s). That means, a class will have one or more constructors.

A constructor can have zero or more parameters. A constructor can be *overloaded*, meaning, you can have several constructors all having the same name but different number/type of parameters.

A **destructor** is also a special method that is invoked automatically when an object is *deleted* or goes out of scope. It also has the same name as the class but prefixed with a tilde (~). Destructors are typically used for freeing memory allocated to objects and/or for performing close-up operations such as displaying summary reports.

2.5 Polymorphism

Polymorphism means many forms. The term applies to methods that have the *same* name in a class hierarchy but are implemented differently. A method is said to be polymorphic if it behaves differently in the base and the derived classes. This feature allows two or more classes in a class hierarchy to use the same method name, but each class implements it differently.

For example, in Figure 2.8, the class `Shape` uses the `Draw()` method to draw a shape. The derived classes, `Rectangle`, `Circle` and `Polygon`, also uses the `Draw()` method, but they draw different shapes (rectangle, circle or polygon). So we say the `Draw()` method in `Rectangle`, `Circle` and `Polygon` overrides the `Draw()` method in `Shape`.

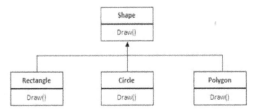

Figure 2.8: Polymorphism

Polymorphism comes in two flavours:

Compile time polymorphism refers to binding overloaded methods at *compile* time. This process is called *early binding*. Overloaded methods have the same name but have different number and/or type of parameters. They behave differently depending on the number/type of parameters. (Note that method *overloading* is not the same as method *overriding*.)

Runtime polymorphism refers to binding methods that have the same name in the base and derived classes. This binding occurs at *run-time* and the process is called *late binding*. The methods in the derived classes *override* the method in the base class, thus stopping the inheritance.

2.6 Interfaces

A class must expose its services (methods) if it wants other classes to access them. That is, it must publish its services. Interfaces are used for this purpose. The interface (class) tells what services it provides to other classes. For example, if an Employee object wants to know the name of its department, it can send the EmpNo to a Dept object which can then access the department name and pass it to the Employee object.

Interfaces declare properties, methods and events (interface members). It is the responsibility of the inheriting classes to implement the methods. They are used to provide a standard structure for the inheriting classes.

Abstract classes can be used for the same purpose, but they are used mainly when the number of members that need to be inherited is small. The classes that inherit the methods must implement them.

2.7 Object Interaction

In object-based systems, objects must interact to perform useful business functions. Objects interact by passing (sending) messages to one another. Passing messages is similar to calling methods and supplying parameters. The called object implements the method and passes the results to the calling object. Figure 2.9 illustrates the idea of message passing.

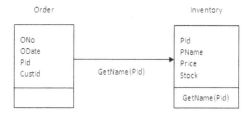

Figure 2.9: Message passing

2.8 Coding for Objects

As C# is an object-oriented language, writing code is slightly different from writing code for procedure-oriented languages such as C/C++. To use an object, first create it using the class template. Then to access a variable/method, prefix it with a dot. The code below illustrates the idea.

18

```
class student        // define class student
{
    string name;     // data member
    int age;

    public static display_name()   // method member
    {
        Console.WriteLine("Name:" + name);
    }

    public static display_age()
    {
        Console.WriteLine("Name:" + age);
    }

}

student s = new student(); //create object s of type student

s.name;      // access name
s.age        // access age

s.display_name(); // call method display_name()
s.display_age();  // call method display_age()
```

Exercise

1. What are objects and how are they created?

2. List the main benefits of class inheritance.

3. What is an abstract class? How is it useful?

4. What is an interface? How is it different from an abstract class?

5. What is the difference between method overloading and method overriding?

6. What is polymorphism and how is it useful?

7. Identify three classes for a library information system. For each class, list its variables and methods.

8. Write skeleton code to define class employee with variables name and salary and methods display_name() and display_salary() to display the name and salary.

9. How do objects interact with one another?

Chapter 3

C# Basics

Learning Outcomes:

After completing this chapter, the student will be able to

- *Explain the different data types.*
- *Declare variables and constants.*
- *Use arithmetic, relational and Boolean operators.*
- *Form algebraic expressions.*
- *Write assignment statements.*
- *Write input/output statements.*
- *Explain the purpose of namespaces.*
- *Write simple C# programs.*

3.1 Data Types

When you declare variables or constants you must specify their data types. The **data type** tells what type of data (integer, double, string, Boolean, etc.) will be stored in the computer's memory. Some data types require more memory than others. C# uses this information to allocate the correct amount of memory for the variables or constants.

C# supports several data types such as Boolean, byte, integer, long, float, double, character and string. The table below shows the various data types, their ranges, and the amount of memory (in bytes) needed to store them.

Data Type	Alias For	Range of Values
Sbyte	System.SByte	-128 to 127
Byte	System.Byte	0 to 255
Short	System.Int16	-32,768 to 32,767
Ushort	System.UInt16	0 to 65,535
Int	System.Int32	-2,147,483,648 to 2,147,483,647
Uint	System.UInt32	0 to 4,294,967,295
Long	System.Int64	-9,223,372,036,854,775,808 to 9,223,372,036,854,775,807
Ulong	System.UInt64	0 to 18,446,744,073,709,551,615
Float	System.Float	-3.4×10^{38} to $+3.4 \times 10^{38}$
Double	System.Double	$\pm 5.0 \times 10^{-324}$ to $\pm 1.7 \times 10^{308}$
Decimal	System.Decimal	-7.9×10^{28} to 7.9×10^{28}
Char	System.Char	U+0000 to U+FFFF
Bool	System.Boolean	True or false
String	System.String	A sequence of characters
Object	System.Object	A sequence of character(s)

You must choose the appropriate data type for your variables. For example, you can choose the short data type for small integer numbers (positive or negative), int for bigger integer numbers, and long for very large integer numbers. If you only need positive integers (for example, to store the population of a country), you can use the unsigned integer data type uint. For financial calculations, you can choose the decimal data type. For single characters, choose the char data type; for a string of characters, choose the string data type.

3.2 Identifiers

Identifiers are names used to represent variables, labels, class and object names, named constants and functions (methods). An identifier can be 1 to 255 characters long (although in practice it seldom exceeds 25 characters). It is formed by combining upper and/or lower case letters (A-Z, a-z), digits (0-9) and the underscore (_). Special characters such as @, #, *, ?, period (.) and blank (white space) are not allowed in an identifier. An identifier always starts with a letter and may be followed by one or more letters, digits, or underscores.

Here are some examples of correct identifiers:

Correct Identifiers

```
Total
AccountBalance
Interest_rate
Rate_of_return
Root1
```

Here are some examples of incorrect identifiers:

Incorrect Identifiers	**Reason**
Date?	Contains ?
Interest rate	Contains blank
Amount$ Payable	Contains $ and blank
123	Starts with a number
e.one	Contains .
@fsktm.um.edu.my	Contains @ and .
http://www.gci.org	Contains :, / and .

When forming identifiers, the following naming conventions are useful:

1. Use meaningful names. For example, you should use the variable name `total` (or `sum`) to store the total of a set of numbers instead of a variable name `t` (or `s`).

2. If a variable is long, use mixed cases or underscores. For example, you can use the names `TotalPay`, `Total_Pay` or `total_pay` to store the total pay of all the employees in a company.

3. Prefix each identifier with a lowercase prefix to specify its data type. For example, you can use `dblTotal` instead of `Total`.

Note: Most programmers use lowercase letters (with underscore) to name variables.

Keywords

Keywords (or reserved words) are identifiers that have special meaning in C#. So these keywords cannot be used as identifiers. That means you cannot use words such as `Console`, `For`, `Switch`, `WriteLine` and `While` as identifiers. The list of keywords in C# is given below.

abstract	Add	as	ascending
async	Await	base	bool
break	By	byte	case
catch	char	checked	class
const	continue	decimal	default
delegate	descending	do	double
dynamic	else	enum	equals
explicit	extern	false	finally
fixed	float	for	foreach
from	get	global	goto
group	if	implicit	in
int	interface	internal	into
is	join	let	lock
long	namespace	new	null
object	on	operator	orderby
out	override	params	partial
private	protected	public	readonly
ref	Remove	return	sbyte
sealed	select	set	short
sizeof	stackalloc	static	string
struct	switch	this	throw
true	try	typeof	uint
ulong	unchecked	unsafe	ushort
using	value	var	virtual
void	volatile	where	while
yield			

3.3 Variables, Constants and Literals

Variables are identifiers used to access data items stored in the computer's memory. You can say they refer to memory locations. Each memory location can store a piece of data such as a character or a number. The value stored in a memory location can change during program execution. As C# variables are case-sensitive, upper and lowercase letters are not the same. For example, the variables Total, total and totaL are not the same. They are three different variables.

Constants are similar to variables, but their values don't change during program execution. For example, in a program that computes the area of a circle, `radius` would be a variable while `pi` (the value 3.142) would be a constant. To declare constants, you use the keyword `const` before the data type.

Literals are constant values assigned to variables. They can be numeric, character, string, Boolean or other data types.

The below are some examples of variables, constants and literals:

```
Commission
GrossPay
Interest_Rate
Sum_of_x
Sumx2
"acts of chivalry"      // this is a string literal
1234567                 // this is also a numeric literal
'*'                     // this is character literal
false                   // this is a Boolean literal
```

There are also literals with specific meaning. They are called **escape sequences** or **escape characters**. These are especially useful for sending output to the console or printer. The table below gives a list of these escape sequences.

Escape sequence	Character produced	Meaning
\a	Alert/beep	Beep the computer speaker
\b	Backspace	Move to one position to the left
\f	Form feed	Move to the next page
\n	New line	Move to the next line
\r	Carriage return	Move to the beginning of the current line
\t	Horizontal tab	Move to one tab position
\v	Vertical tab	Move a fixed number of lines down
\'	Single quote	Print a single quote
\"	Double quote	Print a double quote
\\	Backslash	Print a backslash

Here are some examples:

```
// Print Hello world! on the next line
Console.WriteLine("\nHello world!");

// Print Hello world! on the next tab position
Console.WriteLine("\tHello world!");

// Print Hello world! on the next page
Console.WriteLine("\fHello world!");

// Print Hi… and beep
Console.WriteLine("\aHi…");

// Print the character \
Console.WriteLine("\\");
```

3.4 Declaring Variables and Constants

To use a variable, you must first declare it. The declaration includes the name of the variable and its data type, e.g., `int` (integer), `double`, and `string`. C# will use this information to allocate the correct amount of memory for the variable. Some data types require more memory than others. For example, a variable of type `double` would require 8 bytes whereas a variable of type `int` would require only 4 bytes.

Variable declaration in C# takes the general form:

```
type var1, var2, …, varn;
```

where `type` refers to data type and `var1` to `varn` are the names of variables separated by a comma. The semicolon terminates the statement.

The following are some examples of variable declaration:

```
string ProductCode;
int Quantity;
double Price;
decimal Amount;
float rate;
char ch;
int x, y, z;          // more than 1 variable of the same type on same line
double rate, salary
```

You can also initialize variables in a declaration statement as follows:

```
double total = 0.00;    // declaring and initializing a variable
int n = 20, m = 5;
char ch = 'a';
string name = "AAA"
```

Constants have fixed values, i.e., their values don't change during program execution. A constant is declared by using the keyword `const` followed by the type and name of the constant, the assignment operator and the value. It takes the general form:

```
const type var = value;
```

The following are some examples of constant declaration:

```
const double Rate = 7.50;
const decimal TotalPay = 99999999.99;

const int BufferSize = 1024;
const string Greetings = "Hello there";
const string WebSite = "http://www.must.edu.my";
```

To distinguish between the different data types, programmers sometimes use certain conventions for naming variables and constants. They prefix them with 3 lowercase letters representing the data type. The following table shows the prefixes for several data types.

Data Type	Prefix	Data Type	Prefix
Bool	bln	decimal	dec
Byte	bte	int	int
Short	shr	Long	lng
Float	flt	String	str
Double	dbl	char	chr

The following are some examples of variable and constant declarations using the above convention:

```
string strProductCode;
int intQuantity;
const double dblRate = 7.50;
bool blnMatch = true;
```

3.5 Operators and Expressions

Operators trigger some computation when applied to operands in an expression. There are several categories of operators: arithmetic, relational, logical, increment and decrement, and assignment operators.

Arithmetic Operators

The arithmetic operators are as follows.

Operator	Action
-	Subtraction (also unary minus)
+	Addition
*	Multiplication
/	Division
%	Remainder (modulus)
>>	Shift bits right
<<	Shift bits left

Here are some examples of arithmetic operations involving integer variables. If $a = 8$, $b = 3$ and $c = 2$, then the expressions on the left column evaluate to the values on the right column. (Spaces may be inserted in an expression for readability.)

Expression	Value
a - b	5
a + b	11
a * b	24
b / c	1.5
a % b	2

Note that there are no implied multiplication operations. That means you cannot write `ab` or `(a)(b)` or `a.b` to mean a times b. You have to write the multiplication operation explicitly as `a*b`.

Relational Operators

The relational operators are as follows:

Operator	Meaning
==	Equal to
<	Less than
>	Greater than

25

<=	Less than or equal to
>=	Greater than or equal to
!=	Not equal to

Note that some operators such as <= and >= have two symbols. C# treats the two symbols as a single operator.

The result of a relational operation is always `true` or `false`. For example, if a = 3, b = 4 and c = 5, then the following holds:

Operation	Result
a > b	will yield the value `false`
a <= c	will yield the value `true`
c >= 5	will yield the value `true`
(a + b) == c	will yield the value `false`
c < (a + b)	will yield the value `true`

Boolean/Logical Operators

The Boolean or logical operators are as follows:

Operator	Meaning
& or &&	Logical AND
	or ||	Logical OR
^	Logical XOR
!	Logical NOT

Note: Although you can use the operators | (&) and || (&&) interchangeably for the logical OR (AND), there is a subtle difference. When you use the two character operators (|| and &&), C# may not evaluate all the operands in an expression. For example, if x and y are Boolean, the expression x & y will yield `false` if x is `false`. It is not necessary to evaluate y. This is not the case when you use the single character operator (| or &) where all the operands will be evaluated. Thus using || and && will yield better performance.

The table below summarizes the results of the various logical operations for the Boolean variables x and y.

x	y	x || y	x && y
true	true	true	true
true	false	true	false
false	true	true	false
false	false	false	false

The result of a logical operation is always `true` or `false`.

Here are some examples of logical expressions given x = `true` and y = `false`.

```
x || y      will yield true     // same as x | y
x && y      will yield false    // same as x & y
!x          will yield false
```

You can combine all the operators (arithmetic, relational and logical) in an expression as in the following examples, given a = 2, b = 3, c = 4 and d = 5:

```
a < b || c < d    will yield true
a > b && c > d    will yield false
a + b >= d * c    will yield false
```

26

Increment and Decrement Operators

C# also provides increment and decrement operators as shown in the table below.

Operator	Meaning
++	Increment variable value by 1
--	Decrement variable value by 1

Here are some examples of increment and decrement operations, given a = 2, b = 3.

```
a++ will yield a=3
b++ will yield b=4
a-- will yield a=1
b-- will yield b=2
```

Other Operators

C# also has other operators as shown below.

Operator	Meaning
is	Tests data/object type
? :	Simple if...else
this	Refers to current object

The `is` operator tests the data type of a variable. The `? :` operator is a simple if...else conditional operator. The `this` operator references the current object.

Example 1
If `i` is of type `int` (integer) and `x` is of type `double`,

```
i is double  will yield the value false
x is double  will yield the value true
```

Example 2
If `sex` is of type `char` and `status` is of type `string`, the statement

```
status = (sex == 'M' ? "Mr " : "Ms");
```

will assign the string `Mr` to status if `sex` is equal to `M`, otherwise it will assign `Ms`.

Example 3
If `small`, `x` and `y` are of type `int`, the statement

```
small = (x <= y ? x : y)
```

will assign the smaller of `x` and `y` to `small`.

Expressions

An expression can take the form of a constant, variable, computation, or formula. It can include blanks to make the code more readable. We have already seen the order of operator precedence in the previous examples. They follow the normal algebraic rules. For example, if an expression involves multiplication, division, addition and subtraction, the multiplication and division operations will be performed first before the addition and subtraction. When the operators have the same precedence (example multiplication and division), evaluation always proceeds from left to right. You can use a pair of parentheses () to force the order of evaluation (expressions within parentheses will always be evaluated first).

Here are some examples of expressions:

```
sum2 / n
(a * b - c) / (d - 2 * e)
((b + 2 - 4 * a * c)) / (2 * a)
50 % 12      // get the remainder of 50 divided by 12
```

Boolean/logical variables are evaluated in a similar way. The operator & has a higher precedence than the operator |. Again, parentheses may be used to force the order of evaluation.

3.6 Assignment Statements

All data must be stored in the computer's memory before they can be used in computations. Each memory location has a physical address, but we use a variable to reference it.

The assignment statement is used to store the result of an expression. It takes the form:

```
variable = expression;
```

It can be interpreted as follows: evaluate the expression on the right-hand side of the operator (=) and assign the result to the variable on the left-hand side. The expression on the right-hand side can be a constant, a literal or an expression. Here are some examples of assignment statements.

```
age = 20;
more = true;
greetings = "Hello there";
MyName = "Maria";
pay  = basic + allowance + hours_worked * rate;
net_pay = pay - 0.12 * pay;
```

The examples below show the contents of the variables 'before' and 'after' the assignment for the first four statements above.

Before		After	
Variable	**Contents of memory**	**Variable**	**Contents of memory**
Age	0	Age	20
More	false	more	true
Greetings		greetings	Hello there
MyName		MyName	Maria

There are also short-hand assignment operators: *=, +=, -= and %=. If these operators are used, the variable on the left-hand side also acts as the first operand in the expression on the right-hand. For example, if x = 8 and y = 5, you will have the following results.

Operator	Example	Equivalent to	Result
*=	x *= y	x = x * y	x will have the value 40
/=	x /= y	x = x / y	x will have the value 1.6
+=	x += y	x = x + y	x will have the value 13
-=	x -= y	x = x - y	x will have the value 3
%=	x %= y	x = x % y	x will have the value 3

3.7 Type Casting & Boxing/Unboxing

You would normally ensure that the data type of the variable on the left-hand side of the assignment operator is the same as the data type of the expression on the right-hand side. If the data types are not the same, there might be errors in the computation e.g., loss of precision. To convert data from one type to another, you could use **type casting**. It takes the form:

```
(data type) variable
```

For example, if x is an integer variable and y is a double variable, then the statement

```
y = (double) x;
```

would convert x to double before assigning it to y.
Similarly, if x and n are integer variables, and y is a double variable, then the statement

```
y = (double) x / n;
```

would convert x to double before dividing it by n and assigning the result to y.
The data type of the variable on the left-hand-side of the assignment operator must be long enough to hold the value of the expression on the right-hand side.

The type casting also applies to a subclass object that is inherited from a super class. (For more information on subclass, superclass and inheritance, see Chapters 2 and 12.) To illustrate, if s is an object of type sub and ss is an object of type sup, and if sub is a subclass of sup, then the statement

```
s = (sub) ss;
```

will cast the super class object ss to the subtype before assigning a reference to s.

C# treats all variables and values as objects. It uses a special data type called object which will accept values of any data type whether they are value or reference type. Sometimes it may be convenient to treat a value type variable as an object. To illustrate, consider the code below.

```
int x = 5;
object y = x;       // box a number
int z = (int) y;    // unbox a number
```

Assigning a value-type variable to an instance of an object is called **boxing**. The reverse, i.e., converting an object type to value-type variable is called **unboxing**.

Normal or ordinary variables are allocated memory on **the stack** whereas instance variables are allocated memory on the **heap**. The memory allocation on the stack and heap for the above code is shown below.

You must be careful when you unbox an instance variable. For example, the code below will result in a compiler error because you are trying to put a long (bigger) value (stored as object in y) into an integer variable (z).

```
long x = 12345;
object y = x;
int z = (int) y;  // unboxing a long
```

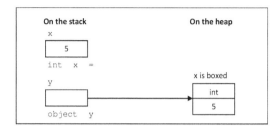

Why do you need stack and heap data structures? C# stores normal variables on the stack as it knows exactly how much memory they need. Instance variables, however, are different. They are created dynamically, on the fly, at runtime. The memory requirements change as instances are created and destroyed (deleted). C# provides a memory manager called **garbage collector** to reclaim memory on the heap when objects are deleted.

3.8 Checking and Unchecking

Variables of different data types require different amounts of memory. For example, an integer variable can store a value of up to 64 bits (8 bytes). The largest number it can store is 2,147,483,647 and the smallest number it can store is -2,147,483,648. If you exceed beyond this range, you will get an overflow error.

Program 3.1 illustrates this.

Program 3.1

```
using System;
using System.Collections.Generic;
using System.Linq;
using System.Text;
using System.Threading.Tasks;

namespace Sample_Programs
{
    class Checking
    {
        static void Main(string[] args)
        {
            int x = 2000000000;
            int y = x + x;          // error occurs here
            Console.WriteLine("Value of y = " + y);
            Console.ReadLine();
        }
    }
}
```

The program will output an incorrect answer:

To overcome this type of error, C# provides the `checked` and `unchecked` types which take the forms:

```
checked (expression)
unchecked (expression)
```

When you use `checked`, the system throws an exception as Program 3.2 illustrates.

Program 3.2

```
using System;
using System.Collections.Generic;
using System.Linq;
using System.Text;
using System.Threading.Tasks;

namespace Sample_Programs
{
    class checking
    {
        static void Main(string[] args)
        {
            int x = 2000000000;
            int y = checked(x + x);
            Console.WriteLine("Value of y = " + y);
            Console.ReadLine();
        }
    }
}
```

When you run this program you will get the below error message in a dialog box:

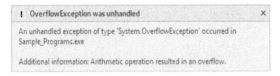

You can catch the error by recoding the program as in Program 3.3.

Program 3.3

```
using System;
using System.Collections.Generic;
using System.Linq;
using System.Text;
using System.Threading.Tasks;
```

31

```
namespace Sample_Programs
{
    class checking
    {
        static void Main(string[] args)
        {
            int x = 2000000000;

            try
            {
                int y = checked(x + x);
            }
            catch (Exception e)
            {
                Console.WriteLine(e);
            }
            Console.ReadLine();
        }
    }
}
```

You will get the same error message as before, but your program will catch the error.

The unchecked simply reverses the effect of checked as in Program 3.4.

Program 3.4

```
using System;
using System.Collections.Generic;
using System.Linq;
using System.Text;
using System.Threading.Tasks;

namespace Sample_Programs
{
    class checking
    {
        static void Main(string[] args)
        {
            int x = 2000000000;
            int y = unchecked(x + x);
            Console.WriteLine("Value of y = " + y);
            Console.ReadLine();
        }
    }
}
```

The code produces wrong result:

32

Note: You can also apply checked/unchecked on a block as in Program 3.5. This has the same effect as the above code.

Program 3.5

```
using System;
using System.Collections.Generic;
using System.Linq;
using System.Text;
using System.Threading.Tasks;

namespace Sample_Programs
{
    class checking
    {
        static void Main(string[] args)
        {
            int x = 2000000000;
            unchecked
            {
                int y = x + x;
                Console.WriteLine("Value of y = " + y);
                Console.ReadLine();
            }
        }
    }
}
```

3.9 Input / Output Statements

Programs typically take input data from users, processes the data, and generate output. The standard input device is the keyboard and the standard output device is the monitor/screen. User enters the input using the keyboard and the program displays the results on the screen. C# provides the Console class (contained in the System namespace) to perform these input/output.

The common methods for reading data from the keyboard are Read() and ReadLine(). These methods allow you to read text data. Read() is used for reading a single character while ReadLine() is used for reading a string of characters terminated by a carriage return (Enter key).

The common methods for sending output to the monitor are Write() and WriteLine(). These methods allow you to display output on the screen. Write() displays the specified output starting at the current cursor position while WriteLine() displays the specified output on the next line.

Program 3.6 illustrates the use of input/output statements.

Program 3.6

```
using System;
using System.Collections.Generic;
using System.Linq;
using System.Text;
using System.Threading.Tasks;

namespace ConsoleApplication1
{
class InputOutput
```

33

```
{
  public static void Main()
  {
      string name;
      int age;
      Console.Write("Enter name: ");   // display message
      name = Console.ReadLine();        // read and store name
      Console.Write("Enter age: ");
      // read age as text, convert it to a 32-bit integer,
      // and store it.
      age = Convert.ToInt32(Console.ReadLine());
      //output on a new line
      Console.WriteLine("\nName: " + name);
      Console.WriteLine("Age: " + age);
  }
 }
}
```

Here is a sample run:

Note: In the above program, `age` is entered as text and then converted to integer using the converter method `ToInt32()` which is part of the `Convert` class. This class also has other converter methods to convert text data to `long`, `double`, `float`, etc.

The + in the statement

```
Console.WriteLine("Age: " + age);
```

is a concatenation operator. It displays the message and prints the value of age after the colon.

You can also use a pair of curly braces { } to specify output items as in the following statement:

```
Console.WriteLine("Age: {0}", age);
```

The curly bracket with the number {0} is called a **placeholder**. The statement displays the same result as before. When placeholders are used, they are numbered {0}, {1}, etc.

For example, in the above program, we could combine the two statements

```
Console.WriteLine("\nName:" + name);
Console.WriteLine("Age: " + age);
```

into a single statement

```
Console.WriteLine("\nName:{0}\nAge: {1}", name, age);
```

to produce the same result.

In this statement, {0} is the placeholder for the first output variable name and {1} is the placeholder for the second output variable age. The escape sequence \n displays the output on a new line.

Message box

You can also display output using a **message box**. To do this, you need to include the namespace System.Windows.Forms which comes with the class MessageBox and the method Show(). Program 3.7 illustrates the use of message box.

Program 3.7

```
using System;
using System.Collections.Generic;
using System.Linq;
using System.Text;
using System.Threading.Tasks;
using System.Windows.Forms;

namespace nsMessageBox
{
    class clsOutput
    {
        static void Main(string[] args)
        {
            string name;
            int age;
            Console.Write("Enter name: ");
            name = Console.ReadLine();
            Console.Write("Enter age: ");
            age = Convert.ToInt32(Console.ReadLine());
            MessageBox.Show("Name: " + name + "    Age: " + age);
            Console.ReadLine();
        }
    }
}
```

When you run the program, the output will appear in a message box as shown below.

A message box can only display a single output. You cannot use escape sequences (e.g., \n, \t) or placeholders ({0}, {1}) to display output in a message box.

3.10 Namespaces

A **namespace** is a collection of related classes (and their methods). It provides unique identifiers for types by placing them in a hierarchical structure. It also provides help for avoiding name clashes between two sets of code. Some of the fundamental programming namespaces in the .NET Framework include:

35

Namespace	Classes Contained
System	Most fundamental classes that are frequently used. For example the class object, from which every other class is derived, is defined in System, as are the primitive data types int, string, double etc.
System.Reflection	Classes that allow examination of the metadata that describes assemblies, objects and types. Also used for COM Interoperability.
System.IO	Input and output, file handling, etc.
System.Collections	Arrays, lists, linked lists, maps and other data structures.
System.Web	Classes that assist in the generation of web pages using ASP+.
System.Net	Classes to make requests over the network and Internet
System.Data	ADO+ classes that make it easy to access data from relational databases and other data sources.
System.WinForms	Classes to display controls for standalone windows applications (as opposed to web).
Microsoft.Win32	Functions which were previously accessible mainly through the Win32 API functions, such as registry access.
System.Activities	The System.Activities namespaces contain all the classes necessary to create and work with activities in Window Workflow Foundation.
System.AddIn	The System.AddIn namespaces contain types used to identify, register, activate, and control add-ins, and to allow add-ins to communicate with a host application.
System.Collections	The System.Collections namespaces contain types that define various standard, specialized, and generic collection objects.
System.Deployment	The System.Deployment namespaces contain types that support deployment of ClickOnce applications.
System.DirectoryServices	The System.DirectoryServices namespaces contain types that provide access to Active Directory from managed code.
System.Dynamic	The System.Dynamic namespace provides classes and interfaces that support Dynamic Language Runtime.
System.IdentityModel	The System.IdentityModel namespaces contain types that are used to provide authentication and authorization for .NET applications.

The classes in the System namespace are shown below.

System

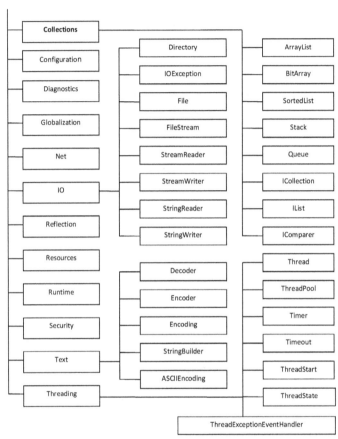

Creating a Namespace

Program 3.8 shows how to create a namespace. To declare a new namespace csharp, you put the reserved word namespace in front of csharp. Curly braces surround the members inside the csharp namespace.

Program 3.8

```
using System;
using System.Collections.Generic;
using System.Linq;
using System.Text;
using System.Threading.Tasks;
```

37

```
namespace csharp   //Namespace declaration
{
    class NameSpaceCS
    {
        public static void Main()
        {
            //Write to console
            Console.WriteLine("csharp namespace");
            Console.ReadLine();
        }
    }
}
```

The program will produce the below output.

You can have any number of namespaces in a program as you want. Program 3.9 shows two namespaces.

Program 3.9

```
using System;
using Mynamespace1;
using Mynamespace2;

namespace Mynamespace1
{
    class firstNspace
    {
        public void fmessage()
        {
            Console.WriteLine("First Namespace");
        }
    }
}

namespace Mynamespace2
{
    class secondNspace
    {
        public void Smessage()
        {
            Console.WriteLine("Second Namespace");
        }
    }
}

class Namespaces
{
    static void Main(string[] args)
    {
        firstNspace fn = new firstNspace();
        secondNspace sn = new secondNspace();
        fn.fmessage();
        sn.Smessage();
```

```
        Console.ReadLine();
    }
}
```

The program will produce the output shown below.

Note: You can avoid prepending namespaces by using a namespace directive as shown in Program 3.9. The directive tells the compiler that the subsequent code is using the names in the specified namespace.

Program 3.10 shows how to create a nested namespace. By placing the code in different sub namespaces, you can keep your code more organized.

Program 3.10

```
using System;
using System.Collections.Generic;
using System.Linq;
using System.Text;
using System.Threading.Tasks;

namespace csharp  //Namespace declaration
{
    namespace csharp2  //Namespace declaration
    {
        class NameSpaceCSS  //Program start class
        {
            public static void Main()
            {
                Console.WriteLine("nested namespaces");
                Console.ReadLine();
            }
        }
    }
}
```

The program will produce the below output.

Exercise

1. List the main data types in C#.

2. Write appropriate declarations, assigning initial values (if any), for each of the following:

   (a) Integer variable: index
       Unsigned integer variable: cust_num
       Double variables: gross, tax, net

   (b) String variables: first, last
       80-element string: message
       String variable: prompt = "ERROR"

   (c) Floating-point variables: root1 = 0.007, root2 = -6.8
       Integer variable: big = 781111222
       Double variable: amount = 999999999.99

3. Given integer variables x, y and z with values 10, 7, 2 respectively, write a program to compute the value of each of the following arithmetic expressions:

   ```
   (a)  x + 2 * y - z
   (b)  x / z - (x * x + y)
   (c)  (x * y) % z
   (d)  5*(x + y + z) - x/z
   (e)  x * y - x * z
   (f)  y * (x + z) * (x - y)
   ```

4. Given integer variables a = 2, b = 5, c = 7 and floating-point variables x = 10.0, y = 10.5, z = 20.0, write a program using type casting to obtain accurate answers for each of the following expressions:

   ```
   (a)  y + a/b
   (b)  a + b * z / a)
   (c)  x + (b / a) * c
   ```

5. Using the values given in question 4, determine the values for each of the following expressions:

   ```
   (a)  a++
   (b)  a < 2 && y > 5.0
   (c)  c >= a
   (d)  a < b || b > c
   (e)  z != 10.0
   (f)  a == 25
   ```

6. Given the following declarations and initial assignments:

   ```
   int i = 4, j = 21, k;
   float x = 94.55, y;
   char a = 'z', b = 't', c = ' ';
   ```

Determine the value of the variable on the left-hand side in the following assignment statements:

```
(a) k = i * j;
(b) y = x + i;
(c) y = k = j;
(d) a = b = c;
(e) i += j;
(f) j -= (k = 5);
```

7. Explore the classes in the System namespace and determine their purpose.

8. What is the purpose of boxing and unboxing an object variable? Illustrate with a simple example.

9. What is the purpose of checked and unchecked? Illustrate with a simple example.

10. Why do you need the data structures stack and heap for storing variables and references to instance variables?

11. What is the purpose of the garbage collector? What will happen if there is no garbage collector?

Chapter 4

Program Control Structures

Learning Outcomes:

After completing this chapter, the student will be able to

- *Explain program control structures*
- *Write programs using **if** and **switch** statements.*
- *Write programs using **for**, **while** and **do** loops.*
- *Use nested loops.*
- *Use **break**, **continue** and **return** statements.*

4.1 Controlling Program Execution

Program control refers to how instructions/statements in a program are executed. Basically there are three program control structures – sequence, selection and repetition. Most programs would require all three control structures.

In the **sequence structure**, the statements are executed sequentially one by one from the beginning to the end. In the **selection (or decision) structure**, the statements are executed based on certain conditions/ tests. For example, if the condition a > b is true control may pass to statement 1; if not, to statement 2. In the **loop (or repetition) structure**, a block of statements is executed repeatedly until a certain condition occurs.

Besides these three control structures, there are also other control structures which change the order of program execution, e.g., exiting a loop prematurely or returning from another function (or subprogram).

C# provides the following program control structures:

- `if` and `switch` for selection/decision structure
- `for`, `while` and `do` for loop/repetition structure
- `break`, `continue`, `return` and `goto` for other structures

4.2 Sequence Structure

In the sequence structure, instructions are executed sequentially, from the beginning to the last statement as shown below:

```
rate = 3.0;                              (S1)
hours = 20;                              (S2)
pay = hours * rate;                      (S3)
Console.WriteLine("Pay = {0}", pay);     (S4)
```

In this code, statement S1 is executed first, then statements S2, S3 and S4. The structure has one *entry* point and one *exit* point as shown below.

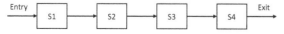

Program 4.1 illustrates the sequence structure. It executes the instructions/statements one by one sequentially from the first to the last.

Program 4.1

```
using System;
using System.Collections.Generic;
using System.Linq;
using System.Text;
using System.Threading.Tasks;

namespace Sample_Program
{
    class Sequence
    {
        static void Main(string[] args)
        {
            int quantity;
            double price, amount;
            quantity = 5;
            price = 2.75;
            amount = price * quantity;
            Console.WriteLine("Amount = $" + amount);
            Console.ReadLine();
        }
    }
}
```

The program produces the following output:

Program 4.2 is another example of this structure. It executes the instructions one by one and displays the results.

Program 4.2

```
using System;
using System.Collections.Generic;
using System.Linq;
using System.Text;
using System.Threading.Tasks;


namespace Sample_Program
{
    class Sequence
    {
        static void Main(string[] args)
        {
            Console.WriteLine("Insert your card");
            Console.WriteLine("Enter your ID number");
            Console.WriteLine("Enter password");
            Console.WriteLine("Thank you");
```

```
                    Console.ReadLine();
        }
    }
}
```

The program produces the following output:

4.3 Selection Structure

The selection or decision structure allows programs to execute instructions in a non-sequential fashion depending on the outcome of certain tests/conditions. In other words, it allows branching. It compares two expressions (or values), and based on the result (`true` or `false`), it branches off to another instruction in the program, which may or may not be the next instruction.

C# provides two types selection structures: `if` and `switch`

❖ **if**

The if structure takes three forms: if, if else, if else if

The first if statement takes the form:

```
if (expression)
        statement;
```

If the expression (condition) evaluates to true, the statement is executed; if not, control passes to the next statement.

The `expression` is usually a comparison, but it can also be a simple numeric expression (e.g., an integer number). The result of the comparison is always a Boolean `true` or `false`. If it is a numeric expression, C# will assign the value `false` if it evaluates to zero and `true` if it evaluates to a non-zero value as shown in the figure below.

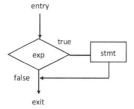

Program 4.3 receives the student's mark from the keyboard, then computes and displays the message Pass if mark is greater than 49. It will not display anything if mark is less than or equal to 49.

Note: C# reads all input data as text/string. As mark is a variable of type integer, the program first converts the (text) data to integer before using it in the computation. The conversion is done using Convert.ToInt32() where Convert is the class and ToInt32() is the method.

Program 4.3

```
using System;
using System.Collections.Generic;
using System.Linq;
using System.Text;
using System.Threading.Tasks;

namespace Sample_Program
{
    class Mark
    {
        static void Main(string[] args)
        {
            int mark;
            Console.Write("Enter your mark: ");
            mark = Convert.ToInt32(Console.ReadLine());
            if (mark > 49)
                Console.WriteLine("Pass");
            Console.ReadLine();
        }
    }
}
```

If you enter the value 74 for mark, the program will display the output:

Note: The if-structure may take the form of a **block** with several statements. In that case, you must enclose all the statements with a pair of curly brackets { } and drop the semicolon as Program 4.4 illustrates.

Program 4.4 receives sales data from the keyboard, then computes and displays the commission. As sales is a numeric variable of type double, the program converts the data to type double using the converter Convert.ToDouble().

Program 4.4

```
using System;
using System.Collections.Generic;
using System.Linq;
using System.Text;
using System.Threading.Tasks;
```

```
namespace Sample_Program
{
    class Commission
    {
        static void Main(string[] args)
        {
            double sales, commission;
            Console.Write("Enter Sales: $");
            sales = Convert.ToDouble(Console.ReadLine());
            if (sales > 1000)
            {
                commission = sales * 0.05;
                Console.WriteLine("Sales= ${0}", sales);
                Console.WriteLine("Commission= ${0}", commission);
                Console.ReadLine();
            }
        }
    }
}
```

If you enter the value 2500 for `sales`, the program will display the following output:

The second `if` statement takes the form:

```
if (expression)
    statement 1;
else
    statement 2;
```

Here, if the `expression` evaluates to `true`, `statement1` is executed; otherwise `statement 2` is executed. Only one of these statements will be executed. (The statements can take the form of blocks.) The figure below illustrates this structure.

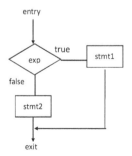

46

Program 4.5 reads data for age (from keyboard) and displays the message `Adult` if the value of `age` is greater than or equal to 18; otherwise it displays thw two messages in the false block.

Program 4.5

```
using System;
using System.Collections.Generic;
using System.Linq;
using System.Text;
using System.Threading.Tasks;

namespace Sample_Program
{
    class Age
    {
        static void Main(string[] args)
        {
            int age;
            Console.Write("How old are you?  ");
            age = Convert.ToInt32(Console.ReadLine());

            if (age >= 18)
            {
                Console.WriteLine("Adult!");
            }
            else
            {
                Console.WriteLine("You are still young.");
                Console.WriteLine("Have fun and enjoy yourself");
            }
            Console.ReadLine();
        }
    }
}
```

If you enter the value 18 for age, you will get the output:

And if you enter the value 16 for age, you will get the output:

Program 4.6 receives input for `grade` and prints the message `Good!` if the grade entered is A, otherwise it prints the message `Not  bad`.

47

Program 4.6

```
using System;
using System.Collections.Generic;
using System.Linq;
using System.Text;
using System.Threading.Tasks;

namespace Sample_Program
{
    class Grade
    {
        static void Main(string[] args)
        {
            char grade;
            Console.Write("Enter your grade (A-F): ");
            grade = Convert.ToChar(Console.ReadLine());
            if (grade == 'A')  // test for grade A
            {
                Console.WriteLine("GOOD!");
            }
            else
            {
                Console.WriteLine("Not bad.");
            }
            Console.ReadLine();
        }
    }
}
```

If you enter A for grade, you will get the output:

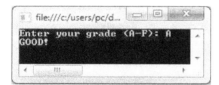

And if you enter D for grade, you will get the output:

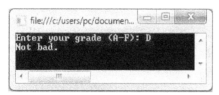

Program 4.7 prompts the user for name and gender. It will test the gender of the person and then displays either Mr. or Ms. along with the name.

Program 4.7

```
using System;
using System.Collections.Generic;
```

```
using System.Linq;
using System.Text;
using System.Threading.Tasks;

namespace Sample_Program
{
    class Status
    {
        static void Main(string[] args)
        {
            string name, sex;
            Console.Write("Please enter your name: ");
            name = Console.ReadLine();
            Console.Write("Please enter your sex: ");
            sex = Console.ReadLine();
            sex = sex.ToLower();
            if (sex == "male")
            {
                Console.WriteLine("Mr. {0}", name);
            }
            else
            {
                Console.WriteLine("Ms. {0}", name);
            }

            Console.ReadLine();
        }
    }
}
```

If the user enters Munir for name, and male for sex, you will get the output:

If the user enters Mary for name, and female for sex, you will get the output:

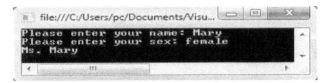

Program 4.8 reads the name of a customer and his/her account balance and displays the message <name>, you are a very good customer if the balance is $10,000 or more and the message <name>, you are not a bad customer if the amount is less than $10,000.

Program 4.8

```
using System;
using System.Collections.Generic;
using System.Linq;
```

49

```
using System.Text;
using System.Threading.Tasks;
namespace Decision
{
    class Acc_balance
    {
        static void Main(string[] args)
        {
            string name;
            double accbal;

            Console.Write("Enter Customer name: ");
            name = Console.ReadLine();
            Console.Write("Enter customer account balance: $");
            accbal = Convert.ToDouble(Console.ReadLine());
            if (accbal >= 10000)
            {
                Console.WriteLine("{0}, you are a very good customer", name);
            }
            else
            {
                Console.WriteLine("{0}, you are not a bad customer", name);
            }
            Console.ReadLine();
        }
    }
}
```

If the user enters Munir for customer name, and $50000 for account balance, you will get the output:

And if the user enters John for customer name, and $4500 for account balance, you will get the output:

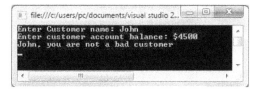

The third if statement takes the form:

```
if (expression 1)
    statement 1;
else if (expression 2)
    statement 2;
else if (expression 3)
```

50

```
    statement 3;
else
    statement 4;
```

Here, expression 1 is evaluated first. If it evaluates to true, statement 1 is executed; otherwise (i.e., false), expression 2 is evaluated. If expression 2 is true, statement 2 is executed; otherwise, expression 3 is evaluated. If it is true, statement 3 is executed; otherwise, statement 4 is executed. Only one of the statements will be executed.

Note: else if is two words; and the last else has no if.

Program 4.9 reads input value for age and displays a message.

Program 4.9

```
using System;
using System.Collections.Generic;
using System.Linq;
using System.Text;
using System.Threading.Tasks;

namespace Sample_Program
{
    class Age
    {
        static void Main(string[] args)
        {
            int age;
            Console.Write("Please enter your age: ");
            age = Convert.ToInt32(Console.ReadLine());
            if (age <= 12)
            {
                Console.WriteLine("You are still a kid.");
            }
            else if (age > 12 && age <= 18)
            {
                Console.WriteLine("You are a teenager.");
            }
            else
            {
                Console.WriteLine("You are an adult.");
            }

            Console.ReadLine();
        }
    }
}
```

If you enter the value 57 for age, the program will display the output:

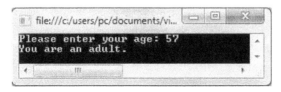

And if you enter the value 17 for age, the program will display the output:

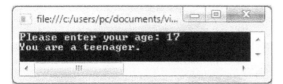

If you enter the value 10 for age, the program will display the output:

Program 4.10 reads a value for mark and displays the message Pass, Fail, Credit or Distinction.

Program 4.10

```
using System;
using System.Collections.Generic;
using System.Linq;
using System.Text;
using System.Threading.Tasks;

namespace Sample_Program
{
    class Mark
    {
        static void Main(string[] args)
        {
            int mark;
            string grade;
            Console.Write("Please enter your mark: ");
            mark = Convert.ToInt32(Console.ReadLine());
            if (mark < 50)
            {
                grade = "Fail";
            }
            else if (mark < 60)
            {
                grade = "Pass";
            }
            else if (mark < 70)
            {
                grade = "Credit";
            }
            else
            {
                grade = "Distinction!";
            }
            Console.WriteLine("Your grade is {0}", grade);
            Console.ReadLine();
        }
```

```
        }
}
```

If you enter the value 77 for mark, you will get the output:

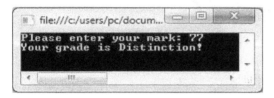

If you enter the value 65 for mark, you will get the output:

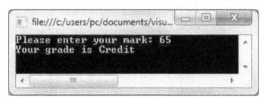

And if you enter the value 55 for mark, you will get the output:

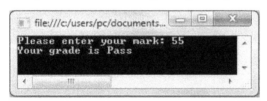

Program 4.11 reads a character from the keyboard and checks if the character is an alphabet. If it is, it checks whether it is a lowercase or uppercase character and displays an appropriate message.

Program 4.11

```
using System;
using System.Collections.Generic;
using System.Linq;
using System.Text;
using System.Threading.Tasks;

namespace Sample_Program
{
    class Char_Check
    {
        static void Main(string[] args)
        {
            char ch;
            Console.Write("Enter a character: ");
            ch = Convert.ToChar(Console.ReadLine());
```

53

```
if (Char.IsLetter(ch) && Char.IsLower(ch))
{
    Console.WriteLine("The character is lowercase");
}
else if (Char.IsLetter(ch) && Char.IsUpper(ch))
{
    Console.WriteLine("The character is uppercase");
}
else
{
    Console.WriteLine("The character is not an alphabet
    character");
}
    Console.ReadLine();
```

If you enter r, you will get the output:

If you enter the R, you will get the output:

If you enter the 7, you will get the output:

Note: When using `if`, `else if` statements you need to keep in mind the following points:

- An `if` can have 0 or 1 else and it must come after any `else if`.
- An `if` can have 0 to many else if and they must come before the `else`.
- Once an `else if` succeeds, none of the remaining `else if` or `else` will be tested.

54

❖ switch

The `switch` structure is an alternative to the `if-else` `if` structure. It provides a neater solution for simple cases. It takes the form:

```
switch (expression)
{
    case expression 1: statement 1;

    case expression 2: statement 2;

    ...

    case expression n: statement n;

    default: last statement;
}
```

The `switch` statement (like the `if-else` `if` statement) executes only one of the cases (assuming there is a `break` statement at the end of each case) as the figure below illustrates.

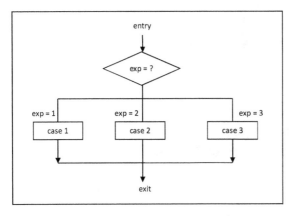

Program 4.12 illustrates the switch statement. First, it evaluates `myChoice`. If it evaluates to 1, it executes `statement1` (case 1); if 2, it executes `statement2` (case 2), and so on. If `myChoice` doesn't evaluate to any of the specified cases, control passes to the `default` case. The `break` statement at the end of each case is used to exit from the switch block. The `break` statement can be used anywhere in the block.

Program 4.12

```
using System;
using System.Collections.Generic;
using System.Linq;
using System.Text;
using System.Threading.Tasks;

namespace Sample_Program
{
    class Switch
    {
```

55

```
static void Main(string[] args)
{
    int myChoice;
    Console.Write("Please make your selection: ");
    myChoice = Convert.ToInt32(Console.ReadLine());

    switch (myChoice)
    {
        case 1:
            Console.WriteLine("Stop");
            break;

        case 2:
            Console.WriteLine("Ready to go");
            break;

        case 3:
            Console.WriteLine("Go");
            break;

        default:
            Console.WriteLine("Undecided");
            break;
    }
        Console.ReadLine();
    }
}
```

If you enter the value 3 for myChoice, you will get the output:

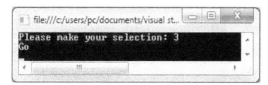

And if you enter the value 5 for myChoice, you will get the output:

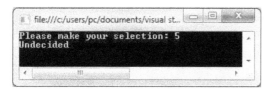

Program 4.13 displays the appropriate grade depending on the value of Mark. Note that we have used the if...else if statement in the first part to test mark instead of the switch statement. This is because switch cannot be used for testing complex cases. It can only be used if the expression evaluates to a character, string or integer.

Program 4.13

```
using System;
using System.Collections.Generic;
```

```csharp
using System.Linq;
using System.Text;
using System.Threading.Tasks;

namespace Sample_Program
{
    class Mark
    {
        static void Main(string[] args)
        {
            int mark;
            char grade;
            Console.Write("Please enter your mark: ");
            mark = Convert.ToInt32(Console.ReadLine());
            if (mark >= 70 && mark <= 100)
                grade = 'A';
            else if (mark >= 60 && mark < 70)
                grade = 'B';
            else if (mark >= 50 && mark < 60)
                grade = 'C';
            else if (mark >= 40 && mark < 50)
                grade = 'D';
            else
                grade = 'F';

            switch (grade)
            {
                case 'A':
                    Console.WriteLine("You got a distinction");
                    break;
                case 'B':
                    Console.WriteLine("You got a credit");
                    break;
                case 'C':
                    Console.WriteLine("You got a pass");
                    break;
                case 'D':
                    Console.WriteLine("You got a weak pass");
                    break;
                case 'F':
                    Console.WriteLine("You failed");
                    break;
                default:
                    break;
            }
            Console.ReadLine();
        }
    }
}
```

If you enter 80 for mark, you will get the output:

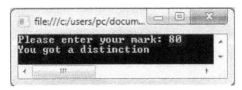

And if you enter 35 for mark, you will get the output:

Program 4.14 is similar to the previous program but uses `switch` for testing the cases.

Program 4.14

```
using System;
using System.Collections.Generic;
using System.Linq;
using System.Text;
using System.Threading.Tasks;

namespace Sample_Program
{
    class SwitchGrade
    {
        static void Main(string[] args)
        {
            char grade;
            Console.Write("Enter student grade: ");
            grade = Convert.ToChar(Console.ReadLine());

            switch (grade)
            {
                case 'A':
                    Console.WriteLine("Excellent!");
                    break;
                case 'B':
                case 'C':
                    Console.WriteLine("Well done");
                    break;
                case 'D':
                    Console.WriteLine("You passed");
                    break;
                case 'F':
                    Console.WriteLine("Better try again");
                    break;
                default:
                    Console.WriteLine("Invalid grade");
                    break;
            }
            Console.WriteLine("Your grade is  {0}", grade);
            Console.ReadLine();
        }
    }
}
```

If you enter A for grade, you will get the output:

58

And if you enter K for grade, you will get the output:

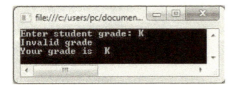

Program 4.15 lists the number of students taking Arts- and Science-based courses. Note that the same statements are executed for both cases A and B. Similarly, the same set of statements is executed for cases C, E, P and M.

Program 4.15

```
using System;
using System.Collections.Generic;
using System.Linq;
using System.Text;
using System.Threading.Tasks;

namespace Sample_Program
{
    class Course
    {
        static void Main(string[] args)
        {
            string courseCode;
            int i, totalArts = 0, totalScience = 0;
            const int n = 5;  // n is a constant
            Console.WriteLine("A - Accounting, B - Business, C - Computing");
            Console.WriteLine("E - Engineering, M - Medicine, P - Pharmacy");

            for (i = 1; i <= n; i++)
            {
                Console.Write("\nEnter course code: ");
                courseCode = Console.ReadLine();
                courseCode = courseCode.ToUpper();
                switch (courseCode)
                {
                    case "A":
                    case "B":
                        totalArts += 1;
                        break;

                    case "C":
                    case "E":
                    case "P":
                    case "M":
                        totalScience += 1;
```

```
                    break;
            default:
                    Console.WriteLine("Invalid Code!");
                    break;
            }
            Console.WriteLine("Total in Arts Stream = {0}",totalArts);
            Console.WriteLine("Total in Science Stream = {0}",totalScience);
        }
        Console.ReadLine();
    }
  }
}
```

Here is a sample run:

```
A - Accounting, B - Business, C - Computing
E - Engineering, M - Medicine, P - Pharmacy
Enter course code: a
Total in Arts Stream = 1
Total in Science Stream = 0

Enter course code: b
Total in Arts Stream = 2
Total in Science Stream = 0

Enter course code: c
Total in Arts Stream = 2
Total in Science Stream = 1

Enter course code: e
Total in Arts Stream = 2
Total in Science Stream = 2

Enter course code: b
Total in Arts Stream = 3
Total in Science Stream = 2
```

Program 4.16 is similar to the previous program but uses longer strings for the case expressions.

Program 4.16

```
using System;
using System.Collections.Generic;
using System.Linq;
using System.Text;
using System.Threading.Tasks;

namespace Sample_Program
{
    class SwitchSelect
    {
        static void Main(string[] args)
        {
            string myInput;
            int myInt;

        begin:
            Console.Write("Enter a number between 1 and 3: ");
            myInput = Console.ReadLine();
            myInt = Int32.Parse(myInput);
```

60

```
switch (myInt)      //switch with integer type
{
    case 1:
        Console.WriteLine("Your number is {0}", myInt);
        break;
    case 2:
        Console.WriteLine("Your number is {0}", myInt);
        break;
    case 3:
        Console.WriteLine("Your number is {0}", myInt);
        break;
    default:
        Console.WriteLine("Your number {0}, is not
                          between 1 and 3.", myInt);
        goto begin;  // branch to the label begin
}

decide:
    Console.Write("Type \"continue\" to go on or \"quit\" to stop: ");
    myInput = Console.ReadLine();

    switch (myInput) //switch with string type
    {
        case "continue":
            goto begin;
        case "quit":
            Console.WriteLine("Bye");
            break;
        default:
            Console.WriteLine("Your input {0}is incorrect.", myInput);
            goto decide;  // branch to the label decide
    }
    Console.ReadLine();
        }
    }
}
```

Here is a sample run:

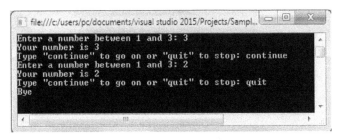

Note: This program uses the unconditional `goto` <label> statement. Executing this statement will transfer control to the statement specified by the label (begin). As much as possible, programmers should avoid using the `goto` statement as it can lead to spaghetti code that is hard to understand and debug.

The following rules apply to the `switch` statement:

- The expression in a `switch` statement must have an integral or enumerated type.

61

- You can have any number of case statements within a switch. Each case is followed by the value to be compared to and a colon.

- The expression for a case must be the same data type as the variable in the switch, and it must be a constant or a literal.

- When the variable being switched on is equal to a case, the statements following that case will execute until a break statement is reached.

- When a `break` statement is reached, the switch terminates, and the flow of control passes to the next line following the switch statement.

- Not every case needs to contain a break. If no break appears, the flow of control will fall through to subsequent cases until a break is reached.

- A `switch` statement may have an optional default case, which must appear at the end of the switch. The default case can be used for performing a task when none of the cases is true. No break is needed in the default case.

4.4 Loop Structure

The loop or repetition structure is used to repeatedly execute a block of statements until a specified condition occurs. When the loop terminates, program control passes to the next statement following the loop.

The loop structure takes the forms: `for, do…while, while`

❖ for

The `for` loop uses a special numeric variable to control the number of repetitions. This variable is called *loop index* or *loop counter*. The `for` statement takes the form:

```
for (initialization; test; update)
{
    statement;
}
```

The `initialization` part or section is used to initialize the loop index. It can also include initialization of other variables. This part is performed just *once at the start or beginning of the loop iteration*.

The `test` (or condition) part determines whether the loop execution should continue. If the `test` evaluates to `false` (zero), the loop is terminated; if it evaluates to `true` (not zero), the `statement(s)` in the block is executed. The test is performed at the *beginning of each loop iteration*.

The `update` part is used to increment (or decrement) the loop counter. This part is executed at the *end of each loop iteration*. This part, like the initialization part, can also include update operations on other variables.

The figure below illustrates the `for` loop.

Note: The `for` loop uses the loop index to control the loop. That means you cannot modify the value of the loop index within the loop. The user can *read* the loop index value, but not modify.

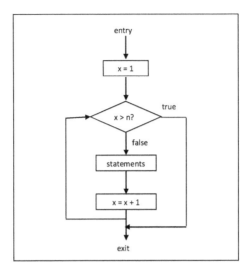

Program 4.17 illustrates the use of for loop to display a set of integer numbers and their squares.

Program 4.17

```
using System;
using System.Collections.Generic;
using System.Linq;
using System.Text;
using System.Threading.Tasks;

namespace LoopStrucure
{
    class square
    {
        static void Main(string[] args)
        {
            int x, xsquare;
            Console.WriteLine(" x     xsquare");
            for (x = 0; x < 7; x++)
            {
                xsquare = x * x;
                Console.WriteLine(" {0}     {1} ", x, xsquare);
            }
            Console.ReadLine();
        }
    }
}
```

The program produces the following output:

Program 4.18 is similar to Program 4.17, but uses an increment of 2.

Program 4.18

```
using System;
using System.Collections.Generic;
using System.Linq;
using System.Text;
using System.Threading.Tasks;
namespace Loop
{
    class Square
    {
        static void Main(string[] args)
        {
            int x, xsquare;
            Console.WriteLine(" x     xsquare");

            for (x = 0; x < 7; x += 2)    //x is incremented by 2
            {
                xsquare = x * x;
                Console.WriteLine(" {0}     {1} ", x, xsquare);
            }
            Console.ReadLine();
        }
    }
}
```

The program produces the following output:

Program 4.19 uses the for loop to print n=7 asterisks (*).

Program 4.19

```
using System;
using System.Collections.Generic;
using System.Linq;
using System.Text;
using System.Threading.Tasks;
```

```
namespace LoopStrucure
{
    class Line
    {
        static void Main(string[] args)
        {
            int i;
            const int n = 7;
            for (i = 1; i <= n; i++)
            {
                //leave space after each *, print on same line
                Console.Write("* ");
            }
            Console.ReadLine();
        }
    }
}
```

The program produces the following output:

Program 4.20 reads a list of integer values into array x (arrays are discussed in Chapter 6), adds 10 to each, then displays the resulting values.

Program 4.20

```
using System;
using System.Collections.Generic;
using System.Linq;
using System.Text;
using System.Threading.Tasks;

namespace LoopStrucure
{
    class addNumber
    {
        static void Main(string[] args)
        {
            int i;
            const int n = 5;
            int[] x = new int[n];   // Create an array

            for (i = 0; i < n; i++)
            {
                Console.Write("Enter an integer: ");
                x[i] = Convert.ToInt32(Console.ReadLine());
            }
            Console.WriteLine();

            for (i = 0; i < n; i++)
            {
                x[i] = x[i] + 10;
```

```
                    .Write("{0} ", x[i]);
            }
                    .ReadLine();
        }
    }
}
```

If you enter the values 1, 2, 3, 4, 5 for the array elements the program will display the following output:

Program 4.21 calculates and prints the average of a set of integer numbers.

Program 4.21

```
using System;
using System.Collections.Generic;
using System.Linq;
using System.Text;
using System.Threading.Tasks;

namespace LoopStrucure
{
    class calculate
    {
        static void Main(string[] args)
        {
            const int n = 5;
            int i, x, sum = 0;
            float avg;

            for (i = 1; i <= n; i++)
            {
                    .Write("Enter an integer: ");
                x =        .ToInt32(     .ReadLine());
                sum = sum + x;   //accumulate total
            }
            avg = sum / n;   //calculate average
                .WriteLine("\nAverage = {0}", avg);
                .ReadLine();
        }
    }
}
```

If you enter the numbers 11, 21, 31, 41, 51, the program will output the following result:

Program 4.22 allows the user to enter the product name, price and quantity for 5 products and then calculates and displays the total amount spent along with other details.

Program 4.22

```
using System;
using System.Collections.Generic;
using System.Linq;
using System.Text;
using System.Threading.Tasks;
namespace LoopStrucure
{
    class Product
    {
        static void Main(string[] args)
        {
            string pname;
            double price,amt, sum=0;
            int i, qty,n=5;
            Console.Write("\t\t\t\tProduct Name\tPrice\tQuantity\tAmount");
            Console.WriteLine();
            for (i = 1; i <= n; i++)
            {
                Console.Write("Enter product name: ");
                pname = Console.ReadLine();
                Console.Write("Enter price: ");
                price = Convert.ToDouble(Console.ReadLine());
                Console.Write("Enter quantity: ");
                qty = Convert.ToInt32(Console.ReadLine());
                amt = price * qty;
                sum = sum + amt;
                Console.WriteLine("\t\t\t\t{0}\t\t{1}\t{2}\t\t{3}",pname, price,
                                                        qty,amt);
            }
            Console.WriteLine();
            Console.WriteLine("\t\t\t\tTotal Amount =${0}", sum);
            Console.ReadLine();
        }
    }
}
```

Here is a sample run.

67

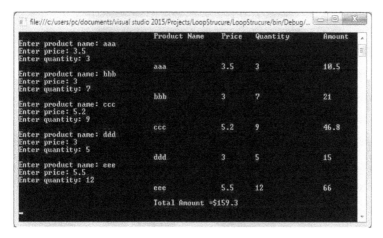

```
file:///c:/users/pc/documents/visual studio 2015/Projects/LoopStrucure/LoopStrucure/bin/Debug/...

                    Product Name    Price    Quantity       Amount
Enter product name: aaa
Enter price: 3.5
Enter quantity: 3
                    aaa             3.5      3              10.5
Enter product name: bbb
Enter price: 3
Enter quantity: 7
                    bbb             3        7              21
Enter product name: ccc
Enter price: 5.2
Enter quantity: 9
                    ccc             5.2      9              46.8
Enter product name: ddd
Enter price: 3
Enter quantity: 5
                    ddd             3        5              15
Enter product name: eee
Enter price: 5.5
Enter quantity: 12
                    eee             5.5      12             66
                    Total Amount =$159.3
```

Programs 4.23 reads the names and marks of n=5 students from the keyboard and computes their grades (0-49 = F, 50-64 = C, 65-79 = B, 80-100 = A). It also calculates the average, minimum and maximum marks.

Program 4.23

```csharp
using System;
using System.Collections.Generic;
using System.Linq;
using System.Text;
using System.Threading.Tasks;

namespace LoopStrucure
{
    class Grade
    {
        static void Main(string[] args)
        {
            int n = 5, sum = 0, max = 0, min = 101, i, mark;
            string name, grade;
            double average;
            Console.Write("\t\t\t\tEXAMINATION REPORT");
            Console.Write("\n\n\t\t\t\tNo.\tStudent Name\tMark\tGrade");

            for (i = 1; i <= n; i++)
            {
                Console.Write("\nEnter Student Name: ");
                name = Console.ReadLine();
                Console.Write("Enter Student Mark: ");
                mark = Convert.ToInt32(Console.ReadLine());
                if (mark <= 49)
                    grade = "F";
                else if (mark >= 50 && mark <= 64)
                    grade = "C";
                else if (mark >= 65 && mark <= 79)
                    grade = "B";
                else if (mark >= 80 && mark <= 100)
                    grade = "A";
                else
                    grade = "Out of range";
```

68

```
        sum = sum + mark;

        if (max < mark)
            max = mark;
        if (min > mark)
            min = mark;
        Console.WriteLine("\t\t\t\t{0}\t{1}\t\t{2}\t{3}", i, name,
                                                mark, grade);
    }

    average = sum / n;
    Console.WriteLine("\t\t\t\tThe Average Mark is " +
                                Math.Round(average, 2));
    Console.WriteLine("\t\t\t\tThe Minimum Mark is " + min);
    Console.WriteLine("\t\t\t\tThe Maximum Mark is " + max);
    Console.ReadLine();
    }
  }
}
```

Here is a sample run.

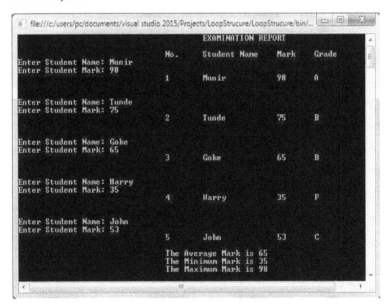

Nested **for** loops

A **for** loop may contain one or more for loops. Such loops are called *nested* loops. A two-level nested loop takes the form:

```
for (initialization1; test1; update1)
{
    for (initialization2; test2; update2)
```

```
    {
        statement;
    }
}
```

In a nested loop, each loop has its own initialization, test/condition and update operations. The inner loop is the body of the outer loop. As such, the inner will not be executed if the outer loop test is false.

The loop index for the inner loop must be different from the loop index of the outer loop. For example, if the outer loop uses the index i, the inner loop cannot use i as its loop index. It must use another loop index say j.

Program 4.24 uses two nested loops to print a pattern of asterisks (*).

Program 4.24

```
using System;
using System.Collections.Generic;
using System.Linq;
using System.Text;
using System.Threading.Tasks;

namespace LoopStrucure
{
    class Display
    {
        static void Main(string[] args)
        {
            int i, j;
            const int m = 5;
            const int n = 6;
            Console.WriteLine("Printing Pattern");
            for(i = 1; i <= m; i++)
            {
                Console.WriteLine(); // print a blank line
                for(j = i + 1; j <= n; j++)
                    Console.Write("*");
            }
            Console.ReadLine();
        }
    }
}
```

The program produces the following output:

Program 4.25 is another example of nested loops to print a different pattern of asterisks.

70

Program 4.25

```
using System;
using System.Collections.Generic;
using System.Linq;
using System.Text;
using System.Threading.Tasks;

namespace LoopStrucure
{
    class display
    {
        static void Main(string[] args)
        {
            int i, j;
            const int m = 5;
            Console.WriteLine("Printing Pattern");
            for (i = 1; i <= m; i++)
            {
                Console.WriteLine();
                for (j = 1; j <= i; j++)
                    Console.Write("* ");
            }
            Console.ReadLine();
        }
    }
}
```

The program produces the following output:

Program 4.26 is another example of nested loops. It prints a multiplication table.

Program 4.26

```
using System;
using System.Collections.Generic;
using System.Linq;
using System.Text;
using System.Threading.Tasks;

namespace LoopStrucure
{
    class MultiplyTable
    {
        static void Main(string[] args)
        {
            int i, j;
            const int n = 12;
            const int m = 6;
```

71

```
Console.WriteLine("\t\tMultiplication Table\n");
Console.WriteLine("\t{0}\t{1}\t{2}\t{3}\t{4}\t{5}\n",1,
                                  2, 3, 4, 5, 6);

for (i = 1; i <= n; i++)
{
    Console.Write("{0}", i);
    for (j = 1; j <= m; j++)
    {
        Console.Write("\t{0}", i * j);
    }
    Console.WriteLine();
}
Console.ReadLine();
    }
  }
}
```

Here is the program output:

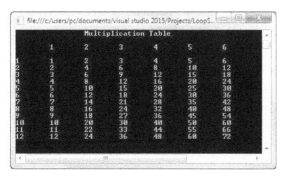

❖ do...while

The do loop is similar to the for loop except that it is controlled by testing a condition instead of using a loop index. The condition is tested at the *end* of each loop iteration (unlike in the for loop). The body of the loop is executed as long as the condition is true. The loop terminates when the condition is false.

It takes the general form:

```
do
{
    statement;
} while (condition);
```

The figure below illustrates this loop structure.

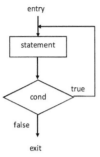

entry

statement

cond → true

false

exit

Program 4.27 reads a value for `timeleft` and executes the loop as long as the value of `timeleft` is greater than or equal to 1. It decrements the value of `timeleft` by 1 each time through the loop. When the loop ends, it displays the message Blast off!

Program 4.27

```
using System;
using System.Collections.Generic;
using System.Linq;
using System.Text;
using System.Threading.Tasks;

namespace LoopStrucure
{
    class Display
    {
        static void Main(string[] args)
        {
            int timeleft;
            Console.Write("Please specify the timeleft: ");
            timeleft = Convert.ToInt32(Console.ReadLine());
            do
            {
                timeleft = timeleft - 1;
                Console.WriteLine("{0}", timeleft);

            } while (timeleft > 1);  // condition is tested
            Console.WriteLine("Blast off!");
            Console.ReadLine();
        }
    }
}
```

If you enter the value 10 for Timeleft, the program will display the following output:

Program 4.28 computes the average of a set of numbers entered from the keyboard. The program tests each number (x) entered. If it is positive, it adds to the sum and increments the counter (n) by 1. If the number entered is -1 (or any negative number), the loop terminates.

Note: The program uses the Boolean variable more to determine if the loop should continue. As long as the value of more is true, the loop executes; otherwise (i.e., if false), the loop terminates.

Program 4.28

```csharp
using System;
using System.Collections.Generic;
using System.Linq;
using System.Text;
using System.Threading.Tasks;
namespace LoopStrucure
{
    class Loop
    {
        static void Main(string[] args)
        {
            int x, n = 0;
            float sum = 0, avg = 0;
            bool more;
            more = true;
            //read and accumulate total if input is +ve
            do
            {
                Console.Write("Enter a positive integer (-1 to exit): ");

                x = Convert.ToInt32(Console.ReadLine());
                if (x <= 0)
                {
                    more = false;
                }
                else
                {
                    sum = sum + x;   //accumulate total
                    n = n + 1;       //increment counter
                }
            } while (more);
            avg = sum / n;           //calculate average
            Console.WriteLine("\nAverage = {0} ", avg);
            Console.ReadLine();
        }
    }
}
```

Here is a sample run:

```
Enter a positive integer (-1 to exit): 4
Enter a positive integer (-1 to exit): 2
Enter a positive integer (-1 to exit): 3
Enter a positive integer (-1 to exit): 76
Enter a positive integer (-1 to exit): 31
Enter a positive integer (-1 to exit): -1

Average = 23.2
```

Program 4.29 uses a do...while loop to display a specified number of sharp (#) characters.

Program 4.29

```csharp
using System;
using System.Collections.Generic;
using System.Linq;
using System.Text;
using System.Threading.Tasks;

namespace LoopStrucure
{
    class doWhileLoop
    {
        static void Main(string[] args)
        {
            int count = 9;
            do
            {
                Console.Write("# ");
                count = count - 1;
            } while (count > 0);
            Console.WriteLine();
            Console.ReadLine();
        }
    }
}
```

Here is the program output:

```
# # # # # # # # #
```

Program 4.30 uses do...while loop to continuously check if the PIN entered by the user is correct. The user is given three attempts to enter the PIN correctly; otherwise, it will terminate with the message "Invalid PIN". The break; statement is used to exit from the loop.

Program 4.30

```csharp
using System;
using System.Collections.Generic;
using System.Linq;
using System.Text;
using System.Threading.Tasks;
```

75

```
namespace LoopStrucure
{
    class pin
    {
        static void Main(string[] args)
        {
            string psw;
            int test = 0;
            do
            {
                Console.Write("Enter PIN: ");
                psw = Console.ReadLine();
                test += 1;

                if (test >= 3)
                {
                    Console.WriteLine("Invalid PIN!");
                    Console.WriteLine("Please check with customer service");
                    break;
                }
            } while (psw != "@must");
            Console.ReadLine();
        }
    }
}
```

Here is a sample output for incorrect PIN:

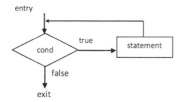

❖ while

The while loop is similar to do...while loop. It takes the form

```
while (condition)
{
   statement;
}
```

The figure below illistrates this loop structure.

```
              entry
                |
                v
              ┌─────┐      true    ┌───────────┐
              │ cond│────────────> │ statement │
              └─────┘              └───────────┘
                |
              false
                |
                v
              exit
```

76

Here, the condition is evaluated first. If it is true (not zero), the statement block is executed; if it is false (zero), the statement block is skipped. The code below illustrates this.

```
while((amount > 0) && (amount <= balance))
{
    balance = balance - amount;
    Console.WriteLine("Please take your cash " + amount);
}
```

The body of the while loop will only execute if the compound condition is true (i.e., if the value of amount is positive *and* is less than or equal to balance).

Program 4.31 uses a while loop to continuously print the message number n times.

Program 4.31

```
using System;
using System.Collections.Generic;
using System.Linq;
using System.Text;
using System.Threading.Tasks;

namespace LoopStrucure
{
    class message
    {
        static void Main(string[] args)
        {
            int i = 1;
            const int n = 7;

            while (i <= n)
            {
                Console.WriteLine("Message number {0} ", i);
                i++;
            }
            Console.ReadLine();
        }
    }
}
```

Here is the program output:

77

4.5 Other Branching Commands

C# also provides other branching commands to prematurely end a for, do...while, or while loop, to end further testing of a switch block or if...else if statement, or to exit from a set of deeply nested loops.

These commands are as follows:

break   Ends for, while, do...while loops or switch, if...else if immediately.

continue Ends the *current* loop cycle immediately.

goto   Transfers control to the labelled statement.

return   Exits from a function.

Program 4.32 illustrates how the break command works. The break terminates the loop, and passes control to the first statement after the loop. When i reaches the value 5, the loop terminates.

Program 4.32

```
using System;
using System.Collections.Generic;
using System.Linq;
using System.Text;
using System.Threading.Tasks;

namespace Exit_Loop
{
    class breakCommand
    {
        static void Main(string[] args)
        {
            int i = 1;

            while (i <= 15)
            {
                if (i == 5)
                    break;
                Console.WriteLine("{0}", i++);
            }
            Console.ReadLine();
        }
    }
}
```

The program produces the following output:

78

Program 4.33 illustrates how the `continue` command works. The `continue` statement skips the current loop cycle, but not the loop. The program displays the value of i only if it is odd. The expression i%2 gives the remainder of i divided by 2. If the remainder is 0, it is an even number.

Program 4.33

```
using System;
using System.Collections.Generic;
using System.Linq;
using System.Text;
using System.Threading.Tasks;

namespace Exit_Loop
{
    class test
    {
        static void Main(string[] args)
        {
            int i;
            for (i = 1; i <= 20; i++)
            {
                if ((i % 2) == 0)   // test if i is even
                    continue;  // continue loop if i is even
                Console.Write(" {0} ", i);
            }
            Console.ReadLine();
        }
    }
}
```

Here is the program output:

Program 4.34 illustrates how the goto command works. When it is executed, control will immediately pass to the labelled statement.

Program 4.34

```
using System;
using System.Collections.Generic;
using System.Linq;
using System.Text;
using System.Threading.Tasks;
namespace Exit_Loop
{
    class gotoCommand
    {
        static void Main(string[] args)
        {
            string myInput;
            int myInt;
        begin:
```

```
        Console.Write("Please enter a number between 1 and 3: ");
        myInput = Console.ReadLine();
        myInt = Convert.ToInt32(myInput);

        //switch with integer type
        switch (myInt)
        {
            case 1:
                Console.WriteLine("Your number is 1");
                break;
            case 2:
                Console.WriteLine("Your number is 2");
                break;
            case 3:
                Console.WriteLine("Your number is 3");
                break;
            default:
                Console.WriteLine("Your number is not between 1 and 3");
                goto begin;
        }

    decide:
        Console.Write("Type \"continue\" to go on or \"quit\" to stop: ");
        myInput = Console.ReadLine();

        //switch with string type
        switch (myInput)
        {
            case "continue":
                goto begin;
            case "quit":
                Console.WriteLine("Bye");
                break;
            default:
                Console.WriteLine("Your input {0} is incorrect.",myInput);
                goto decide;
        }
        Console.ReadLine();
    }
}
}
```

Here is the program output:

4.6 Infinite Loops

You can write an infinite loop by making the condition in the `for`, `do` or `while` loop `true`. To exit the loop, you can use the `break` statement.

Program 4.35 illustrates an infinite loop. It will exit the loop only if you guess the number correctly. Otherwise, it will loop indefinitely!

Program 4.35

```
using System;
using System.Collections.Generic;
using System.Linq;
using System.Text;
using System.Threading.Tasks;
namespace Exit_Loop
{
    class Guessing_game
    {
        static void Main(string[] args)
        {
            int guess;

            Console.WriteLine("This is a guessing game.");
            Console.WriteLine("Guess a number between 2 and 12.");
            Console.WriteLine("See if it matches with what I am thinking.");

            do
            {
                Console.Write("\nGuess a number (2-12): ");
                guess = Convert.ToInt32(Console.ReadLine());
                if (guess == 9)
                {
                    Console.WriteLine(" {0} is a good guess", guess);

                    break;
                }
                else
                {
                    Console.WriteLine(" {0} is a bad guess - try again", guess);
                }
            } while (true);  // infinite loop

            Console.ReadLine();
        }
    }
}
```

Here is a sample run:

```
This is a guessing game.
Guess a number between 2 and 12.
See if it matches with what I am thinking.

Guess a number (2-12): 4
 4 is a bad guess - try again

Guess a number (2-12): 7
 7 is a bad guess - try again

Guess a number (2-12): 11
 11 is a bad guess - try again

Guess a number (2-12): 12
 12 is a bad guess - try again

Guess a number (2-12): 9
 9 is a good guess
```

Program 4.36 is similar to the previous example except that it uses the `for` loop. It will exit the loop only if the user guesses the number correctly. Otherwise, the loop will execute indefinitely!

Program 4.36

```csharp
using System;
using System.Collections.Generic;
using System.Linq;
using System.Text;
using System.Threading.Tasks;

namespace Infinite_Loop
{
    class Program
    {
        static void Main(string[] args)
        {
            int guess;
            Console.WriteLine("This is a guessing game.");
            Console.WriteLine("Guess a number between 2 and 12.");
            Console.WriteLine("See if it matches with what I am thinking.");

            for ( ; ; ) // infinite loop
            {
                Console.Write("\nGuess a number (2-12): ");
                guess = Convert.ToInt32(Console.ReadLine());
                if (guess == 9)
                {
                    Console.WriteLine(" {0} is a good guess",guess);

                    break;
                }
                else
                {
                    Console.WriteLine(" {0} is a bad guess - try again", guess);
                }
            }
            Console.ReadLine();
        }
    }
}
```

Here is a sample run:

Which loop to use?

We have looked at three loop structures – for, do...while and while. Which one should you choose and when? Generally speaking: use the for loop if you know exactly how many times you want to execute a loop; use the while loop if you need to test the condition at the *beginning* of each loop iteration; use the do...while loop if you want to execute the loop at *least* once.

Exercise

1. Review the program control structures in this chapter. Do you need all these control structures to write a complex program?

2. Write a program that will read the name of a customer and his/her account balance and display the message <name>, you are a very good customer if the balance is 50,000 or more and the message <name>, you are not a bad customer if the amount is less than 50,000.

3. Modify the program in question 2 and display the message as follows:

   <name>, you are an excellent customer if the balance is greater than or equal to 100,000;
   <name>, you are a good customer if the balance is greater than or equal to 50,000 but less than 100,000;
   <name>, you are not a bad customer if the balance is less than 50,000.

4. Do question 3 using the switch...case structure.

5. Write if...else if statement that will cause the computer to beep if the user enters a number between 15 to 25.

6. What is wrong with the following code?

```
if (loan > balance)
  msg = "You have overdrawn"
else
  msg = "You still have balance";
```

7. Rewrite the following nested `if` statement using a single `if` with a logical operator:

```
if (A > 3)
  if (B > 10)
    Ans = "Yes";
```

8. What will happen if every `case` in a `switch` structure fails and there is no `default` option?

9. Write a `for` loop that will go on reading integer values until the user enters a negative number.

10. Write a nested `do` loop where the statements in the inner loop are executed five times for every execution of the outer loop.

11. What is the difference between a `do...while` loop and a `while` loop?

12. How many times will the following loop execute?

```
int i = 10;
while (i >= 1)
  i = i - 1;
```

13. Write a program with nested loops to multiply two matrices. Test your program using three sets of test data. (Hint: you will need three nested loops to multiply two matrices.)

14. What is the purpose of the `?:` operator? Give an example.

15. Write a program that will print the message `Good guess` if the user guesses correctly the total or sum of points obtained when a pair of dice is thrown, and the message `Bad guess - Try again!` if the number guessed is not correct. Terminate the loop only if the guess is correct.

16. Write a program that will count the number of odd numbers in a one-dimensional array containing integer numbers.

17. Given student names and their marks for the course C#.NET. Write a program to:

a) Calculate the grade (0-49 = F, 50-59 = D, 60-69 = C, 70-79 = B, 80-100 = A).

b) Calculate the average and standard deviation.

c) Calculate the maximum, minimum and range.

18. Trace the output for the program given below.

```
using System;
class array
{
  public static void Main()
  {
    int i, n = 10;
```

```
int []x = new int [10];
for (i=0; i<n; i++)
{
    x[i] = i;
    Console.Write("{0}  ", x[i]);
}
}
}
```

19. Write a program to generate the following patterns:

     (a)   (b)   (c)

```
*******    *******    *******
******     ******     ******
*****      *****       *****
****       ****        ****
***        ***         ***
**         **          **
*          *           *
```

Chapter 5

Built-In Methods

Learning Outcomes:

After completing this chapter, the student will be able to

- *Explain why built-in methods are important.*
- *List some categories of built-in methods.*
- *Use math, string, data conversion, character, and date/time methods.*
- *Generate random numbers.*
- *Apply format methods.*

5.1 Built-in Methods

A **method (or function)** is a small program that performs a specific task such as calculating the square root of a number, converting a string from uppercase to lower case, converting data from one type to another. C# provides several **built-in methods** to simplify programming. The built-in methods are also called **library** or **predefined methods**. You can use these methods as often as you want anywhere in your program.

A method may have zero or more **parameters**. The parameters *receive* input values from the calling method. (They may also be used to return or send output values to the calling method as you will see in the next chapter). The method uses the parameter values to compute the desired result which is then passed or returned to the calling method via a return statement.

A method may be called in three ways: using a single statement, as an expression on the right-hand side of an assignment statement, or as an expression in a write statement.

C# system provides several categories of built-in methods such as the following:

- Mathematical methods
- Random methods
- String methods
- Data Conversion methods
- Character methods
- Date/Time methods
- Formatting methods

5.2 Mathematical Methods

Mathematical methods perform mathematical calculations such as taking the square root of a number or generating a random number. There are many methods in this category. Here is a partial list.

List of mathematical methods

Method	Purpose
Abs(x)	Returns the absolute value of x. The absolute value is the positive equivalent of the argument.

`Acos(x)`	Returns the angle whose cosine is the specified number.
`Asin(x)`	Returns the angle whose sine is the specified number.
`Atan(x)`	Returns the angle whose tangent is the specified number.
`Atan2(x,y)`	Returns the angle whose tangent is the quotient of two specified numbers.
`BigMul(x,y)`	Produces the full product of two 32-bit numbers.
`Ceiling(x)`	Returns the smallest integral value that is greater than or equal to the specified decimal number.
`Cos(x)`	Returns the cosine of x, expressed in radians.
`Cosh(x)`	Returns the hyperbolic cosine of the specified angle.
`DivRem(x,y,z)`	Calculates the quotient of two 32-bit signed integers and also returns the remainder in an output parameter.
`E`	Represents the natural logarithmic base, specified by the constant, e.
`Equals(x,y)`	Determines whether the specified object instances are considered equal.
`Exp(x)`	Returns the value of e raised to the power of x.
`Floor(x)`	Returns the largest integer less than or equal to the specified decimal number.
`Log(x)`	Returns the natural (base e) logarithm of a specified number.
`Log10(x)`	Returns the base 10 logarithm of a specified number.
`Max(x,y)`	Returns the larger of two specified numbers.
`Min(x,y)`	Returns the smaller of two specified numbers.
`PI`	Represents the ratio of the circumference of a circle to its diameter, specified by the constant.
`Pow(x,y)`	Returns a specified number raised to the specified power.
`ReferenceEquals(x,y)`	Determines whether the specified object instances are the same instance.
`Round(x [,dp])`	Returns the rounded value of x, rounded to the specified number of decimal places (dp).
`Sign(x)`	Returns a value indicating the sign of a number.
`Sin(x)`	Returns the sine of x, expressed in radians.
`Sinh(x)`	Returns the hyperbolic sine of the specified angle.
`Sqrt(x)`	Returns the square root of a specified number.
`Tan(x)`	Returns the argument's tangent value, expressed in radians.
`Tanh(x)`	Returns the hyperbolic tangent of the specified angle.
`Truncate(x)`	Calculates the integral part of a specified decimal number.

Here are some examples of mathematical methods:

Expression	Result
`Ceiling(4.8)`	5
`Exp(3)`	20.086
`Floor(4.8)`	4
`Log(2,2)`	1
`Log10(10)`	1
`Pow(3,2)`	9
`Round(3.1421, 2)`	3.14
`Round(5.7)`	6
`Sign(-3)`	-1
`Sqrt(25)`	5
`Pow(3,Math.Sqrt(4))`	9

Note: A method may also be nested within another method as shown in the last example.

Program 5.1 uses of several mathematical methods. Mathematical methods must be prefixed with the Math class followed by a period (.). For example, to calculate the square root of x, you must write Math.Sqrt(x). The last statement illustrates nested methods.

Program 5.1

```
using System;
using System.Collections.Generic;
using System.Linq;
using System.Text;
using System.Threading.Tasks;

namespace Built_In_Functions
{
    class MathsFunc
    {
        static void Main(string[] args)
        {
            double x = 4;
            double y = 2;
            Console.WriteLine("Given x = 4 & y = 2");
            Console.WriteLine("Square root of x = {0}", Math.Sqrt(x));
            Console.WriteLine("Tan(x) = {0}", Math.Tan(x));
            Console.WriteLine("x power y = {0}", Math.Pow(x, y));
            Console.WriteLine("y power of square root x = {0}", Math.Pow(y,
                                                        Math.Sqrt(x)));
            //Console.ReadLine();
        }
    }
}
```

The program produces the following output:

```
Given x = 4 & y = 2
Square root of x = 2
Tan(x) = 1.15782128234958
x power y = 16
y power of square root x = 4
```

Program 5.2 checks if two integer numbers entered from the keyboard are equal.

Program 5.2

```
using System;
using System.Collections.Generic;
using System.Linq;
using System.Text;
using System.Threading.Tasks;

namespace Built_In_Functions
{
    class MathsFunc
    {
        static void Main(string[] args)
        {
            int x, y;
```

88

```
Console.Write("Enter x: ");
x = Convert.ToInt32(Console.ReadLine());
Console.Write("Enter y: ");
y = Convert.ToInt32(Console.ReadLine());

if (Math.Equals(x, y))
{
    Console.WriteLine("The values are equal!");
}
else
{
    Console.WriteLine("The values are not equal x = {0},
                       y = {1}",x, y);
}
Console.ReadLine();
        }
    }
}
```

If you enter the numbers 65 and 77 for x and y respectively, the program will produce the output:

And if you enter 25 for both x and y, the program will produce the output:

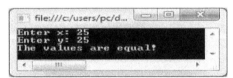

Program 5.3 calculates the areas and circumferences of circles given the radii 2.5, 3.1, 5.2, 7.2, 8.3, and displays the output to 2 decimal places.

Program 5.3

```
using System;
using System.Collections.Generic;
using System.Linq;
using System.Text;
using System.Threading.Tasks;

namespace Built_In_Functions
{
    class MathsFunc
    {
        static void Main(string[] args)
        {
            int i, n = 5;
            double area, radius, circum;
            Console.Write("\t\tThis Program will calculate Area and
```

89

```
                                      Circumference of 5 circles");
        .WriteLine();
        .Write("\n\t\t\tNo.\tRadius\tArea\t\tCircumference");
        .WriteLine();

    for (i = 1; i <= n; i++)
    {
            .Write("Enter Radius: ");
        radius =        .ToDouble(        .ReadLine());
        area =      .PI * radius * radius;
        circum = 2 *     .PI * radius;
            .WriteLine("\t\t\t{0}\t{1}\t{2}\t\t{3}", i,
        radius,     .Round(area, 2),     .Round(circum, 2));
    }
        .ReadLine();
    }
}
}
```

The program will produce the following output:

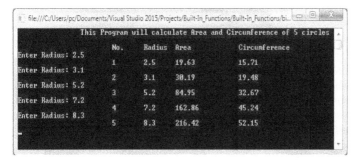

5.3 Random Number Generators

C# provides several random number generator methods. A partial list is as follows:

List of random methods

Method	Purpose
Next()	Returns an integer random number.
Next(1,u)	Returns an integer random number between 1 and u.
NextBytes	Fills the elements of a specified array of bytes with random numbers.
NextDouble	Returns a random number between 0.0 and 1.0.

Program 5.4 generates several random numbers. First it first creates an object of type Random. Then it uses the object to generate the random numbers. The method Next() is used to generate integer random numbers while NextDouble() is used to generate double random numbers between 0 and 1.

Program 5.4

```
using System;
using System.Collections.Generic;
using System.Linq;
using System.Text;
using System.Threading.Tasks;

namespace Built_In_Functions
{
    class RandomFunc
    {
        static void Main(string[] args)
        {
            int rn1, rn2;
            double rn3;
            Random rObj = new Random(); //create a Random object
            rn1 = rObj.Next(); // generate integer random no.
            rn2 = rObj.Next(2, 12); // number between 2 and 12
            rn3 = rObj.NextDouble(); // number between 0 and 1
            Console.WriteLine(rn1);
            Console.WriteLine(rn2);
            Console.WriteLine(Math.Round(rn3, 4)); // round to 4 dp
            Console.ReadLine();
        }
    }
}
```

Here is a sample run:

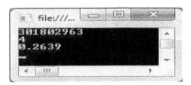

Program 5.5 generates 50 unique (not repeated) integer random numbers in the range [1000, 9999]. Then it determines how many of these fall in the ranges 1000-2499, 2500-4999, 5000-7499 and 7500-9999. It also shows how many of these are even numbers and how many are divisible by 5.

Program 5.5

```
using System;
using System.Collections.Generic;
using System.Linq;
using System.Text;
using System.Threading.Tasks;

namespace Built_In_Functions
{
    class RandomFunc
    {
        static void Main(string[] args)
        {
            int i, even = 0, n = 50;
            int[] c = new int[5];
            Random randObj = new Random();//create a Random object
            int[] x = new int[50];
```

91

```
for (i = 0; i < n; i++)
{
    if (i % 5 == 0)
        Console.WriteLine();
    x[i] = randObj.Next(1000, 9999);
    Console.Write("\t{0}", x[i]);
    if (x[i] % 2 == 0)
        even = even + 1;
    if (x[i] % 5 == 0)
        c[0] = c[0] + 1;
    if (x[i] >= 1000 && x[i] <= 2499)
        c[1] = c[1] + 1;
    if (x[i] >= 2500 && x[i] <= 4999)
        c[2] = c[2] + 1;
    if (x[i] >= 5000 && x[i] <= 7499)
        c[3] = c[3] + 1;
    if (x[i] >= 7500 && x[i] <= 9999)
        c[4] = c[4] + 1;
}
Console.WriteLine();
Console.WriteLine("\n\tNumbers that falls between 1000-2499 = {0}",
                    c[1]);
Console.WriteLine("\n\tNumbers that falls between 2500-4999 = {0}",
                    c[2]);
Console.WriteLine("\n\tNumbers that falls between 5000-7499 = {0}",
                    c[3]);
Console.WriteLine("\n\tNumbers that falls between 7500-9999 = {0}",
                    c[4]);
Console.WriteLine("\n\n\tNumbers Even numbers = {0}", even);
Console.WriteLine("\n\tNumbers divisible by 5 = {0}", c[0]);
Console.ReadLine();
        }
    }
}
```

Here is a sample run:

Program 5.6 simulates the sum of points (2 to 12) on a pair of dice. If the user guesses the sum correctly, it displays the message "Good guess - Congratulations!" or the message "Bad guess - Try again" if the guess is wrong. The program terminates when the user makes a correct guess within a maximum of 5 attempts.

Program 5.6

```csharp
using System;
using System.Collections.Generic;
using System.Linq;
using System.Text;
using System.Threading.Tasks;

namespace Built_In_Functions
{
    class RandomFunc
    {
        static void Main(string[] args)
        {
            int low = 2, high = 12, guess, i, n = 5,x;

            Random rdObj = new Random();//create a Random object
            x = rdObj.Next(low, high);
            for (i = 1; i <= n; i++)
            {
                Console.Write("Guess a number between 2 and 12 please! ");
                guess = Convert.ToInt32(Console.ReadLine());
                if (guess == x)
                {
                    Console.WriteLine("Good Guess Congratulation!");
                    break;
                }
                else
                {
                    Console.WriteLine("Try Again!");
                }
            }
            Console.ReadLine();
        }
    }
}
```

Here is a sample run:

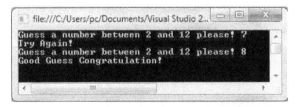

Program 5.7 illustrates how to randomly generate a 7-character long password from the characters A-Z, a-z, 0-9, %, $, #, and @.

Program 5.7

```
using System;
using System.Collections.Generic;
using System.Linq;
using System.Text;
using System.Threading.Tasks;

namespace Built_In_Functions
{
    class RandomFunc
    {
        static void Main(string[] args)
        {
            string pchar =
            "ABCDEFGHIJKLMNOPQRSTUVWXYZabcdefghijklmnopqrstuvwxyz0123456789$#%@";
            string pword = "";
            int i, j, x;
            var random = new Random();
            Console.Write("\tRandomly Generated Passwords");
            Console.WriteLine();
            Console.WriteLine("\n\tNo.\tPassword");
            for (i = 1; i < 11; i++)
            {
                for (j = 1; j < 8; j++)
                {
                    x = random.Next(0, 66);
                    pword = pword + pchar.Substring(x, 1);
                }
                Console.WriteLine("\t{0}\t{1}", i, pword);
                pword = "";
            }
            Console.ReadLine();
        }
    }
}
```

Here is a sample run:

5.4 String Methods

String methods perform operations on strings, e.g., calculating the length of a string, converting a string from lower case to uppercase, or locating a substring in a given string. C# provides several string methods. A partial list is as follows:

94

List of string methods

Method	Purpose
Char	Gets the property at a specified character position in this instance.
Compare	Compares two string objects.
CompareTo	Compares this instance with a specified object.
Concat	Concatenates one or more instances of string, or the string representations of the values of one or more instances of object.
Contains	Returns a value indicating whether the specified string object occurs within this string.
Copy	Create a new instance of string with the same values of one or more instances of object.
CopyTo	Copies a specified number of characters from a specified position in this instance to a specified position in an array of Unicode characters.
IndexOf	Returns the index of the first occurrence of the specified string in this instance.
Insert	Inserts a specified instance of string object at a specified index position in this instance.
Length	Gets the number of characters in this instance.
PadLeft	Right-aligns the characters in this instance, padding on the left with spaces or a specified Unicode character for a specified total length.
PadRight	Left-aligns the characters in this string, padding on the right with spaces or a specified Unicode character, for a specified total length.
Remove	Deletes a specified number of characters from this instance beginning at a specified position.
Replace	Replaces all occurrences of a specified Unicode character or string in this instance, with another specified Unicode character or string.
Reverse	Returns string in the reverse order.
Split	Identifies the substrings in this instance that is delimited by one or more characters specified in an array, and then places the substrings into a string array.
Substring	Retrieves a substring from this instance. The substring starts at a specified character position and has a specified length.
ToCharArray	Copies the characters in a specified substring in this instance to a Unicode character array.
ToLower	Returns string converted to lowercase.
ToString	Converts the value of this instance to a string.
ToUpper	Returns string in all uppercase letters. If any character in the argument is already uppercase, no change takes place for that character.
Trim	Removes all occurrences of a set of specified characters from the beginning and end of this instance.

Below are some examples of string methods:

Expression	Result
Compare("good", "bad")	1
ToLower("ETHICAL ISSUES")	ethical issues
ToUpper("ETHICAL issues")	ETHICAL ISSUES
Copy("Hello")	Hello
Length("Hello")	5
Equals("good", "bad")	false
Concat("Hi", "there!")	Hithere!

Program 5.8 uses several string methods. String methods must be prefixed with the class `string`. For example, to compare two strings, you will write `string.Compare()`.

Program 5.8

```
using System;
using System.Collections.Generic;
using System.Linq;
using System.Text;
using System.Threading.Tasks;

namespace Built_In_Functions
{
    class StringFunc
    {
        static void Main(string[] args)
        {
            string string1 = "Hello";
            string string2 = "Good Morning";
            string strCopy;
            bool strEquals;
            int strComp;
            strComp = string.Compare(string1, string2);
            strCopy = string.Copy(string1);
            strEquals = string.Equals(string1, string2);
            string1 = string1.ToLower();
            string2 = string2.ToUpper();
            Console.WriteLine(strComp);
            Console.WriteLine(strCopy);
            Console.WriteLine(strEquals);
            Console.WriteLine(string1);
            Console.WriteLine(string2);
            Console.ReadLine();
        }
    }
}
```

The program produces the following output:

Program 5.9 uses several string methods to:
- count the number of occurrences of character 'a' in a string
- replace all occurrences of 'a' with 'A' in a string
- remove all embedded blanks in a string
- right-justify a string

It uses the following test strings:
```
"It is a nice and beautiful day"
"Time and tide waits for no man"
"It is a small, small world"
```

Program 5.9

```
using System;
using System.Collections.Generic;
```

```
using System.Linq;
using System.Text;
using System.Threading.Tasks;

namespace Built_In_Functions
{
    class StringFunc
    {
        static void Main(string[] args)
        {
            string rep1, rep2, rep3, emb1, emb2, emb3;
            int cnt = 0, i = 0, n = 3;
            string[] str = new string[3] { "It is a nice and beautiful day",
              "Time and tide waits for no man", "It is a small, small world" };
            string str1 = "It is a nice and beautiful day";
            string str2 = "Time and tide waits for no man";
            string str3 = "It is a small, small world";
            rep1 = str1.Replace('a', 'A');
            rep2 = str2.Replace('a', 'A');
            rep3 = str3.Replace('a', 'A');
            emb1 = str1.Replace(" ", "");
            emb2 = str2.Replace(" ", "");
            emb3 = str3.Replace(" ", "");

            for (i = 0; i < n; i++)
            {
                foreach (char a in str[i])
                {
                    if (a == 'a')
                        cnt++;
                }
            }

            Console.WriteLine();
            Console.WriteLine("The numbers of a's in the given string is {0}",
                                                                        cnt);
            Console.WriteLine("\n\nThe Replacement of 'a' with 'A'
                              are: \n{0}\n{1}\n{2}", rep1, rep2, rep3);
            Console.WriteLine("\n\nResult of the removal of all Embedded
                              blanks are: \n{0}\n{1}\n{2}", emb1, emb2, emb3);
            Console.WriteLine();
            Console.WriteLine();
            Console.WriteLine("Right Justification of the strings:");
            Console.WriteLine(str1.PadLeft(35, '*'));
            Console.WriteLine(str2.PadLeft(35, '*'));
            Console.WriteLine(str3.PadLeft(35, '*'));
            Console.ReadLine();
        }
    }
}
```

The program produces the following output:

```
file:///C:/Users/pc/Documents/Visual Studio 2015/Projects/B...

The numbers of a's in the given string is 10

The Replacement of 'a' with 'A' are:
It is A nice And beAutiful dAy
Time And tide wAits for no mAn
It is A smAll, smAll world

Result of the removal of all Embedded blanks are:
Itisaniceandbeautifulday
Iimeandtidewaitsfornoman
Itisasmall,smallworld

Right Justification of the strings:
*****It is a nice and beautiful day
*****Time and tide waits for no man
*********It is a small, small world
```

5.5 Data Conversion Methods

Data conversion methods change the data from one data type to another. Data conversion methods must be prefixed with the class `Convert`. C# provides several data conversion methods. A partial list is as follows:

List of conversion methods

Method	Purpose
ToBase64String	Converts an array of 8-bit unsigned integers to its equivalent string representation that is encoded with base-64 digits.
ToBoolean	Converts the value to an equivalent Boolean value.
ToByte	Converts the value of this instance to an equivalent 8-bit unsigned integer.
ToChar	Converts the value to an equivalent Unicode character.
ToDateTime	Converts the value to an equivalent DateTime.
ToDecimal	Converts the value to an equivalent Decimal number.
ToDouble	Converts the value to an equivalent double-precision floating-point number.
ToInt16	Converts the value to an equivalent 16-bit signed integer.
ToInt32	Converts the value to an equivalent 32-bit signed integer.
ToInt64	Converts the value to an equivalent 64-bit signed integer.
ToSByte	Converts the specified Boolean value to the equivalent 8-bit signed integer.
ToString	Converts the value to an equivalent string.
ToSingle	Converts the value to an equivalent single-precision floating-point number.
ToUInt16	Converts the specified Boolean value to the equivalent 16-bit unsigned integer.
ToUInt32	Converts the specified Boolean value to the equivalent 32-bit unsigned integer.
ToUInt64	Converts the specified Boolean value to the equivalent 64-bit unsigned integer.

Program 5.10 uses several data conversion methods. C# treats all input data as text (even if they are numeric). The statement `Console.ReadLine()` reads input data. Then it converts the data to the specified data type using a converter method. For example, the statement:

```
age = Convert.ToInt32(Console.ReadLine());
```

reads `age` as text, then converts it to 32 bit integer.

98

Similarly, the statement:

```
grade = Convert.ToChar(Console.ReadLine());
```

reads grade as text, then converts it to character.

Program 5.10

```
using System;
using System.Collections.Generic;
using System.Linq;
using System.Text;
using System.Threading.Tasks;

namespace Built_In_Functions
{
    class ConversionsFunc
    {
        static void Main(string[] args)
        {
            string name;
            int age;
            char grade;
            Console.Write("Enter your name: ");
            name = Console.ReadLine();
            Console.Write("Enter your age: ");
            age = Convert.ToInt32(Console.ReadLine());
            Console.Write("Enter your grade: ");
            grade = Convert.ToChar(Console.ReadLine());
            Console.WriteLine("\nHello {0}, you are {1} years old!
                You scored {2} in your exam.", name, age, grade);
            Console.ReadLine();
        }
    }
}
```

Here is a sample run:

Program 5.11 reads name, price and quantity of item purchased, calculates the amount spent and displays it.

Program 5.11

```
using System;
using System.Collections.Generic;
using System.Linq;
using System.Text;
using System.Threading.Tasks;
```

99

```
namespace Built_In_Functions
{
    class Compute_Amount
    {
        static void Main(string[] args)
        {
            string item;
            int quantity;
            double price, amount;
            Console.Write("Enter item name: ");
            item = Console.ReadLine();
            Console.Write("Enter price: $");
            price = Convert.ToDouble(Console.ReadLine());//convert to Double
            Console.Write("Enter quantity: ");
            quantity = Convert.ToInt32(Console.ReadLine());//convert to Integer
            amount = price * quantity;
            Console.WriteLine("\nItem name: " + item);
            Console.WriteLine("Price: $" + price);
            Console.WriteLine("Quantity: " + quantity);
            Console.WriteLine("Amount: $" + amount);
            Console.ReadLine();
        }
    }
}
```

Here is a sample run:

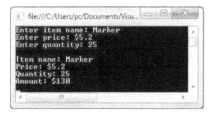

5.6 Character Methods

Character methods tests if a character is a digit, letter, punctuation, etc. C# provides several character methods. A partial list is as follows:

List of character methods

Method	Purpose
MaxValue	Represents the largest possible value of a Char.
MinValue	Represents the smallest possible value of a Char
CompareTo	Compares this instance to a specified object and returns an indication of their relative.
Equals	Returns a value indicating whether this instance is equal to a specified object.
IsControl	Indicates whether a specified Unicode character is categorized as a control character.
IsDigit	Indicates whether a Unicode character is categorized as a decimal digit.
IsLetter	Indicates whether a Unicode character is categorized as an alphabetic letter.
IsLower	Indicates whether a Unicode character is categorized as a lowercase letter.
IsNumber	Indicates whether a Unicode character is categorized as a decimal digit or hexadecimal number.

100

IsPunctuation	Indicates whether a Unicode character is categorized as a punctuation mark.
IsSeparator	Indicates whether a Unicode character is categorized as a separator character.
IsSymbol	Indicates whether a Unicode character is categorized as a symbol character.
IsUpper	Indicates whether a Unicode character is categorized as an uppercase letter.
Parse	Converts the value of the specified string to its equivalent Unicode character.
ToLower	Converts the value of a Unicode character to its lowercase equivalent.
ToString	Converts the value of this instance to its equivalent string representation.
ToUpper	Converts the value of a Unicode character to its uppercase equivalent.

Program 5.12 uses several character methods. Character methods must be prefixed with the class Char. Note that characters are enclosed with single quotes (').

Program 5.12

```
using System;
using System.Collections.Generic;
using System.Linq;
using System.Text;
using System.Threading.Tasks;
namespace Built_In_Functions
{
    class CharFunc
    {
        static void Main(string[] args)
        {
            char chA = 'A';
            char ch1 = '1';
            Console.WriteLine(chA.CompareTo('B'));
            Console.WriteLine(chA.Equals('A'));
            Console.WriteLine(Char.GetNumericValue(ch1));
            Console.WriteLine(Char.IsControl('\t'));
            Console.WriteLine(Char.IsDigit(ch1));
            Console.WriteLine(Char.IsLetter(','));
            Console.WriteLine(Char.IsLower('u'));
            Console.WriteLine(Char.IsNumber(ch1));
            Console.WriteLine(Char.IsSymbol('+'));
            Console.WriteLine(Char.Parse("S"));
            Console.WriteLine(Char.ToLower('M'));
            Console.WriteLine('x'.ToString());
            Console.ReadLine();
        }
    }
}
```

The program produces the following output:

101

Program 5.13 is similar to Program 5.11. It reads a character and checks if the character is an alphabet or digit and displays an appropriate message.

Program 5.13

```
using System;
using System.Collections.Generic;
using System.Linq;
using System.Text;
using System.Threading.Tasks;

namespace Built_In_Functions
{
    class Classifier
    {
        static void Main(string[] args)
        {
            char ch;
            Console.Write("Enter a character: ");
            ch = Convert.ToChar(Console.ReadLine());
            if (Char.IsLetter(ch) && Char.IsLower(ch))
            {
                Console.WriteLine("The character is lowercase alphabet letter");
            }
            else if (Char.IsLetter(ch) && Char.IsUpper(ch))
            {
                Console.WriteLine("The character is uppercase alphabet letter");
            }
            else if (Char.IsDigit(ch))
            {
                Console.WriteLine("The character is a digit");
            }
            else
            {
                Console.WriteLine("The character is not an alphabet or digit");
            }
            Console.ReadLine();
        }
    }
}
```

If you enter 'a', you will get the output:

```
Enter a character: a
The character is a lowercase alphabet letter
```

If you enter 'A', you will get the output:

If you enter 7, you will get the output:

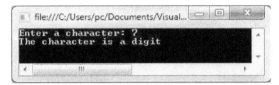

And if you enter any character other than a digit or alphabet, you will get the output:

5.7 Date/Time Methods

C# provides several date/time methods such as for retrieving system date, calculating the difference between two dates, and converting date to text. Here is a partial list.

Date/time methods

Method	Purpose
Date	Gets the date component of this instance.
Day	Gets the day of the month represented by this instance.
DayOfWeek	Gets the day of the week represented by this instance.
DayOfYear	Gets the day of the year represented by this instance.
Hour	Gets the hour component of the date represented by this instance.
Millisecond	Gets the milliseconds component of the date represented by this instance.
Minute	Gets the minute component of the date represented by this instance.
Month	Gets the month component of the date represented by this instance.
Now	Gets a DateTime that is the current local date and time on this computer.
Second	Gets the seconds component of the date represented by this instance.
Year	Gets the year component of the date represented by this instance.
Add	Adds the value of the specified TimeSpan to the value of this instance.
AddDays	Adds the specified number of days to the value of this instance.
AddHours	Adds the specified number of hours to the value of this instance.
AddMilliseconds	Adds the specified number of milliseconds to the value of this instance.
AddMinutes	Adds the specified number of minutes to the value of this instance.

103

The following list gives a partial list of format specifier with examples applied to an arbitrary date value `DateTime.Now`, which exposes the current date and time information.

Format Specifier	Current Culture	Example Output
D	en-US	4/10/2002
D	en-NZ	10/04/2002
D	de-DE	10.04.2002
D	en-US	Tuesday, April 23, 2002

Program 5.14 shows how to set and format the current time. The method `Now` from the class `DateTime` returns the system time.

Program 5.14

```
using System;
using System.Collections.Generic;
using System.Globalization; // Remember to add this namespace
using System.Linq;
using System.Text;
using System.Threading; // Remember to add this namespace
using System.Threading.Tasks;

namespace Built_In_Functions
{
    class DateTimeFunc
    {
        static void Main(string[] args)
        {
            DateTime dt = DateTime.Now;
            // Set the CurrentCulture property to U.S. English.
            Thread.CurrentThread.CurrentCulture = new CultureInfo("en-US");
            // Display dt, formatted using the ShortDatePattern
            // and the CurrentThread.CurrentCulture.
            Console.WriteLine(dt.ToString("d"));
            // Create a CultureInfo object for German in Germany.
            CultureInfo ci = new CultureInfo("de-DE");
            // Display dt, formatted using the ShortDatePattern
            // and the CultureInfo object.
            Console.WriteLine(dt.ToString("d", ci));
            Console.ReadLine();
        }
    }
}
```

Here is the program output:

Program 5.15 displays the current date and the next day's date.

Program 5.15

```
using System;
using System.Collections.Generic;
using System.Globalization;
using System.Linq;
using System.Text;
using System.Threading;
using System.Threading.Tasks;

namespace Built_In_Functions
{
    class DateTimeFunc
    {
        static void Main(string[] args)
        {
            Thread.CurrentThread.CurrentCulture = new CultureInfo("en-US");
            DateTime dt = DateTime.Now;
            Console.WriteLine("Today is {0}", DateTime.Now.ToString("d"));
            // This code increments dt by one day.
            dt = dt.AddDays(1);
            Console.WriteLine("Tomorrow is {0}", dt.ToString("d"));
            Console.ReadLine();
        }
    }
}
```

Here is the program output:

Program 5.16 shows how to format a date.

Program 5.16

```
using System;
using System.Collections.Generic;
using System.Globalization;
using System.Linq;
using System.Text;
using System.Threading;
using System.Threading.Tasks;

namespace Built_In_Functions
{
    class DateTimeFunc
    {
        static void Main(string[] args)
        {
            DateTime dt = DateTime.Now;
            DateTimeFormatInfo dfi = new DateTimeFormatInfo();
            CultureInfo ci = new CultureInfo("de-DE");

            // Make up a new custom DateTime pattern, for demonstration.
```

105

```
dfi.MonthDayPattern = "MM-MMMM, ddd-dddd";
// Use the DateTimeFormat from the culture associated
// with the current thread.
Console.WriteLine(dt.ToString("d"));
Console.WriteLine();
Console.WriteLine(dt.ToString("m"));

// Use the DateTimeFormat from the specific
// culture passed.
Console.WriteLine();
Console.WriteLine(dt.ToString("d", ci));
// Use the settings from the DateTimeFormatInfo
// object passed.
Console.WriteLine();
Console.WriteLine(dt.ToString("m", dfi));

// Reset the current thread to a different culture.
Thread.CurrentThread.CurrentCulture = new CultureInfo("fr-BE");

Console.WriteLine();
Console.WriteLine(dt.ToString("d"));
Console.ReadLine();
        }
    }
}
```

Here is a sample run:

5.8 Format Methods

Format methods convert object values to strings using specified formats. They can also be used to control the appearance of output when sent to the screen or printer. For example, you can use format methods to display a dollar sign, a percent sign, comma, and specify the number of decimal places.

List of format methods

Method	Purpose
Format(IFormatProvider, String, Object)	Replaces the format item or items in a specified string with the string representation of the corresponding object. A parameter supplies culture-specific formatting information.
Format(IFormatProvider, String, Object, Object)	Replaces the format items in a specified string with the string representation of two specified objects. A parameter supplies culture-specific formatting information.
Format(IFormatProvider, String, Object, Object, Object)	Replaces the format items in a specified string with the string representation of three specified objects. An parameter supplies culture-specific formatting information.

106

`Format(IFormatProvider, String, Object[])`	Replaces the format items in a specified string with the string representations of corresponding objects in a specified array. A parameter supplies culture-specific formatting information.
`Format(String, Object)`	Replaces one or more format items in a specified string with the string representation of a specified object.
`Format(String, Object, Object)`	Replaces the format items in a specified string with the string representation of two specified objects.
`Format(String, Object, Object, Object)`	Replaces the format items in a specified string with the string representation of three specified objects.
`Format(String, Object[])`	Replaces the format item in a specified string with the string representation of a corresponding object in a specified array.

Program 5.17 illustrates how to insert a decimal value into a string to display it to user as a single string. Format methods are prefixed with the class string.

Program 5.17

```
using System;
using System.Collections.Generic;
using System.Linq;
using System.Text;
using System.Threading.Tasks;

namespace Format_Method
{
    class Program
    {
        static void Main(string[] args)
        {
            decimal item_price = 25.36m;
            string s;
            s = string.Format("The price is {0} per kilo.", item_price);
            Console.WriteLine(s);
            Console.ReadLine();
        }
    }
}
```

Here is a sample run:

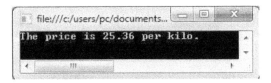

You can also format the value differently as in Program 5.18.

Program 5.18

```
using System;
using System.Collections.Generic;
using System.Linq;
using System.Text;
using System.Threading.Tasks;
```

```
namespace Format_Method
{
    class Program
    {
        static void Main(string[] args)
        {
            decimal item_price = 25.36m;
            string s;
            s = string.Format("The price is ${0:C2} per kilo.", item_price);
            Console.WriteLine(s);
            Console.ReadLine();
        }
    }
}
```

Here is a sample run:

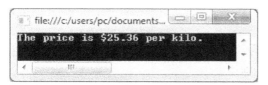

Program 5.19 illustrates how to control alignment and spacing. The placeholder {0} in the format string is a format item. The 0 is the index of the object whose string value will be inserted at that position. Indexes always start at 0. If the object to be inserted is not a string, the `ToString` method will be called to convert it to string before inserting it in the result string.

Program 5.19

```
using System;
using System.Collections.Generic;
using System.Linq;
using System.Text;
using System.Threading.Tasks;

namespace Format_Method
{
    class Program
    {
        static void Main(string[] args)
        {
            string stmt;
            decimal weight = 20.4m;
            stmt = string.Format("The weight is {0}kilo.", weight);
            Console.WriteLine(stmt);
            Console.ReadLine();
        }
    }
}
```

Here is a sample run:

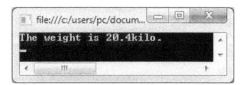

You can have as many format items and as many objects in the object list as your program requires, as long as the index of every format item has a matching object in the object list.

Program 5.20 shows how to use two format items and two objects in the object list.

Program 5.20

```csharp
using System;
using System.Collections.Generic;
using System.Linq;
using System.Text;
using System.Threading.Tasks;

namespace Format_Method
{
    class Program
    {
        static void Main(string[] args)
        {
            string stmt;
            stmt = string.Format("At {0}, the speed is {1}km/h.",
                                    DateTime.Now, 68.5);
            Console.WriteLine(stmt);
            Console.ReadLine();
        }
    }
}
```

Here is a sample run:

You can follow the index in a format item with a format string to control how an object is formatted.

Program 5.21 applies the "D" format string to the first object {0:d} and "t" format string to the second object {0:t} in the object list.

Program 5.21

```csharp
using System;
using System.Collections.Generic;
using System.Linq;
using System.Text;
using System.Threading.Tasks;
```

```
namespace Format_Method
{
    class Program
    {
        static void Main(string[] args)
        {
            string stmt;
            stmt = string.Format("It is now {0:D} at {0:t}", DateTime.Now);
            Console.WriteLine(stmt);
            Console.ReadLine();
        }
    }
}
```

Here is a sample run:

Program 5.22 uses the `Format (String, Object)` method to embed an individual's age in the middle of a string. This example is similar to Program 5.17 except that it uses a loop structure.

Program 5.22

```
using System;
using System.Collections.Generic;
using System.Linq;
using System.Text;
using System.Threading.Tasks;

namespace Format_Method
{
    class Program
    {
        static void Main(string[] args)
        {
            string output;
            int years;
            DateTime birthdate = new DateTime(2002, 7, 28);
            DateTime[] dates = { new DateTime(2016, 8, 16),
                new DateTime(2013, 7, 28), new DateTime(2009, 10, 16),
                new DateTime(2011, 7, 27), new DateTime(2015, 5, 27) };

            foreach (DateTime dateValue in dates)
            {
                TimeSpan interval = dateValue - birthdate;

                // Get approx.number of years, without accounting for leap years.
                years = ((int)interval.TotalDays) / 365;

                // See if adding the number of years exceeds dateValue.
                if (birthdate.AddYears(years) <= dateValue)
                {
                    output = string.Format("You are now {0} years old.", years);
                    Console.WriteLine(output);
                }
```

110

```
            else
            {
                output = string.Format("You are now {0} years
                                old.", years - 1);
                Console.WriteLine(output);
            }
            Console.ReadLine();
        }
    }
}
```

Here is a sample run:

Program 5.23 uses the `Format(String, Object, Object)` method to display time and temperature data stored in a generic `Dictionary <TKey, TValue>` object. Note that the format string has three format items, although there are only two objects to format. This is because the first object in the list (date and time) is used by two format items: The first format item displays the time, and the second displays the date.

Program 5.23

```
using System;
using System.Collections.Generic;
using System.Linq;
using System.Text;
using System.Threading.Tasks;

namespace Format_Method
{
    class Program
    {
        static void Main(string[] args)
        {
            string info;
            Dictionary<DateTime, double> temperature_Info = new
                            Dictionary<DateTime, double>();
            temperature_Info.Add(new DateTime(2016, 8, 1, 14, 0, 0), 72.52);
            temperature_Info.Add(new DateTime(2015, 10, 1, 10, 0, 0), 18.61);
            Console.WriteLine("Temperature Information:\n");

            foreach (var item in temperature_Info)
            {
                info = string.Format("Temperature at {0,8:t} on
                                {0,9:D}: {1,5:N1}°C", item.Key, item.Value);
                Console.WriteLine(info);
            }
            Console.ReadLine();
        }
    }
```

111

```
        }
}
```

Here is a sample run:

All standard numeric format strings except "D" (which is used with integers only), "G", "R", and "X" allow a precision specifier that defines the number of decimal digits in the result string.

Program 5.24 illustrates the use of standard numeric format strings to control the number of decimal digits in the result string.

Program 5.24

```csharp
using System;
using System.Collections.Generic;
using System.Linq;
using System.Text;
using System.Threading.Tasks;

namespace Format_Method
{
    class Program
    {
        static void Main(string[] args)
        {
            string stmt;
            object[] values = { 1303, 1754.67235, 15426.14 };
            foreach (var value in values)
            {
                stmt = string.Format("{0,12:C2}    {0,12:E3}    {0,12:F4}
                                     {0,12:N3}    {1,12:P2}\n", Convert.ToDouble(value),
                          Convert.ToDouble(value) / 10000);
                Console.WriteLine(stmt);
            }
            Console.ReadLine();
        }
    }
}
```

Here is a sample run:

112

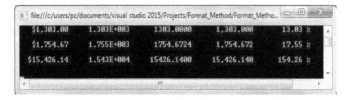

C# doesn't convert an array of integers to an object array; therefore you have to perform the conversion yourself before calling the `Format(String, Object[])` method. Program 5.25 illustrates this.

Program 5.25

```
using System;
using System.Collections.Generic;
using System.Linq;
using System.Text;
using System.Threading.Tasks;

namespace Format_Method
{
    class Program
    {
        static void Main(string[] args)
        {
            int i, total = 0, num;
            Random rnd = new Random();
            int[] numbers = new int[4];
            for ( i = 0; i <= 2; i++)
            {
                num = rnd.Next(100);
                numbers[i] = num;
                total += num;
            }

            numbers[3] = total;
            object[] values = new object[numbers.Length];
            numbers.CopyTo(values, 0);
            Console.WriteLine("{0} + {1} + {2} = {3}", values);
            Console.ReadLine();
        }
    }
}
```

Here is a sample run:

Program 5.26 calculates the areas and circumferences of circles given the radii 5, 4.5, 5.2, 3.1, and 2.5. This example is similar to Program 5.3 except that format method is used to round the output to 4 decimal places.

113

Program 5.26

```
using System;
using System.Collections.Generic;
using System.Linq;
using System.Text;
using System.Threading.Tasks;

namespace Format_Method
{
    class Program
    {
        static void Main(string[] args)
        {
            int i, n = 5;
            double area, radius, circum;
            Console.Write("\t\tThis Program will calculate Area and
                            Circumference of 5 circles");
            Console.WriteLine();
            Console.Write("\n\t\t\tNo.\tRadius\tArea\t\tCircumference");
            Console.WriteLine();
            for (i = 1; i <= n; i++)
            {
                Console.Write("Enter Radius: ");
                radius = Convert.ToDouble(Console.ReadLine());
                area = Math.PI * radius * radius;
                circum = 2 * Math.PI * radius;
                Console.WriteLine("\t\t\t{0}\t{1}\t{2}\t\t{3}", i,
                            radius, string.Format("{0:F4}",area),
                            string.Format("{0:0.0000}",circum));
            }
            Console.ReadLine();
        }
    }
}
```

Here is a sample run:

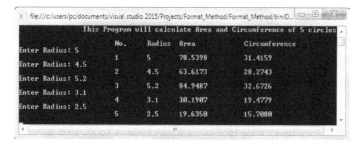

5.9 Sample Programs

Program 5.27 demonstrates several built-in string methods – Length, PadLeft and PadRight. The Length method counts the number of characters in strInput. The PadLeft method right-aligns the characters in strInput, the PadRight method left-aligns the characters in strInput.

114

Program 5.27

```csharp
using System;
using System.Collections.Generic;
using System.Linq;
using System.Text;
using System.Threading.Tasks;

namespace Sample_Programs
{
    class Program
    {
        static void Main(string[] args)
        {
            string strInput, strPadLeft, strPadRight;
            int str;

            Console.Write("Enter a String: ");
            strInput = Console.ReadLine();
            str = strInput.Length;   //calculate length

            //left-aligns the characters
            strPadRight = strInput.PadRight(20, '*');

            //right-aligns the characters
            strPadLeft = strInput.PadLeft(20, '*');

            //print the output
            Console.WriteLine("Length of string is: {0}", str);
            Console.WriteLine("String using PadRight: {0}", strPadRight);

            Console.WriteLine("String using PadLeft : {0}", strPadLeft);

            Console.ReadLine();
        }
    }
}
```

Here is a sample output:

Program 5.28 uses the method Replace() to replace all occurrences of a specified Unicode character or string with another specified Unicode character or string .

Program 5.28

```csharp
using System;
using System.Collections.Generic;
using System.Linq;
using System.Text;
using System.Threading.Tasks;
```

115

```
namespace Sample_Programs
{
    class ReplaceMethod
    {
        static void Main(string[] args)
        {
            string str = "Hello World!";
            string chReplace, strReplace;
            chReplace = str.Replace('o', 'a');
            strReplace = str.Replace("Hello", "My");
            Console.WriteLine("Original string: Hello World\n");
            Console.WriteLine("Replace character 'o' with
                                'a':\n{0}\n", chReplace);
            Console.WriteLine("Replace string \"Hello\" with
                                \"My\":\n{0}\n", strReplace);
            Console.ReadLine();
        }
    }
}
```

Here is the program output:

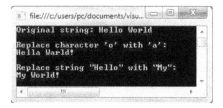

Program 5.29 calculates the average and standard deviation of a set of 20 integer random numbers between 100 and 200.

Program 5.29

```
using System;
using System.Collections.Generic;
using System.Linq;
using System.Text;
using System.Threading.Tasks;

namespace Sample_Programs
{
    // Generates 20 integer random numbers between lo (100)
    // and hi (200), then calculates the average and std dev.

    class RandomMaths
    {
        static void Main(string[] args)
        {
            int hi = 200, lo = 100;
            int rn, n = 20;
            double total = 0.0, sqTotal = 0.0;
            double result = 0.0;
            Random randObj = new Random();// create Random object
            for (int i = 1; i <= n; i++)
            {
                // generate a random number between lo and hi
```

116

```
                rn = randObj.Next(lo, hi);
                Console.Write("{0}   ", rn);
                // skip to next line if more than 5 numbers
                if (i % 5 == 0)
                    Console.WriteLine();
                total += rn;
                sqTotal += rn * rn;
            }
            // calculate the average
            result = total / n;
            Console.WriteLine("\nAverage = {0}", result);
            // calculate the standard deviation
            result = Math.Sqrt(sqTotal / n - result * result);
            Console.WriteLine("Standard deviation = {0}", Math.Round(result, 2));
            Console.ReadLine();
        }
    }
}
```

Here is a sample run:

Program 5.30 illustrates several mathematical methods.

Program 5.30

```
using System;
using System.Collections.Generic;
using System.Linq;
using System.Text;
using System.Threading.Tasks;

namespace Sample_Programs
{
    class MathsFunc
    {
        static void Main(string[] args)
        {
            double x = 0.1;
            double sqrNumber;
            double sinNumber;
            double logNumber;
            Console.Write("x\tSqrt(x)\tSin(x)\tLog10(x)\n");
            while (x < 0.6)
            {
                sqrNumber = Math.Sqrt(x);   //square root function
                sinNumber = Math.Sin(x);    //sine function
                logNumber = Math.Log10(x);  //base 10 logarithm
                                            //print the result
                Console.Write("{0}\t{1}\t{2}\t{3}\n", x,
                Math.Round(sqrNumber, 2), Math.Round(sinNumber, 2),
                Math.Round(logNumber, 2));
```

117

```
                x += 0.1; // x = x + 0.1
            }
            Console.ReadLine();
        }
    }
}
```

Here is the program output:

Program 5.31 generates n (10) unique integer random numbers between lo (1) and hi (20), then sorts and displays the numbers in ascending order of magnitude.

Program 5.31

```
using System;
using System.Collections.Generic;
using System.Linq;
using System.Text;
using System.Threading.Tasks;

namespace Sample_Programs
{
    // generates n (10) unique integer random numbers between
    // lo (1) and hi (20), then sorts and displays the numbers.
    class Technique
    {
        static void Main(string[] args)
        {
            int lo = 1, hi = 20, n = 10, count = 0, rand, temp;
            int[] x = new int[n];
            bool match;
            Random randNumber = new Random();// create a Random object

            do  // generate random numbers
            {
                rand = randNumber.Next(lo, hi);
                match = false;
                for (int i = 0; i < count; i++)
                {
                    if (rand == x[i])
                    {
                        match = true;
                        break;
                    }
                }
                if (!match)
                {
                    x[count] = rand;
                    count += 1;
                }
            } while (count < n);
```

```
// sort the numbers
for (int i = 0; i < n - 1; i++)
{
    for (int j = i + 1; j < n; j++)
    {
        if (x[i] > x[j])
        {
            temp = x[i];
            x[i] = x[j];
            x[j] = temp;
        }
    }
}
// print the sorted numbers
for (int i = 0; i < n; i++)
    Console.Write("{0}  ", x[i]);
Console.ReadLine();
}
}
}
```

Here is a sample run:

Exercise

1. Write a program that calculates the monthly payment of a loan of $3,000 at 5% interest over three years. Use suitable format for your output.

2. Write a program that causes the numeric value in the variable Amount to be displayed as a dollar value.

3. Simulate a table-tennis match between two players, A and B, given that A has a 0.6 chance of winning each point. Simulate 5 games and determine the winner (i.e., the one who wins 3 games first).

4. Generate 200 unique integer random numbers in the range [100, 999]. Then determine:

   (a) How many of these fall in the ranges 100-249, 250-499, 500-749 and 750-999
   (b) How many of these are (a) even numbers and (b) divisible by 5.
   (c) Sort and display the numbers in ascending order of magnitude.

5. Given a string less than 80 characters long, write a program to (a) right-justify, (b) center-justify and (c) count the number of a's and A's.

6. Generate 100 integer random numbers in the range 1 to 100 in array x[10, 10]. Then calculate the sum of all:

   (a) the diagonal elements,

119

(b) the square of the numbers in the even rows (i.e., rows 0, 2, 4, 6, 8),

(c) the square root of the numbers in the odd columns (i.e., columns 1, 3, 5,7, 9).

7. Compute and display x, Sqrt(x), Log10(x) for x = 1, 2, ..., 20.

Chapter 6

Programmer-defined Methods

Learning Outcomes:

After completing this chapter, the student will be able to

- *Explain programmer-defined methods.*
- *Call methods and return values.*
- *Write code for methods.*
- *Call method as statement or expression.*
- *Pass arguments by value, ref (reference) and out (output).*
- *Write recursive methods.*
- *Write code for delegates.*

6.1 Why Programmer-defined Methods?

In the previous chapter, we learned how to use built-in methods (functions) provided by the C# library. The C# library, however, doesn't provide all the methods that we (programmers) need. That means we must write our own methods. This chapter tells how to do this. The methods we write are called **programmer-defined methods**.

Using methods (whether built-in or ours) has many advantages. We can write code once and use it as many times as we want. Using methods also helps us to structure complex programs into manageable chunks in the form of methods. This helps us (and others) to read and understand our code better. It also helps us to debug (remove errors) our program more easily.

6.2 Defining Methods

To use a method you must first define it. The definition takes the form:

```
static method_type method_name(parameter_list)
{
  variable declaration

  return expression
}
```

where:
- `method_type` is any valid data type
- `method_name` is any valid identifier
- `parameter_list` is a list of parameters separated by commas
- `variable declaration` is a list of variables declared within the method
- `return` is a reserved word
- `expression` is the value returned by the method to the calling method

The method_type indicates the *type* of value the method will return. The return value can be any valid data type such as int, double, float, char, etc. If you do not specify the return type, the method will return an integer value by default.

If a method doesn't return any value to the calling method, it is said to be of type void. Since the void type method does not return any value, the expression part in the return statement could be dropped.

The method_name is the name of the method. The parameter-list contains the parameters the method needs for *receiving* input *from* the calling method or for *sending* output *to* the calling method. The parameters must be separated by commas. The parameter type tells what type of type of data the parameter will hold.

The data type of every parameter in the parameter-list must be specified. The parameter-list takes the form:

type var_1, type var_2, ..., type var_n

If a method has no parameters (i.e., when the parameter-list is empty), only the method_name() is written, but the parentheses are still required.

Here are some examples of correct and incorrect method declarations.

```
static float average2(float x, float y)    // correct

static long cube(int i)                     // correct

static char response(char ch)               // correct

static void Main()         // correct; void parameter list

static void main()       //incorrect case; Main, not main

static float average3(float x1, x2, x3)  // incorrect; data type
                                          // missing for x2, x3

static square(int x1, x2; float y1)  // incorrect; has ;
                                      // data type missing for x2

static char convert(char ch, int a, b)    // incorrect;
                                           // data type missing for b
```

Program 6.1 receives two integer values from Main() and returns the larger of the two using the method FindMax(). The access specifier public before FindMax() tells that the method can be accessed from outside the class using a class instance.

Program 6.1

```
using System;
using System.Collections.Generic;
using System.Linq;
using System.Text;
using System.Threading.Tasks;

namespace Function_Example
{
    class Program
    {
        public static int FindMax(int num1, int num2)
        {
```

122

```
        int result; // local variable declaration
        if (num1 > num2)
            result = num1;
        else
            result = num2;

        return result;
    }

    static void Main(string[] args)
    {
        int x = 40, y = 50;
        Console.WriteLine("The larger of the numbers is: {0}",
                                              FindMax(x, y));
        Console.ReadLine();
    }
  }
}
```

The program produces the following output:

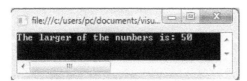

Note:

(1) The methods in a class can appear in any order, but program execution will always start at Main().

(2) The body of each method must be enclosed between a pair of curly braces { }.

(3) A method cannot be defined within another method (i.e., methods cannot be nested). All methods operate at the same level.

(4) The number, type and order of *arguments* in the *calling* method must correspond to the number, type and order of *parameters* in the *called* method.

(5) Sometimes the arguments in the calling method are called *actual parameters* and the parameters in the called method are called *formal parameters*.

6.3 Calling Methods

When a method calls another method, the computer temporarily suspends the current method and branches off to execute the called method. After the called method terminates, program control returns to the calling method as shown in Figure 6.1. The program control flow is as follows:

1) Program starts at Main().
2) Main() calls MyMethod() and passes control to it.
3) MyMethod() executes; upon completion, it passes control back to Main().
4) Main() resumes from where it stopped.

The arrows show the flow of control between `Main()` and `MyMethod()`.

Flow of control between Main() and MyMethod()

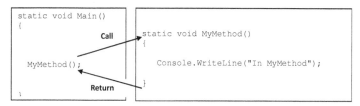

A method call consists of the method name followed by a list of arguments to be passed to the (corresponding) parameters in the called method. The number, type and order of arguments passed must correspond to the number, type and order of parameters in the called method. An argument can be an explicit value, a variable name, an expression, or another method call.

A method can be called in three ways:

1) As a standalone statement as below:

```
method_name(argument list);
```

2) As an expression appearing on the *right-hand side* of the assignment operator (=):

```
variable = method_name(argument list);
```

3) As an expression in a `Write()` or `WriteLine()` statement/method:

```
Console.WriteLine(method_name(argument list));
```

[This is an example of nested methods: the `WriteLine()` method provided by C# contains the programmer-defined method `method_name()`.]

We will discuss each of these in the sequel.

❖ **Method Call as a Statement**

A method call may take the form of a statement. Program 6.2 illustrates method call as a statement. To call `displayWage()` from `Main()`, we use the statement:

```
displayWage(rate1, hours1);
```

This is what happens when `Main()` calls `displayWage()`: `Main()` passes the arguments `rate1` and `hours1` to the corresponding parameters `rate2` and `hours2` in `displayWage()`. The arrows below show the passing of arguments to parameters.

124

Program 6.2

```
using System;
using System.Collections.Generic;
using System.Linq;
using System.Text;
using System.Threading.Tasks;

namespace Function_Example
{
    // Program to illustrate method call as a statement
    class Program
    {
        static void Main(string[] args)
        {
            // rate1 and hours1 are local this method
            double rate1 = 5.00;
            int hours1 = 25;
            displayWage(rate1, hours1);  // call as statement
            Console.ReadLine();
        }

        static void displayWage(double rate2, int hours2)
        {   // rate2 and hours2 are local this method
            Console.WriteLine("Wage earned = ${0}", rate2 *
                                    (Convert.ToDouble(hours2)));
        }
    }
}
```

Here is the program output:

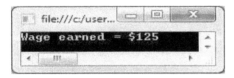

When displayWage() is called, the following actions take place:

1. The values of *arguments* rate1 and hours1 in Main() are passed to the corresponding *parameters* rate2 and hours2 in displayWage().

2. The statements in displayWage() are executed using the parameter values in rate2 and hours2. The method computes and displays the value of the expression rate2*hours2. It does not return any value to Main().

When a calling method passes *copies* of *arguments* to the corresponding *parameters* in a called method, we call this **passing by value**. If the parameters in the called method changes, they will have no effect on the arguments in the calling method. Thus, in our example, changing rate2 or hours2 in displayWage() will not change rate1 or hours1 in Main(). This is because each pair has its own scope: rate1 and hours1 are local to Main() and hence visible only in Main(). Similarly, rate2 and hours2 are local to displayWage() and hence visible only in displayWage(). That is, *arguments* are local the *calling method* while *parameters* are local to the *called method*. That is what *passing by value* means.

125

Note: The *names* of arguments and parameters need not be the same. For example, we could have used the *same* names for both arguments and parameters and the result would be the same. Thus, if we replace rate2 with rate1 and hours2 with hours1 in displayWage() we will have the same result.

In Program 6.3 Main() passes argument n (whose value is entered from the keyboard) to parameter m in RndNumber() which then prints m random numbers.

Program 6.3

```
using System;
using System.Collections.Generic;
using System.Linq;
using System.Text;
using System.Threading.Tasks;

namespace Function_Example
{
    // Program to illustrate method call as a statement
    class Program
    {
        static void Main(string[] args)
        {
            int n;
            Console.Write("How many number do you want to generate? ");

            n = Convert.ToInt32(Console.ReadLine());
            RndNumber(n); //call the function
            Console.ReadLine();
        }

        static void RndNumber(int m)
        {
            int i, x;
            Random rndObj = new Random();
            for (i = 1; i <=m; i++)
            {
                x = rndObj.Next();
                Console.Write("\n{0}", x);
            }
        }
    }
}
```

If you enter 10 the program will produce the output:

The called method may be defined anywhere in the class – before or after Main(). The order is not important. In Program 6.4, the called method is defined before Main(). The output is the same as that of Program 6.2.

Program 6.4

```
using System;
using System.Collections.Generic;
using System.Linq;
using System.Text;
using System.Threading.Tasks;

namespace Function_Example
{
    // Program to illustrate method call as a statement
    class Program
    {
        static void displayWage(double rate2, int hours2)
        {
            Console.WriteLine("Wage earned = ${0}", rate2 *
                                    (Convert.ToDouble(hours2)));
            Console.ReadLine();
        }
        static void Main(string[] args)
        {
            double rate1 = 5.00;
            int hours1 = 25;
            displayWage(rate1, hours1);
        }
    }
}
```

The keyword void prefixed to a method tells that it does not return any value to the calling method. If the called method does not return any value, the expression part in the return statement or even the entire return statement can be dropped.

Note: It is not always necessary for a calling program to pass arguments to a called method program. For example, in Program 6.5, Main() calls StudentDetails() to display student information but it doesn't pass any value.

Program 6.5

```
using System;
using System.Collections.Generic;
using System.Linq;
using System.Text;
using System.Threading.Tasks;

namespace Function_Example
{
    // Program to illustrate method call as a statement
    class Program
    {
        static void StudentDetails()
        {
            string name = "Munir", program="IT",
                        phone="08011112222",gender="Male";
            int age = 27;
            Console.WriteLine("Name: {0}\nProgram: {1}\nGender:
                {2}\nPhone: {3}\nAge: {4}", name,program,gender,phone,age);
```

127

```
        }
        static void Main(string[] args)
        {
            StudentDetails();
            Console.ReadLine();
        }
    }
}
```

The program produces the output:

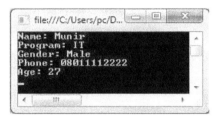

❖ **Method Call as an Expression**

Here, the method is called within an expression (appearing on the right-hand side of the assignment operator =). Program 6.6 illustrates this.

Program 6.6

```
using System;
using System.Collections.Generic;
using System.Linq;
using System.Text;
using System.Threading.Tasks;

namespace Function_Example
{
    // Illustrates method call as an expression
    class SquareMethod
    {
        static void Main(string[] args)
        {
            int xsq, x = 10;

            Console.WriteLine("x = {0}", x);
            xsq = square(x);    // call as expression
            Console.WriteLine("Square of x = {0}", xsq);
            Console.ReadLine();
        }

        static int square(int y)
        {
            y = y * y;
            return y;
        }
    }
}
```

128

The program produces the output:

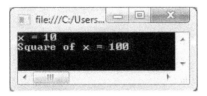

In Program 6.6, the value 10 is passed to the parameter y in the square() method. When the statement y = y * y; is executed, the value of y changes to 100, which is then returned to Main(). The value of x(10) remains unchanged since only a copy of x is passed to y.

Note: In Program 6.6, square() is declared as type int because it returns an integer value to Main().

You can also call a method using an *instance* of a class. Program 6.7 illustrates this. This example is similar to program 5.1 except that we are calling the method through an instance of the class.

Program 6.7

```
using System;
using System.Collections.Generic;
using System.Linq;
using System.Text;
using System.Threading.Tasks;

namespace Function_Example
{
    // Illustrates method call as an expression
    class GetBiggerNum
    {
        static void Main(string[] args)
        {
            // local variable declaration
            int x = 50, y = 94, result;

            GetBiggerNum gn = new GetBiggerNum(); // class instance

            result = gn.FindMax(x, y); //calling FindMax method
            Console.WriteLine("Max value is : {0}", result);
            Console.ReadLine();
        }

        public int FindMax(int num1, int num2)
        {
            int ans; // local variable declaration
            ans = Math.Max(num1, num2);
            return ans;
        }
    }
}
```

The program produces the following output:

129

You can also call a `public` method from another class by using a class instance. Program 6.8 illustrates this. The `Main()` method creates an instance of the class `GetBiggerNum`. Then it calls the method `FindMax()`. Here called method is attached to an *instance* of the class, not to the class itself.

Program 6.8

```
using System;
using System.Collections.Generic;
using System.Linq;
using System.Text;
using System.Threading.Tasks;

namespace Function_Example  // Illustrates method call as expression
{
    class Program
    {
        static void Main(string[] args)
        {
            // local variable declaration
            int x = 800, y = 500, result;
            GetBiggerNum gn = new GetBiggerNum(); //create class instance

            result = gn.FindMax(x, y); //calling the FindMax method
            Console.WriteLine("Max value is : {0}", result);
            Console.ReadLine();
        }
    }

    class GetBiggerNum
    {
        public int FindMax(int num1, int num2)
        {
            // local variable declaration
            int ans;
            ans = Math.Max(num1, num2);
            return ans;
        }
    }
```

The program produces the following output:

130

A method call can appear within a `Write/WriteLine` statement. For example, in Program 6.6, we could drop the statement

```
xsq = square(x);
```

and call the method directly from within the `WriteLine` as follows:

```
Console.WriteLine("Square of x = {0}", square(x));
```

Similarly, in Program 6.7, we could drop the statement

```
result = gn.FindMax(x, y);
```

and call the method directly as follows:

```
Console.WriteLine("Max value is : {0}", gn.FindMax(x, y));
```

6.4 Passing Arguments to Methods

A method can pass arguments to the corresponding parameters in another method (within its scope). The *called* method receives these arguments in its parameters and performs the desired calculation. The *number, type and order of arguments* passed must correspond to the *number, type and order of parameters* in the called method. Otherwise, there will be errors.

In C#, the calling method can pass arguments to the parameters in the called method in three ways:

- **by value**
- **by ref** (short for **reference**)
- **by out** (short for **output**)

❖ **Passing arguments by value**

When an argument is passed by value, only a *copy* of the argument is passed to the parameter in the called method. If the called method changes the parameter value, it will have no effect on the argument in the calling method. This is because the parameter is *local* to the called method. It is not visible to the calling method. Program 6.9 illustrates this.

Program 6.9

```
using System;
using System.Collections.Generic;
using System.Linq;
using System.Text;
using System.Threading.Tasks;

namespace Function_Example
{
    class CallByValue
    {
        static void Main(string[] args)
        {
            int x = 12;
            Print(x);
            Console.WriteLine("Value of x in Main() = " + x);
```

131

```
                .ReadLine();
    }

    static void Print(int x)
    {
        x = 2 * x;    // this x's scope is local
                .WriteLine("Value of x in Print() = " + x);
    }
  }
}
```

The program produces the following output:

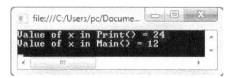

Program 6.10 swaps two integer values using the swap () method.

Program 6.10

```
using System;
using System.Collections.Generic;
using System.Linq;
using System.Text;
using System.Threading.Tasks;

namespace Function_Example
{
    class PrimaryValue
    {
        static void Main(string[] args)
        {
            //variable declaration
            int a = 100, b = 200;
                .WriteLine("Before swap, value of a : {0}", a);
                .WriteLine("Before swap, value of b : {0}", b);
            swap(a, b); // calling a function to swap the values
                .WriteLine("\nAfter swap, value of a : {0}", a);
                .WriteLine("After swap, value of b : {0}", b);
                .ReadLine();
        }

        static void swap(int x, int y)
        {
            int temp;
            temp = x; // save the value of x
            x = y;    // put y into x
            y = temp; // put temp into y
        }
    }
}
```

The program produces the following output:

132

Note that the arguments in the calling method had not changed even though the value of parameters in the called method had changed.

Program 6.11 simulates the sum of points on a pair of dice and asks the user to guess the sum. It uses the method genNum() to generate a random number for sum. If the user guesses it correctly, it displays the message "Good guess - Congratulations!" or the message "Bad guess - Try again" if the guess is wrong. The program terminates when the user makes a correct guess within a maximum of 5 attempts.

Program 6.11

```
using System;
using System.Collections.Generic;
using System.Linq;
using System.Text;
using System.Threading.Tasks;

namespace Function_Example
{
    class CallByValue
    {
        static void Main(string[] args)
        {
            int x, low = 2, high = 12, k, i, n = 5;
            for (i = 1; i <= n; i++)
            {
                Console.Write("Guess a number between 2 and 12 please! ");
                k = Convert.ToInt32(Console.ReadLine());
                x = genNum(low, high);
                if (k == x)
                {
                    Console.WriteLine("Good Guess Congratulation!");
                    break;
                }
                else
                {
                    Console.WriteLine("Try Again!");
                }
            }
            Console.ReadLine();
        }

        static int genNum(int x, int y)
        {
            int z;
            Random rdObj = new Random();
            z = rdObj.Next(x, y);
            return z;
        }
    }
}
```

The program produces the following output:

Program 6.12 uses two methods - `area1()` and `circum1()` - to calculate the area and circumference of circles for different values for radii: 7.5,7,12, 7.7, 23.5. The output is rounded to 4 decimal places.

Program 6.12

```csharp
using System;
using System.Collections.Generic;
using System.Linq;
using System.Text;
using System.Threading.Tasks;

namespace Function_Example
{
    class CalculateValue
    {
        static void Main(string[] args)
        {
            int i, n = 5 ;
            double radius, area, circumference;
            Console.Write("\t\t\tNo.\tRadius\tArea\t\tCircumference");
            Console.WriteLine();

            for (i = 1; i <= n; i++)
            {
                Console.Write("Enter Radius: ");
                radius = Convert.ToDouble(Console.ReadLine());
                area = area1(radius);
                circumference = circum1(radius);
                Console.WriteLine("\t\t\t{0}\t{1}\t{2}\t{3}", i, radius,
            string.Format("{0:F4}", area), string.Format("{0:F4}", circumference));
            }
            Console.ReadLine();
        }

        static double area1(double radius)
        {
            return Math.PI * radius * radius;
        }

        static double circum1(double radius)
        {
            return 2 * Math.PI * radius;
        }
    }
}
```

134

The program produces the following output:

	No.	Radius	Area	Circumference
Enter Radius: 7.5				
	1	7.5	176.7146	47.1239
Enter Radius: 7				
	2	7	153.9380	43.9823
Enter Radius: 12				
	3	12	452.3893	75.3982
Enter Radius: 7.7				
	4	7.7	186.2650	48.3805
Enter Radius: 23.5				
	5	23.5	1734.9445	147.6549

❖ **Passing arguments by ref (reference)**

When you pass arguments by `ref`, the parameters in the called method uses the *same* memory locations as the arguments in the calling method. There are no separate copies for parameters. That means if we make any changes to the parameters the arguments will also change. Program 6.13 illustrates this.

Note: (a) the arguments passed must have some values and (b) the keyword `ref` must appear in both places.

Program 6.13

```
using System;
using System.Collections.Generic;
using System.Linq;
using System.Text;
using System.Threading.Tasks;

namespace Function_Example
{
    class CallByRef
    {
        static void Main(string[] args)
        {
            int x = 12;
            Console.WriteLine("Value of x in Main() before call = "+ x);
            Show(ref x); // call by reference
            Console.WriteLine("Value of x in Main() after call = " + x);
            Console.ReadLine();
        }

        static void Show(ref int x)
        {
            x = 2 * x;
            Console.WriteLine("Value of x in Show = " + x);
        }
    }
}
```

The program produces the following output:

135

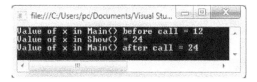

Program 6.14 illustrates this.

Program 6.14

```
using System;
using System.Collections.Generic;
using System.Linq;
using System.Text;
using System.Threading.Tasks;

namespace Function_Example
{
    class CallByRef
    {
        static void Main(string[] args)
        {
            int a = 100, b = 200; //variable declaration

            Console.WriteLine("Before swap, value of a : {0}", a);
            Console.WriteLine("Before swap, value of b : {0}", b);

            swap(ref a, ref b); //calling function to swap values

            Console.WriteLine("\nAfter swap, value of a : {0}", a);
            Console.WriteLine("After swap, value of b : {0}", b);
            Console.ReadLine();
        }
        static void swap(ref int x, ref int y)
        {
            int temp;
            temp = x; // save the value of x
            x = y;    // put y into x
            y = temp; // put temp into y
        }
    }
}
```

The program produces the following output:

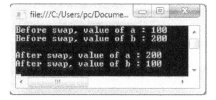

Note that changing the values inside `swap()` also changes the values in `Main()`.

❖ Passing arguments by out (output)

When we pass arguments by out, the arguments need not have any assigned values. Our purpose here is to *receive* output from the called method. Output parameters are similar to reference parameters, except that they transfer data *out* of a method rather than *into* it. Program 6.15 illustrates passing value by out.

Program 6.15

```
using System;
using System.Collections.Generic;
using System.Linq;
using System.Text;
using System.Threading.Tasks;

namespace Function_Example
{
    class CallByOut
    {
        static void Main(string[] args)
        {
            int x;
            Show7(out x);
            Console.WriteLine("Value of x in Main() after call = " + x);
            Console.ReadLine();
        }

        static void Show7(out int x)
        {
            x = 7;
            Console.WriteLine("Value of x in Show7() = " + x);
        }
    }
}
```

Here is the program output:

Output parameters have no assigned values. They are useful when you want a method to return more than one value unlike the `return` statement which returns only one value. Program 6.16 illustrates this.

Program 6.16

```
using System;
using System.Collections.Generic;
using System.Linq;
using System.Text;
using System.Threading.Tasks;

namespace Function_Example
{
    class CallByOut
    {
        static void Main(string[] args)
```

137

```
    {
        int a, b; // variable declaration
        getValues(out a, out b); // calling a function to get the values
        Console.WriteLine("\nAfter method call, value of a: {0}", a);
        Console.WriteLine("After method call, value of b: {0}", b);
        Console.ReadLine();
    }

    static void getValues(out int x, out int y)
    {
        Console.Write("Enter the first integer value: ");
        x = Convert.ToInt32(Console.ReadLine());
        Console.Write("Enter the second integer value: ");
        y = Convert.ToInt32(Console.ReadLine());
    }
  }
}
```

Here is the program output:

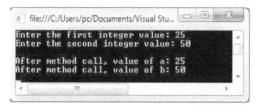

Mixing Arguments/Parameters

You can mix the argument/parameter types in a method call. For example, to calculate the area and circumference of a circle, you can call `radius` by value, and `area` and `circumference` by `out` as Program 6.17 illustrates.

Program 6.17

```
using System;
using System.Collections.Generic;
using System.Linq;
using System.Text;
using System.Threading.Tasks;

namespace Function_Example
{
    class Mixed
    {
        static void Main(string[] args)
        {
            double radius = 7, circum, area;
            Circle(radius, out circum, out area);
            Console.WriteLine("Area = " + area);
            Console.WriteLine("Circumference = " + circum);
            Console.ReadLine();
        }
```

138

```
static void Circle(double radius, out double circum, out double area)
    {
        area = 3.14 * radius * radius;
        circum = 2 * 3.14 * radius;
    }
    }
}
```

Here is program output:

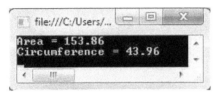

6.5 Method Types & Return Values

In addition to returning by output and reference, you can also return a single value using the `return` statement. In this case, the method type and value returned must be of the same data type (e.g. `int`, `double`). That means, a method of type `double` must return a `double` value; a method of type `string` must return a string value; a method of type `void` doesn't return any value.

The `return` statement in the called method takes the form:

```
return expression;
```

In the case of `void` type methods, the `expression` part or even the entire statement can be dropped.

Program 6.18 illustrates the use of `return` statement.

Program 6.18

```
using System;
using System.Collections.Generic;
using System.Linq;
using System.Text;
using System.Threading.Tasks;

namespace Function_Example
{
    class ChangeCase
    {
        static void Main(string[] args)
        {
            string x, change;
            Console.Write("Please enter a lower-case sentence: ");
            x = Console.ReadLine();
            change = upper(x);    // x is a string
            Console.WriteLine("\nThe upper-case equivalent is: {0}", change);
            Console.ReadLine();
        }
```

```
        static string upper(string y)
        {
            y = y.ToUpper();
            return y;   // y must be a string
        }
    }
}
```

Here is a sample run:

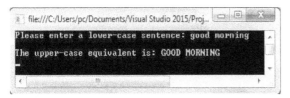

Program 6.19 illustrates the void type method. It does not return any value.

Program 6.19

```
using System;
using System.Collections.Generic;
using System.Linq;
using System.Text;
using System.Threading.Tasks;

namespace Function_Example
{
    class Compute
    {
        static void Main(string[] args)
        {
            int a = 2, b = 3;
            sum(a, b);
            Console.ReadLine();
        }

        static void sum(int x, int y)
        {
            Console.WriteLine("Sum = {0}", x + y);
            // no return statement
        }
    }
}
```

Here is the program output:

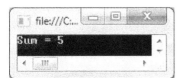

140

6.6 Recursive Methods

A **recursive** method is one that calls itself. To illustrate, consider the factorial of a natural number, which is given by

```
factorial(n)  = 1                    for n = 0
              = n * factorial(n-1)   for n > 0
```

If n=0, the value of factorial(n)=1. This is the *anchor* condition for the method. In recursion, you must always have an anchor, otherwise the method would not terminate. If n>0, the method calls itself recursively.

Program 6.20 computes the factorial of n recursively.

Program 6.20

```
using System;
using System.Collections.Generic;
using System.Linq;
using System.Text;
using System.Threading.Tasks;

namespace Function_Example
{
    // Factorial(n) computation using recursion

    class Factorial
    {
        static void Main(string[] args)
        {
            long fact;
            int n;
            Console.Write("Enter number: ");
            n = Convert.ToInt32(Console.ReadLine());
            fact = factorial(n);
            Console.WriteLine("The factorial of {0} = {1}", n, fact);
            Console.ReadLine();
        }

        static long factorial(int x)
        {
            if (x < 1)
                return 1;
            else
                return (x * factorial(x - 1));
        }
    }
}
```

Here is a sample run:

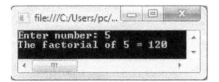

```
file:///C:/Users/pc/...
Enter number: 5
The factorial of 5 = 120
```

141

The *fibonacci sequence* 1, 1, 2, 3, 5, 8, 13, 21, ... where each number after the first two is the sum of the two preceding numbers can also be generated using recursion. Program 6.21 uses a recursive method to generate the fibonacci sequence up to n.

Program 6.21

```
using System;
using System.Collections.Generic;
using System.Linq;
using System.Text;
using System.Threading.Tasks;

namespace Function_Example
{
    // Fibonacci sequence using recursion
    class Fibonacci
    {
        static void Main(string[] args)
        {
            int fact;
            int n;
            Console.Write("Enter n for fibonacci sequence: ");
            n = Convert.ToInt32(Console.ReadLine());
            fact = fibonacci(n);
            Console.WriteLine("\nFibonacci({0}) = {1}", n, fact);
            Console.ReadLine();
        }

        static int fibonacci(int x)
        {
            int fn;
            if ((x == 0) || (x == 1))
                return 1;
            else
            {
                fn = fibonacci(x - 1) + fibonacci(x - 2);
                return fn;
            }
        }
    }
}
```

Here is a sample output:

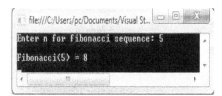

Why do we need recursion? For example, we could compute the factorial of a number without using recursion just as easily as in Program 6.22.

142

Program 6.22

```
using System;
using System.Collections.Generic;
using System.Linq;
using System.Text;
using System.Threading.Tasks;

namespace Function_Example
{
    // Factorial(n) computation without using recursion
    class WithoutRecursion
    {
        static void Main(string[] args)
        {
            long fact;
            int n;
            Console.Write("Enter a small integer: ");
            n = Convert.ToInt32(Console.ReadLine());
            fact = factorial(n);
            Console.WriteLine("\nFactorial({0}) = {1}", n, fact);
            Console.ReadLine();
        }

        static long factorial(int x)
        {
            long fact = x;
            for (int i = x - 1; i > 1; i--)
                fact = fact * i;
            return fact;
        }
    }
}
```

Here is a sample output:

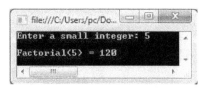

While it is possible to write programs without using recursion, some programs are most easily written easily using recursion, for example, the **Hanoi tower game** problem.

The Hanoi Tower Game

In this game, there are three pegs L, W and R (for Left, Work and Right) and a set of disks of varying sizes. Initially, all the disks are in peg L, and they are arranged from the biggest at the bottom to the smallest at the top (as shown in figure below). The task is to transfer the disks, one by one, from peg L to peg R using the work peg W given the rule that at any instant the disks at each peg must always be arranged from the biggest at the bottom to the smallest at the top.

The Hanoi tower

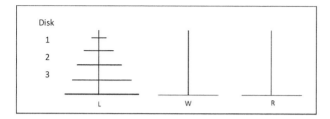

Without using recursion, writing code to solve this problem is not easy. But with recursion, it is rather easy. Program 6.23 uses a recursive method to solve the Hanoi Tower Game Problem. The algorithm for moving n disks from L to R, using W works as follows:

1. If n=1, move the single disk from L to R and stop.
2. Move the top n-1 disks from L to W, using R as work.
3. Move the remaining disk from L to R.
4. Move the n-1 disks from W to R, using L as work.

Program 6.23

```
using System;
using System.Collections.Generic;
using System.Linq;
using System.Text;
using System.Threading.Tasks;

namespace Function_Example
{
    class Hanoi
    {
        public void transfer(int n, char from, char to, char work)
        {
            if (n == 1)
            {
                Console.WriteLine("Move disk 1 from peg {0} to peg
                                  {1}", from, to);
            }
            else
            {
                // move n-1 disks from source to work
                transfer(n - 1, from, work, to);
                Console.WriteLine("Move disk {0} from peg {1} to peg
                                  {2}", n, from, to);
                //move n-1 disks from work to destination
                transfer(n - 1, work, to, from);
            }
        }

        static void Main(string[] args)
        {
            int n;
            Console.Write("Enter number of disks: ");
            n = Convert.ToInt32(Console.ReadLine());
```

144

```
        Hanoi h = new Hanoi();
        if (n > 0)
            h.transfer(n, 'L', 'R', 'W');
        Console.ReadLine();
    }
  }
}
```

Here is a sample output:

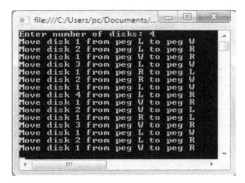

6.7 Delegates

A **delegate** is a type that enables you to store references to functions (methods). It is similar to the function pointer in C/C++. Its declaration takes the form of a function but it has no function body. To use a delegate, you prefix it with the keyword delegate as follows:

```
access_modifier type delegate_name(parameter_list);
```

where:

- access_modifier is the scope of the delegate (e.g., public)
- type is the return type (e.g., double)
- delegate_name is the name of the delegate
- parameter_list is the list of parameters

Once the delegate is declared, you can declare variables of that type and initialize them to reference any function that has the same signature as the delegate. Then you can call the function by using the delegate variable as if it was a function.

Delegates are used widely for handling events in Windows applications. Delegates can be single-cast or multi-cast. A **single-cast delegate** calls a single method when it is invoked (called) and may return a value. A **multi-cast delegate** calls more than one method when it is invoked. In this case, the methods are called in order every time it is invoked. A multicast delegate may not return any value.

Program 6.24 uses a delegate to call add() or multiply() depending on what the user selects.

145

Program 6.24

```
using System;
using System.Collections.Generic;
using System.Linq;
using System.Text;
using System.Threading.Tasks;

namespace Function_Example
{
    class UseDelegate
    {
        delegate int tads(int x, int y);

        static int add(int x, int y)
        {
            return x + y;
        }

        static int multiply(int x, int y)
        {
            return x * y;
        }

        static void Main(string[] args)
        {
            tads dg;
            int x, y;
            string input;
            Console.Write("Enter first integer number: ");
            x = Convert.ToInt32(Console.ReadLine());
            Console.Write("Enter second integer number: ");
            y = Convert.ToInt32(Console.ReadLine());
            Console.WriteLine("Enter A to add and M to multiply");
            input = Console.ReadLine();
            if (input.ToUpper() == "A")
                dg = new tads(add);
            else
                dg = new tads(multiply);
            Console.WriteLine("Answer = {0}", dg(x, y));
            Console.ReadLine();
        }
    }
}
```

Here is a sample run:

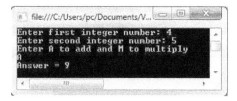

Program 6.25 uses delegate to call and calculate the area of a rectangle() or triangle().

Program 6.25

```
using System;
using System.Collections.Generic;
using System.Linq;
using System.Text;
using System.Threading.Tasks;

namespace Delegate_Example
{
    delegate double area(double x, double y);

    class clsDelegate
    {
        static double rectangle(double length, double width)
        {
            return length * width;
        }

        static double triangle(double bas, double height)
        {
            return 0.5 * bas * height;
        }

        static void Main(string[] args)
        {
            double rec, tri;
            area a;

            a = new area(rectangle);
            rec = a(5.0, 7.0);
            Console.WriteLine("Area of rectangle = {0}", rec);

            a = new area(triangle);
            tri = a(5.0, 4.0);
            Console.WriteLine("Area of triangle = {0}", tri);
            Console.ReadLine();
        }
    }
}
```

Here is the program output:

Program 6.26 demonstrates the declaration, instantiation and use of delegates to reference methods that takes an integer parameter and returns an integer value.

Program 6.26

```
using System;
using System.Collections.Generic;
using System.Linq;
using System.Text;
```

```
using System.Threading.Tasks;

delegate int NumberChanger(int n);

namespace Delegate_Example
{
    class TestDelegate
    {
        static int num = 10;
        public static int AddNum(int p)
        {
            num += p;
            return num;
        }

        public static int MultNum(int q)
        {
            num *= q;
            return num;
        }
        public static int getNum()
        {
            return num;
        }

        static void Main(string[] args)
        {
            //create delegate instances
            NumberChanger nc1 = new NumberChanger(AddNum);
            NumberChanger nc2 = new NumberChanger(MultNum);

            //calling the methods using the delegate objects
            nc1(25);
            Console.WriteLine("Value of Num: {0}", getNum());
            nc2(5);
            Console.WriteLine("Value of Num: {0}", getNum());
            Console.ReadLine();
        }
    }
}
```

Here is the program output:

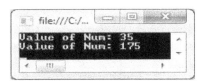

Multicast Delegates

Delegate objects can be composed using the "+" operator. A composed delegate calls delegates that it was composed from. Only delegates of the same type can be composed. The "-" operator can be used to remove a delegate from a composed delegate.

By using this property you can create an invocation list to call methods when a delegate is invoked. This is called multicasting a delegate. Program 6.27 illustrates this.

148

Program 6.27

```csharp
using System;
using System.Collections.Generic;
using System.Linq;
using System.Text;
using System.Threading.Tasks;

delegate int NumberChanger(int n);

namespace Delegate_Example
{
    class TestDelegate
    {
        static int num = 10;
        public static int AddNum(int p)
        {
            num += p;
            return num;
        }

        public static int MultNum(int q)
        {
            num *= q;
            return num;
        }

        public static int getNum()
        {
            return num;
        }

        static void Main(string[] args)
        {
            //create delegate instances
            NumberChanger nc;
            NumberChanger nc1 = new NumberChanger(AddNum);
            NumberChanger nc2 = new NumberChanger(MultNum);
            nc = nc1;
            nc += nc2;

            //calling multicast
            nc(5);
            Console.WriteLine("Value of Num: {0}", getNum());
            Console.ReadLine();
        }
    }
}
```

Here is the program output:

149

Exercise

1. Given an array of integers. Write a method to compute the minimum and maximum.

2. Given an array and its size, write a method that computes the average and standard deviation of the elements in the array.

3. Given the principal, interest rate and number of years, calculate the interest.

4. Given the radius of a circle, write methods to calculate its area and circumference.

5. Given the coordinates of a triangle ((x1, y1), (x2, y2), (x3, y3)), write a method to compute its area. (Hint: Area = x1*y2 + x2*y3 + x3*y1 - y1*x2 - y2*x3 - y3*x1)

6. Given a sentence, write a method to remove all the embedded blank spaces.

7. Write a method to simulate a table-tennis game where one player has a 70 percent chance of winning each point.

8. Give an example of a method call by mixing value, reference and output parameters.

9. Write a program using a delegate with two functions that will return the maximum and minimum of two integer numbers.

Chapter 7

Arrays

Learning Outcomes:

After completing this chapter, you will be able to

- *Explain the purpose of arrays*
- *Work with one and two-dimensional arrays*
- *Work with jagged arrays.*
- *Use collections.*
- *Write simple programs using arrays.*

7.1 Why Arrays?

In the previous chapters, we used variables to store single data items. But in many applications we need to store and process a set of related data items, such as marks obtained by students or a list of contacts. This is where array comes in.

An array is a collection of memory locations to store related data items. All the items in the array are referenced by a common name and a subscript/index is used to reference each item in the array. For example, you can declare an array called `mark` to store the marks obtained by students in a course and use a subscript, say i, to specify the mark of the i-th student in the array by `mark[i]`. By changing the value of i, you can access any or all the items in the array.

7.2 One-Dimensional Arrays

An array with one subscript is called a one-dimensional array. It is declared as follows:

```
type[] var_name = new type[size];
```

where:
- `type` refers to the base type (`int`, `char`, `float`, etc.) of the array, which is the type of each element in the array.
- `[]` indicates that it is an array variable.
- `var_name` specifies the name of the array.
- `[size]` refers to the size of the array, i.e., the number of items it will hold.

Here are some examples of one-dimensional array declarations.

```
int[] mark = new int[30];        // mark can hold 30 integers
double[] x = new double[50];     // x can hold 50 doubles
char[] ch = new char[20];        // ch can hold 20 characters
string[] name = new string[10];  // name can hold 10 strings
```

The subscript/index of an array always starts from 0 and ends with `size-1`. It is enclosed between a pair of square brackets (`[]`). The first statement above tells that `mark` is as an integer array of `size` 30. The individual elements of the array are `mark[0]`, `mark[1]`,..., `mark[29]`.

Initializing Arrays

There are at least three methods of declaring and initialing arrays:

First Method

We have seen one method in the above statements. When an object is created using the keyword `new`, the system automatically initializes all numeric variables to 0, character and string variables to `null`, and Boolean variables to `false`. The statement below illustrates this.

```
float[] height = new float[5];
```

Internally, it looks something like this:

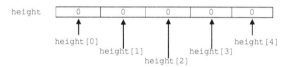

Second Method

Another way is by declaring and initializing the array as in the statement below:

```
int[] myArray = {1, 2, 3, 4, 5};
```

Internally, it looks something like this:

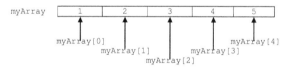

This form does not use the keyword `new`. The array name is `myArray` which is of type `int`. The square brackets `[]` indicate that it is an array variable. The initial values of the array are literals enclosed between a pair of curly braces (`{}`). The system automatically figures out the size of the array (in this case 5).

Third Method

This form combines the previous two as in the following statement:

```
int[] myArray = new int[5] {1, 2, 3, 4, 5};
```

Note that the size of the array must match the number of the elements in the array. Here are some examples of array initialization.

```
int[] id = {1, 2, 3, 4, 5, 6, 7};
float[] x = new float[5] {5.5, 4.4, 3.3, 2,2, 1.1};
```

152

```
char[] vowel = {'a', 'e', 'i', 'o', 'u'};
string[] city = {"Kuala Lumpur", "Tokyo", "Singapore", "Paris", "London",
                 "Bangkok"};
```

The first statement declares id as an array of type int and assigns the values 1, 2, ..., 7 to id[0], id[1], ..., id[6].

The second statement declares x as an array of type float and assigns the values 5.5 to x[0], 4.4 to x[2], ..., 1.1 to x[4].

The third statement assigns characters a, e, etc. to vowel[0], vowel[1], etc. respectively. Characters are enclosed between a pair of single quotes (').

The fourth statement is similar to the third. Strings are enclosed between a pair of double quotes (").

Accessing array elements

We will give some examples on how to declare and access arrays elements.

Program 7.1 declares and initializes the integer array variable number. It uses a for loop with index i to access the array elements and compute and store the total in variable total. Not that the loop index i runs from 0 to 4 (not from 1 to 5).

Program 7.1

```
using System;
using System.Collections.Generic;
using System.Linq;
using System.Text;
using System.Threading.Tasks;

namespace Arrays
{
    class Total
    {
        static void Main(string[] args)
        {
            int[] number = { 9, 6, 20, 5, 12 };
            int sum = 0;
            for (int i = 0; i < 5; i++)
                sum += number[i];   // accumulate the total
            Console.WriteLine("Total = {0}", sum);
            Console.ReadLine();
        }
    }
}
```

Here is the program output:

Note: You will normally use the for loop to access every element of an array.

153

Program 7.2 performs the same task as Program 7.1, but using a function. The Main() function passes the array y to function get_Total() which then computes and returns the total (total).

Program 7.2

```
using System;
using System.Collections.Generic;
using System.Linq;
using System.Text;
using System.Threading.Tasks;

namespace Arrays
{
    class Total
    {
        static void Main(string[] args)
        {
            int total;
            int[] y = { 9, 6, 20, 5, 12 };
            total = getTotal(y);
            Console.WriteLine("Total = {0}", total);
            Console.ReadLine();
        }

        static int getTotal(int[] intArray)
        {
            int sum = 0;
            for (int i = 0; i < 5; i++)
                sum += intArray[i];
            return sum;
        }
    }
}
```

Here is the program output:

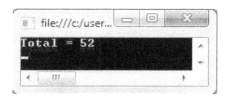

Program 7.3 uses a function to display elements of an array. The Main() function passes the array weekdays to the function DisplayDays() which then display the days of the week.

Program 7.3

```
using System;
using System.Collections.Generic;
using System.Linq;
using System.Text;
using System.Threading.Tasks;

namespace Array
{
    class Display
```

154

```
    {
        static void DisplayDays(string[] days)
        {
          int i;
          for(i = 0; i < days.Length; i++)
              Console.Write(days[i] + "{0}", i < days.Length - 1 ? " " : "");
        }

        static void Main(string[] args)
        {
          string[] weekdays = {"Mon","Tue","Wed","Thu","Fri","Sat"};
          DisplayDays(weekdays);
          Console.ReadLine();
        }
    }
}
```

Here is a sample run:

Program 7.4 uses a function to compute the average of integer values. The Main() function passes the array balance and size to the function getAverage() which then computes and returns the average (avg).

Program 7.4

```
using System;
using System.Collections.Generic;
using System.Linq;
using System.Text;
using System.Threading.Tasks;

namespace Array_Function
{
    class Array
    {
        double getAverage(int[] arr, int size)
        {
            int i;
            double avg;
            int sum = 0;
            for (i = 0; i < size; ++i)
                sum += arr[i];
            avg = (double)sum / size;
            return avg;
        }

        static void Main(string[] args)
        {
            Array app = new Array();

            // an int array with 5 elements
            int[] balance = new int[] { 1000, 2, 3, 17, 50 };
```

155

```
double avg;

// pass pointer to the array as an argument
avg = app.getAverage(balance, 5);
//output the returned value
Console.WriteLine("Average value is: {0} ", avg);
Console.ReadLine();
        }
    }
}
```

Here is a sample run:

Program 7.5 declares and initializes the array n using a `for` loop with index `i` to access successive elements of the array.

Program 7.5

```
using System;
using System.Collections.Generic;
using System.Linq;
using System.Text;
using System.Threading.Tasks;

namespace Arrays
{
    class Initialize
    {
        static void Main(string[] args)
        {
            int[] n = new int[10]; // n is an array of 10 integers
            int i;

            for (i = 0; i < 10; i++)
            {
                n[i] = i + 100;
                Console.WriteLine("Element[{0}] = {1}", i, n[i]);
            }
            Console.ReadLine();
        }
    }
}
```

Here is the program output:

156

Searching an array

You can use a for loop and an if statement to search an item in an array. Program 7.6 searches for the smallest value in the array balance. First, it assumes that the smallest value is in balance[0] and assigns it to the variable small. Then it compares small with the rest of the values in balance, one at a time. If the value compared is smaller than the value in small, it is assigned to small and the process is continued. This will place the smallest value in small.

Program 7.6

```
using System;
using System.Collections.Generic;
using System.Linq;
using System.Text;
using System.Threading.Tasks;

namespace Array
{
    // Find the smallest number in an array
    class Smallest
    {
        static void Main(string[] args)
        {
            double[] balance = { 100.0, 23.0, 700.0, 0.14, 999.0 };
            double small = balance[0];
            int i;
            for (i = 0; i < 5; i++)
                if (small > balance[i])
                    small = balance[i];
            Console.WriteLine("Smallest value = {0}", small);
            Console.ReadLine();
        }
    }
}
```

Here is the program output:

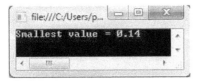

Program 7.7 is similar to Program 7.6 except that it displays the smallest number and the average of all the numbers in array x (rounded to 2 decimal places).

157

Program 7.7

```
using System;
using System.Collections.Generic;
using System.Linq;
using System.Text;
using System.Threading.Tasks;
namespace Arrays
{
    class Smallest_Avg
    {
        static void Main(string[] args)
        {
            double[] x = { 100.0, 23.0, 700.0, 0.14, 999.0, 666.6, 123.45 };
            int i, n = 7;
            double sum = 0, avg, min = 1000;
            for (i = 0; i < n; i++)
            {
                if (min > x[i])
                    min = x[i];
                sum = sum + x[i];
            }
            avg = sum / n;
            Console.WriteLine("Smallest Num. = {0}", min);
            Console.WriteLine();
            Console.WriteLine("Average = {0}", Math.Round(avg, 2));
            Console.ReadLine();
        }
    }
}
```

Here is the program output:

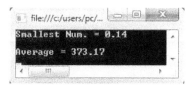

Program 7.8 generate n=100 integer random numbers between 100 and 999 in array x. Then prompts user to enter an integer number from the keyboard. The program search for a match in x, if there is a match, it display the message "Match found at position..." otherwise "No match found" if there is no match.

Program 7.8

```
using System;
using System.Collections.Generic;
using System.Linq;
using System.Text;
using System.Threading.Tasks;

namespace Arrays
{
    class Search
    {
        static void Main(string[] args)
        {
```

158

```
int i, n = 100, z;
int[] x = new int[n];
Boolean match = false;
var ObjRnd = new Random();
Console.Write("Enter a number between 100 to 999: ");
z = Convert.ToInt32(Console.ReadLine());

for (i = 0; i < n; i++)
{
    if (i % 5 == 0)
        Console.WriteLine();
    x[i] = ObjRnd.Next(100, 999);
    Console.Write("\t{0}", x[i]);
}
for (i = 0; i < n; i++)
{
    if (z == x[i])
    {
        match = true;
        Console.WriteLine("\n\nMatch found at position {0}", i);
        break;
    }
    else
    {
        match = false;
    }
}
if (match==false)
{
    Console.WriteLine("\n\nNo match found");
}
Console.ReadLine();
        }
    }
}
```

Here is the output when there is a match:

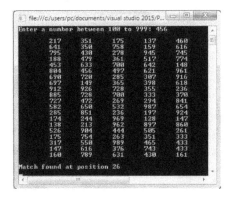

And here is the program output when there is no match:

159

Program 7.9 takes a list of products sold at My Street Shop and a customer purchase and computes and displays a receipt that resembles the one below.

Products

```
     ProdCode              Price (RM)
     AAA                      5.00
     BBB                      7.00
     CCC                      2.30
     DDD                      1.70
     EEE                      9.00
```

Purchase
```
     ProdCode              Quantity
      BBB                      2
      DDD                      4
      EEE                      1
```

Receipt format:

```
              My Street Shop
ProdCode   Quantity   Price   Amount (RM)

BBB           2        7.00      14.00

DDD           4        1.70       6.80

EEE           1        9.00       9.00


Total purchase =RM xxx.xx
```

Program 7.9

```
using System;
using System.Collections.Generic;
using System.Linq;
using System.Text;
using System.Threading.Tasks;

namespace Arrays
{
    class Program
    {
        static void Main(string[] args)
```

160

```
    {
        string[] prodcode = {"AAA", "BBB", "CCC", "DDD", "EEE" };
        double[] price = {5.00, 7.00, 2.30, 1.70, 9.00 };
        string prcode;
        double amount = 0, sum = 0;
        int i,j, qty, n = 5;
        Console.Write("\t\t\t\tMy Street Shop");
        Console.Write("\n\n\t\t\tProdCode\tQuantity\tPrice\tAmount(RM)");

        for (i = 1; i <=n; i++)
        {
            Console.Write("\nEnter ProdCode: ");
            prcode = Console.ReadLine();
            prcode = prcode.ToUpper();
            if (prcode.Equals("EXIT"))
                break;

            Console.Write("Enter Quantity:  ");
            qty = Convert.ToInt32(Console.ReadLine());
            for (j = 0; j < n; j++)
            {
                if (prcode == prodcode[j])
                {
                    amount = qty * price[j];
                    sum = sum + amount;
                    Console.WriteLine("\t\t\t{0}\t\t{1}\t\t{2}\t{3}",prcode,
                                qty,string.Format("{0:F2}",price[j]),
                                    string.Format("{0:F2}",amount));
                }
            }
        }
        Console.WriteLine("\n\t\t\tTotal Purchase =RM{0}",
                                string.Format("{0:F2}",sum));
        Console.ReadLine();
    }
  }
}
```

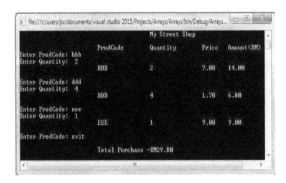

Swapping variables

To swap (exchange) two variables, say num1 and num2, you cannot write statements like below (it won't work).

161

```
num1 = num2;
num2 = num1;
```

The first statement will assign the value of num2 to num1. Now both num1 and num2 will now have the same value. The second statement will not produce the intended result.

To swap the contents of two variables, you need a third variable, say temp, and use three statements as shown below:

```
temp = num1;
num1 = num2;
num2 = temp;
```

Sorting variables

Sorting data e.g., ascending or alphabetical order is a very common data processing activity. There are many algorithms for sorting items in an array with different efficiencies. One algorithm that is easy to understand, but not necessarily efficient, is given below.

• Compare the first element in the list (array) with the second element. If the first element is larger than the second, swap the first and the second so that the smaller of the two occupies the first position. If the first is smaller than the second, it is already in ascending order (so no need to swap).

• Next, compare the first element with the third element and repeat the previous step.

• Continue the process of comparing the first element with all the rest of the elements, swapping whenever an element is smaller than the first. This process will eventually place the smallest element in the first position in the list. This completes the first pass.

• In the next pass, we repeat the process on the reduced list (i.e., without the first element). This would place the next smallest element in the second position.

• Continue the process until we compare (and possibly swap) the second last and the last element.

This algorithm will sort the list with the smallest element occupying the first position and the largest element occupying the last position.

Program 7.10 sorts a list of integers in ascending order of magnitude. The two (nested) for loops do the actual sorting. Index i in the outer loop is used to reference the first element in the list (or reduced list) while index j in the inner loop is used for the second and subsequent elements in the list (or reduced list). That is, for each i (i = 1, 2, ..., n-1), j runs from i+1 to n. The if statement inside the loop performs the swap if the first element is greater than any of the other elements in the list (or reduced list).

Program 7.10

```
using System;
using System.Collections.Generic;
using System.Linq;
using System.Text;
using System.Threading.Tasks;

namespace Array
{
    // Sort a list of n (< max) integer numbers
    class Sort
    {
        static void Main(string[] args)
```

162

```
{
    const int max = 100;
    int size,i,j, temp;
    int[] list = new int[max];
    Console.Write("Enter list size: ");
    size = Convert.ToInt32(Console.ReadLine());
    for (i = 0; i < size; i++)
    {
        Console.Write("Enter next number: ");
        list[i] = Convert.ToInt32(Console.ReadLine());
    }
    for (i = 0; i < size - 1; i++)
    {
        for (j = i + 1; j < size; j++)
        {
            if (list[i] > list[j])
            {
                temp = list[i];         // these three lines
                list[i] = list[j];      // interchange the elements
                list[j] = temp;         // list[i] and list[j]
            }
        }
    }
    Console.WriteLine("\nSorted list: ");
    for (i = 0; i < size; i++)
    {
        Console.Write(" {0} ", list[i]);
    }
    Console.ReadLine();
}
}
}
```

Here is a sample run:

The above exchange-sort algorithm is not computationally efficient. A more efficient algorithm is the bubble sort. Program 7.11 implements this algorithm. Go through the program and figure out how the algorithm works!

Program 7.11

```
using System;
using System.Collections.Generic;
using System.Linq;
using System.Text;
using System.Threading.Tasks;
```

163

```csharp
namespace Array
{
    // Bubble sort
    class Sort
    {
        static void Main(string[] args)
        {
            const int max = 100;
            int size, temp;
            int[] list = new int[max];
            Console.Write("Enter list size: ");
            size = Convert.ToInt32(Console.ReadLine());
            for (int i = 0; i < size; i++)
            {
                Console.Write("Enter next number: ");
                list[i] = Convert.ToInt32(Console.ReadLine());
            }

            // bubble sort algorithm
            for (int i = 1; i < size; i++)
            {
                for (int j = 0; j < size - i; j++)
                {
                    if (list[j] > list[j + 1])
                    {
                        temp = list[j];
                        list[j] = list[j + 1];
                        list[j + 1] = temp;
                    }
                }
            }

            Console.WriteLine("\nSorted list: ");
            for (int i = 0; i < size; i++)
            {
                Console.Write(" {0} ", list[i]);
            }
            Console.ReadLine();
        }
    }
}
```

Here is a sample run:

Param Arrays

C# provides param (parameter) arrays for passing an unknown number of parameters to a method. Program 7.12 illustrates this.

164

Program 7.12

```
using System;
using System.Collections.Generic;
using System.Linq;
using System.Text;
using System.Threading.Tasks;

namespace Array_Function
{
    class Param_Array
    {
        public int AddElements(params int[] arr)
        {
            int sum = 0;
            foreach (int i in arr)
            {
                sum += i;
            }
            return sum;
        }
    }

    class Program
    {
        static void Main(string[] args)
        {
            int sum;
            Param_Array app = new Param_Array();
            sum = app.AddElements(512, 720, 250, 567, 889);
            Console.WriteLine("The sum is: {0}", sum);
            Console.ReadLine();
        }
    }
}
```

Here is a sample run:

foreach

The foreach loop allows you to iterate through an array (collection) so you can process each item in an array. It takes the form:

```
foreach (type variable in array)
{
    statements;
}
```

Here variable holds each element of the array as the statements in the loop are executed. It must be of the same type (or compatible) as the array type. The keyword in is used to specify the array we want to access.

165

In Program 7.13(a), the data type of `person` (string) is the same as the data type of array `names`.

Program 7.13(a)

```
using System;
using System.Collections.Generic;
using System.Linq;
using System.Text;
using System.Threading.Tasks;

namespace Array
{
    class Foreach
    {
        static void Main(string[] args)
        {
            string[] names = { "Peter", "Joe", "Mike" };
            foreach (string person in names)
            {
                Console.WriteLine(" {0} ", person);
            }
            Console.ReadLine();
        }
    }
}
```

Here is the program output:

Program 7.13(a) is equivalent to Program 7.13(b) which uses the `for` loop.

Program 7.13(b)

```
using System;
using System.Collections.Generic;
using System.Linq;
using System.Text;
using System.Threading.Tasks;

namespace Array
{
    class For_Loop
    {
        static void Main(string[] args)
        {
            string[] names = { "Peter", "Joe", "Mike" };
            for (int i = 0; i < 3; i++)
                Console.WriteLine(" {0} ", names[i]);
                Console.ReadLine();
        }
    }
}
```

166

Program 7.14 is similar to Program 7.5 except that it uses foreach to display the elements of the array.

Program 7.14

```
using System;
using System.Collections.Generic;
using System.Linq;
using System.Text;
using System.Threading.Tasks;

namespace Array
{
    class Foreach
    {
        static void Main(string[] args)
        {
            int[] n = new int[10]; // n is an array of 10 integers
            int i;

            //initialize elements of array n
            for ( i = 0; i < 10; i++)
            {
                n[i] = i + 100;
            }

            //output each array element's value
            foreach (int j in n)
            {
                i = j - 100;
                Console.WriteLine("Element[{0}] = {1}", i, j);
            }
            Console.ReadLine();
        }
    }
}
```

Here is the program output:

7.3 Two-Dimensional Arrays

Some applications require two-dimensional arrays consisting of rows and columns. A two-dimensional array has two subscripts (indexes). The first subscript is used to refer the rows and the second subscript to refer to the columns. Its declaration takes the form:

```
type[,] array_name = new type[row, column];
```

The statement below is an example of a two-dimensional array declaration:

```
double[,] x = new double[3,4];
```

It declares x as an array of type `double` with 3 rows and 4 columns as shown below:

COLUMN

		0	1	2	3
		0	1	2	3
	0	[0, 0]	[0, 1]	[0, 2]	[0, 3]
ROW	1	[1, 0]	[1, 1]	[1, 2]	[1, 3]
	2	[2, 0]	[2, 1]	[2, 2]	[2, 3]

You can also initialize a two-dimensional array using two levels of curly brackets. For example, you can initialize array x[3,4] as follows:

```
double[,] x = { {1,2,3,4}, {5,6,7,8}, {9,10,11,12} };
```

Note that each row is enclosed within a pair of curly brackets { } and is separated by a comma.

The above statement will assign values as follows:

```
x[0,0] = 1    x[0,1] =  2    x[0,2] =  3    x[0,3] =  4
x[1,0] = 5    x[0,1] =  6    x[0,2] =  7    x[1,3] =  8
x[2,0] = 9    x[2,1] = 10    x[2,2] = 11    x[2,3] = 12
```

Every element in the array is identified by x[i,j], where x is the name of the array, and i and j are the row and column subscripts.

Accessing Two-Dimensional Arrays

To access a two-dimensional array we must use two subscripts – one for row, one for column. To access all the elements, you need two `for` loops as Program 7.15(a) illustrates. It calculates the average of all elements in the array x. The outer loop index i is used for the row while the inner loop index j is used for the column.

Program 7.15(a)

```
using System;
using System.Collections.Generic;
using System.Linq;
using System.Text;
using System.Threading.Tasks;

namespace Array
{
    // Computes the average of all elements in array x
    class Compute
    {
        static void Main(string[] args)
        {
            float total = 0, average;
            int[,] x = { { 4, 5, 6, 2, 12 }, { 10, 25, 33, 22, 11 },
                         { 21, 32, 43, 54, 65 }, { 3, 2, 1, 5, 6 } };

            for (int i = 0; i < 4; i++)
                for (int j = 0; j < 5; j++)
```

168

```
                    total += x[i, j];

           average = (total / 20);
           Console.WriteLine("Average = {0}", average);
           Console.ReadLine();
       }
   }
}
```

Here is the program output:

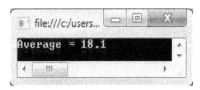

You can also use the `foreach` loop to access all the elements of a two-dimensional array as Program 7.15(b) illustrates.

Program 7.15(b)

```
using System;
using System.Collections.Generic;
using System.Linq;
using System.Text;
using System.Threading.Tasks;

namespace Array
{
    // Computes the average of all elements in array x
    class Compute
    {
        static void Main(string[] args)
        {
            float total = 0, average;

            int[,] x = { { 4, 5, 6, 2, 12 }, { 10, 25, 33, 22, 11 },
                         { 21, 32, 43, 54, 65 }, { 3, 2, 1, 5, 6 } };

            foreach (int value in x)
                total += value;

            average = (total / 20);
            Console.WriteLine("Average = {0}", average);
            Console.ReadLine();
        }
    }
}
```

Here is the program output:

169

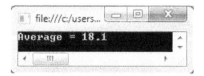

Program 7.16 does the same thing as Program 7.15 but it does by passing array x to the function getAverage(). It will produce the same result.

Program 7.16

```
using System;
using System.Collections.Generic;
using System.Linq;
using System.Text;
using System.Threading.Tasks;

namespace Array
{
    // Compute the average of all the elements in array x
    // by calling a function
    class Compute
    {
        static void Main(string[] args)
        {
            int[,] x = { { 4, 5, 6, 2, 12 }, { 10, 25, 33, 22, 11 },
                        { 21, 32, 43, 54, 65 }, { 3, 2, 1, 5, 6 } };
            float average;
            average = getAverage(x);   // call function
            Console.WriteLine("Average = {0}", average);
            Console.ReadLine();
        }

        static float getAverage(int[,] y)
        {
            float total = 0;
            foreach (int value in y)
                total += value;
            return (total / 20);
        }
    }
}
```

Here is the program output:

Program 7.17 displays the value of every array element in the two-dimensional array x.

Program 7.17

```
using System;
using System.Collections.Generic;
```

170

```csharp
using System.Linq;
using System.Text;
using System.Threading.Tasks;

namespace Array
{
    class Display
    {
        static void Main(string[] args)
        {
            // an array with 5 rows and 2 columns
            int[,] a = new int[5, 2] { { 0, 0 }, { 1, 2 }, { 2, 4 },
                                       { 3, 6 }, { 4, 8 } };
            int i, j;
            // display each array element's value
            for (i = 0; i < 5; i++)
            {
                for (j = 0; j < 2; j++)
                {
                    Console.WriteLine("a[{0},{1}] = {2}", i, j, a[i, j]);
                }
            }
            Console.ReadLine();
        }
    }
}
```

Here is the program output:

7.4 Multi-Dimensional Arrays

A multi-dimensional array has more than two dimensions. Working with multi-dimensional arrays is similar to working with two-dimensional arrays. A three-dimensional array declaration takes the form:

```
type[ , , ] array_name = new type[size1, size2, size3];
```

The above declaration has two commas. An array of four dimensions will have three commas, and so on.

A three-dimensional array uses three subscripts:

The first references the row (size1).
The second references the column (size2).
The third references the dimension (size3).

171

The figure below uses the concept of a page to represent a three-dimensional array [4, 4, 3].

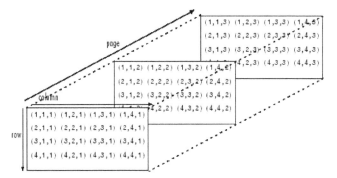

To access the element in the second row, third column of page 2, for example, you use the subscripts (2, 3, 2).

Accessing three-dimensional arrays is similar to accessing two-dimensional arrays. To access all the elements, you will need three subscripts and three for loops as illustrated in Program 7.18.

Program 7.18

```
using System;
using System.Collections.Generic;
using System.Linq;
using System.Text;
using System.Threading.Tasks;

namespace Array
{
    class Display
    {
        static void Main(string[] args)
        {
            int[,,] number = new int[3, 5, 4];
            number[0, 0, 0] = 1;
            number[0, 1, 0] = 2;
            number[0, 2, 0] = 3;
            number[0, 3, 0] = 4;
            number[0, 4, 0] = 5;
            number[1, 1, 1] = 2;
            number[2, 2, 2] = 3;
            number[2, 2, 3] = 4;

            // Loop over each dimension's length.
            for (int i = 0; i < number.GetLength(2); i++)
            {
                for (int y = 0; y < number.GetLength(1); y++)
                {
                    for (int x = 0; x < number.GetLength(0); x++)
                    {
                        Console.Write("{0}",number[x, y, i]);
                    }
                    Console.WriteLine();
                }
                Console.WriteLine();
```

172

```
        }
        Console.ReadLine();
      }
    }
}
```

Here is the program output:

7.5 Jagged Arrays

C# provides jagged arrays, where the rows may be of different sizes. A jagged is also called an array of arrays. The syntax for declaring a jagged array involves specifying sets of [ ] as the code below shows:

```
int[][] jag = new int[2][];
jag[0] = new int[4];
jag[1] = new int[6];
```

In the above code, jag[0] and jag[1] each hold a reference to a one-dimensional array of type int. The first element, jag[0], holds a reference to a one-dimensional array of size 4 and the second, jag[1], holds a reference to another one-dimensional array of size 6.

The code below shows how to loop through all the elements of a jagged array.

```
for (int i = 0; i<jag.Length; i++)
{
    for (int j = 0; j<jag[i].Length; j++)
    {
        Console.WriteLine(jag[i][j]);
    }
}
```

The Length attribute gives the number of items in the array object.

Program 7.19 creates a jagged array with integer random numbers. Then it calculates the sum and average for each row and all elements of the array.

173

Program 7.19

```
using System;
using System.Collections.Generic;
using System.Linq;
using System.Text;
using System.Threading.Tasks;

namespace Array
{
    // Calculates the sum and average of items in a jagged array

    class JaggedArray
    {
        static int sum(int[] intArray)
        {
            int total = 0;
            foreach (int element in intArray)
                total += element;
            return total;
        }

        static int average(int total, int length)
        {
            return (total / length);
        }

        static void Main(string[] args)
        {
            // create a Random object
            Random rObj = new Random();

            int rInt;
            // total number of elements in the jagged array
            int size = 0;
            // sum of the jagged array
            int total = 0;
            int grand_total = 0;

            // create a jagged array
            int[][] jag = new int[3][];

            for (int i = 0; i < 3; i++)
            {
                rInt = rObj.Next(1, 5);
                size += rInt;
                jag[i] = new int[rInt];
            }

            // generate and print the jagged array
            Console.WriteLine("The generated jagged array is");

            for (int i = 0; i < jag.Length; i++)
            {
                Console.Write("[ ");
                for (int j = 0; j < jag[i].Length; j++)
                {
                    rInt = rObj.Next(0, 1000);
                    jag[i][j] = rInt;
                    Console.Write(jag[i][j] + " ");
                }
                Console.WriteLine("]");
            }
```

174

```
Console.WriteLine();

// calculate and print the sum and average of each row
for (int i = 0; i < jag.Length; i++)
{
    total = sum(jag[i]);
    grand_total += total;
    Console.WriteLine("Array[{0}]: Sum = {1}, Average =
                {2}", i, total, average(total, jag[i].Length));
}

// calculate and print the sum and average of the jagged array
Console.WriteLine();
Console.WriteLine("The grand sum for the jagged array is"
                                        + grand_total);
Console.WriteLine("The grand average for the jagged
                array is " + average(grand_total, size));
Console.ReadLine();
        }
    }
}
```

Here is the program output:

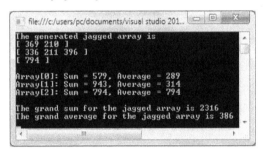

Program 7.20 builds an array whose elements are themselves arrays, each of which has a different size.

Program 7.20

```
using System;
using System.Collections.Generic;
using System.Linq;
using System.Text;
using System.Threading.Tasks;

namespace Array
{
    class JaggedArray
    {
        static void Main(string[] args)
        {
            // Declare the array of two elements:
            int[][] arr = new int[2][];
            int i, j;

            // Initialize the elements:
            arr[0] = new int[5] { 1, 3, 5, 7, 9 };
```

175

```
arr[1] = new int[4] { 2, 4, 6, 8 };

// Display the array elements:
for (i = 0; i < arr.Length; i++)
{
    Console.WriteLine();
    Console.Write("Element({0}): ", i);

    for (j = 0; j < arr[i].Length; j++)
    {
        Console.Write(" {0}{1}", arr[i][j], j ==
                        (arr[i].Length - 1) ? "" : " ");
    }
    Console.WriteLine();
}
Console.ReadLine();
        }
    }
}
```

Here is the program output:

Note that a one-dimensional jagged array can be initialized as in Program 7.21.

Program 7.21

```
using System;
using System.Collections.Generic;
using System.Linq;
using System.Text;
using System.Threading.Tasks;

namespace Array
{
    class JaggedArray
    {
        static void Main(string[] args)
        {
            // a jagged array of 5 array of integers
            int[][] jag = new int[][] { new int[] { 0, 0 },
                        new int[] { 1, 2 }, new int[] { 2, 4 },
                        new int[] { 3, 6 }, new int[] { 4, 8 } };
            int i, j;

            // output each array element's value
            for (i = 0; i < 5; i++)
            {
                for (j = 0; j < 2; j++)
                {
                    Console.WriteLine("jag[{0}][{1}] = {2}", i, j, jag[i][j]);
                }
```

176

```
        }
        Console.ReadLine();
    }
  }
}
```

Here is the program output:

7.6 Collections

Arrays are used to store a set of data items of the same type such as type int, long and double. But arrays can also be used to store a list or collection of any type of object.

C# provides the namespace System.Collections to handle any collection of objects. The namespace contains the class ArrayList which has methods such as Add, Clear, Count, Insert, Remove, Sort, etc.

A **collection** is basically an alternative to an array. However, unlike arrays, you can add and remove items from a list by using an index and the array will resize itself automatically. It also allows dynamic memory allocation, adding, searching and sorting items.

The following are the various commonly used classes of the System.Collection namespace.

Class	Methods	Meaning
	`public virtual void Clear();`	Removes all elements from the Stack.
	`public virtual bool Contains(object obj);`	Determines whether an element is in the Stack.
	`public virtual object Peek();`	Returns the object at the top of the Stack without removing it.
Stack	`public virtual object Pop();`	Removes and returns the object at the top of the Stack.
	`public virtual void Push(object obj);`	Inserts an object at the top of the Stack.
	`public virtual object[] ToArray();`	Copies the Stack to a new array.
	`public virtual void Clear();`	Removes all elements from the Queue.
Queue	`public virtual bool Contains(object obj);`	Determines whether an element is in the Queue.
	`public virtual object Dequeue();`	Removes and returns the object at the beginning of the Queue.

177

	`public virtual void Enqueue(object obj);`	Adds an object to the end of the Queue.
	`public virtual object[] ToArray();`	Copies the Queue to a new array.
	`public virtual void TrimToSize();`	Sets the capacity to the actual number of elements in the Queue.
Hashtable	`public virtual void Add(object key, object value);`	Adds an element with the specified key and value into the Hashtable.
	`public virtual void Clear();`	Removes all elements from the Hashtable.
	`public virtual bool ContainsKey(object key);`	Determines whether the Hashtable contains a specific key.
	`public virtual bool ContainsValue(object value);`	Determines whether the Hashtable contains a specific value.
	`public virtual void Remove(object key);`	Removes the element with the specified key from the Hashtable.

Program 7.22 creates a set of `Employee` objects and stores them in the array `emp[]`. Then it displays the information in employee collection using the `foreach` loop.

Program 7.22

```
using System;
using System.Collections.Generic;
using System.Linq;
using System.Text;
using System.Threading.Tasks;

namespace Array_Function
{
    class Employee
    {
        string name;
        int age;

        public Employee()
        {
            name = "";
            age = 0;
        }

        public void getinfo()
        {
            Console.Write("Enter name: ");
            name = Console.ReadLine();
            Console.Write("Enter age: ");
            age = Convert.ToInt32(Console.ReadLine());
        }

        public void Print()
        {
            Console.WriteLine("\nName: " + name);
            Console.WriteLine("Age:  " + age);
        }
    }

    class FindMain
    {
        static void Main(string[] args)
```

178

```
    {
        Employee[] emp = new Employee[3];

        for (int i = 0; i < 3; i++)
        {
            emp[i] = new Employee();
            emp[i].getinfo();
        }

        foreach (Employee e in emp)
            e.Print();
        Console.ReadLine();
    }

    }
}
```

Here is a sample run:

Program 7.23 is similar to the above but uses the class `ArrayList` and the `Add` method.

Program 7.23

```
using System;
using System.Collections;
using System.Collections.Generic;
using System.Linq;
using System.Text;
using System.Threading.Tasks;

namespace Array_Function
{
    class Employee
    {
        string name;
        int age;

        public Employee(string n, int a)
        {
            this.name = n;
            this.age = a;
        }

        public void Print()
        {
```

179

```
            Console.WriteLine("Name: " + name);
            Console.WriteLine("Age : " + age);
        }
    }

    class ClsMain
    {
        static void Main(string[] args)
        {
            // create array list
            ArrayList emplist = new ArrayList();

            emplist.Add(new Employee("Mei Ling", 25));
            emplist.Add(new Employee("Faizal", 23));
            emplist.Add(new Employee("Munir", 27));
            foreach (Employee emp in emplist)
                emp.Print();
            Console.ReadLine();
        }
    }
}
```

Here is the output:

Program 7.24 adds 10 integer numbers to `ArrayList` and then sorts and displays the values.

Program 7.24

```
using System;
using System.Collections;
using System.Collections.Generic;
using System.Linq;
using System.Text;
using System.Threading.Tasks;

namespace Array_Function
{
    class clsMain
    {
        static void Main(string[] args)
        {
            ArrayList al = new ArrayList();

            Console.WriteLine("Adding some numbers:");
            al.Add(45);
            al.Add(78);
            al.Add(33);
            al.Add(56);
            al.Add(12);
            al.Add(23);
```

180

```
        al.Add(9);
        al.Add(15);
        al.Add(25);
        al.Add(17);
        Console.WriteLine("Capacity: {0} ", al.Capacity);
        Console.WriteLine("Count: {0}", al.Count);
        Console.Write("Content: ");
        foreach (int i in al)
        {
            Console.Write(i + " ");
        }
        Console.WriteLine();
        Console.Write("Sorted Content: ");
        al.Sort();
        foreach (int i in al)
        {
            Console.Write(i + " ");
        }
        Console.WriteLine();
        Console.ReadLine();
    }
}
}
```

Here is the program output:

Program 7.25 uses C# built-in stack method to implement stack operations.

Program 7.25

```
using System;
using System.Collections.Generic;
using System.Linq;
using System.Collections; // namespace for stack operations
using System.Text;
using System.Threading.Tasks;

namespace Data_Structure_Example
{
    class BuiltInStack
    {
        static void find(Stack myStack, string item)
        {
            int position = 0;

            if (myStack.Contains(item))
            {
                System.Collections.IEnumerator myEnum = myStack.GetEnumerator();
                while (myEnum.MoveNext())
                {
                    if ((String)myEnum.Current == item)
```

181

```csharp
            {
                Console.WriteLine("The position of first matched item is
                                  {0}.", position);
                break;
            }
            position++;
        }
    }
    else
        Console.WriteLine("Item not found!");
}
static void Main(string[] args)
{
    string choice;
    Stack stk = new Stack();

    while (true)
    {
        Console.WriteLine();
        Console.WriteLine("P-Push, O-Pop, C-Clear, K-Peek, E - IsEmpty,
                          F - Find, X - Exit");

        Console.Write("Enter your choice: ");
        choice = Console.ReadLine();
        choice = choice.ToUpper();

        if (choice == "X")
            break;

        switch (choice)
        {
            case "P":
                Console.Write("Enter item to push: ");
                stk.Push(Console.ReadLine());
                break;
            case "O":
                if (stk.Count == 0)
                    Console.WriteLine("Stack is empty!");
                else
                    Console.WriteLine(stk.Pop());
                break;
            case "C":
                stk.Clear();
                break;
            case "K":
                if (stk.Count == 0)
                    Console.WriteLine("Stack is empty!");
                else
                    Console.WriteLine(stk.Peek());
                break;
            case "E":
                if (stk.Count == 0)
                    Console.WriteLine("True!");
                else
                    Console.WriteLine("False!");
                break;
            case "F":
                Console.Write("Enter item to search: ");
                find(stk, Console.ReadLine());
                break;
            default:
                Console.WriteLine("Invalid Choice!");
                break;
```

```
                }
            }
            Console.ReadLine();
        }
    }
}
```

Here is a sample run:

Program 7.26 uses C# built-in queue methods to implements the following queue operations:

Add   – adds an item to a queue to the back of the queue

Remove   – removes an item at the head/front of the queue

Length   – computes the length of the queue

Program 7.26

```
using System;
using System.Collections.Generic;
using System.Linq;
using System.Collections; // namespace for queue operations
using System.Text;
using System.Threading.Tasks;

namespace Data_Structure_Example
{
    class BuiltInQueue
    {
        static void Main(string[] args)
```

183

```
        {
            string choice;
            Queue queue = new Queue();

            while (true)
            {
                Console.WriteLine();
                Console.WriteLine("A-Add, R-Remove, L-Length, X- Exit");
                Console.Write("Enter your choice: ");
                choice = Console.ReadLine();
                choice = choice.ToUpper();

                if (choice == "X")
                    break;

                switch (choice)
                {
                    case "A":
                        Console.Write("Enter item to add: ");
                        queue.Enqueue(Console.ReadLine());
                        break;
                    case "R":
                        if (queue.Count == 0)
                            Console.WriteLine("Queue is empty!");
                        else
                            Console.WriteLine(queue.Dequeue());
                        break;
                    case "L":
                        Console.WriteLine("Queue length = {0}", queue.Count);
                        break;
                    default:
                        Console.WriteLine("Invalid Choice!");
                        break;
                }
            }
            Console.ReadLine();
        }
    }
}
```

Here is a sample run:

7.7 Sample Programs

Program 7.27 shows two new functions – ToCharArray and Reverse. It receives a text message from the user, copies the characters to an array using the ToCharArray method, reverses the characters in the array using the Reverse method, then prints the reversed array.

Program 7.27

```
using System;
using System.Collections;
using System.Collections.Generic;
using System.Linq;
using System.Text;
using System.Threading.Tasks;

namespace Array_Function
{
    class clsArray
    {
        static void Main(string[] args)
        {
            string msg;
            Console.Write("Enter a message: ");
            msg = Console.ReadLine();
            char[] amsg = msg.ToCharArray();   // copy msg to array
            Console.WriteLine();
            Console.WriteLine("Display message:");
            Console.WriteLine(amsg);
            Console.WriteLine();
            Array.Reverse(amsg);   // reverse the array amsg
            Console.WriteLine("Display message in reverse order:");
            Console.WriteLine(amsg);
            Console.ReadLine();
        }
    }
}
```

Here is a sample run:

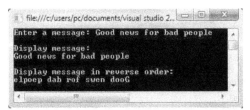

Program 7.28 uses the built-in method Sort to sort items in array x in ascending order of magnitude.

Program 7.28

```
using System;
using System.Collections.Generic;
using System.Text;

namespace Sort_Example
```

185

```
{
  class clsArray
  {
    static void Main(string[] args)
    {
      int[] x = { 9, 8, 7, 6, 5, 4, 3, 2, 1 };
      Array.Sort(x);   // sort the array
      for (int i = 0; i < x.Length; i++)
        Console.Write(x[i] + "  ");
    }
  }
}
```

Here is the output:

Program 7.29 combines the methods in Program 7.27 and Program 7.28. It takes the integer values in list[], reverses the list using the Reverse method, and sorts in ascending order of magnitude using the Sort method.

Program 7.29

```
using System;
using System.Collections.Generic;
using System.Linq;
using System.Text;
using System.Threading.Tasks;

namespace Array_Function
{
  class Sorting
  {
    static void Main(string[] args)
    {
      int[] list = { 34, 72, 13, 44, 25, 30, 10 };
      int[] temp = list;

      Console.Write("Original Array: ");

      foreach (int i in list)
      {
        Console.Write(i + " ");
      }
      Console.WriteLine();

      // reverse the array
      Array.Reverse(temp);
      Console.Write("Reversed Array: ");

      foreach (int i in temp)
      {
        Console.Write(i + " ");
      }
      Console.WriteLine();

      //sort the array
```

186

```
Array.Sort(list);
Console.Write("Sorted Array: ");

foreach (int i in list)
{
    Console.Write(i + " ");
}
Console.WriteLine();
Console.ReadLine();
    }
  }
}
```

Here is the program output:

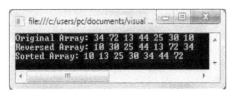

Exercise

1. Given a set of integers in array x[20], determine how many of these elements are (i) positive, (ii) negative and (iii) zero.

2. Given a set of integers in array x[20]. Determine the average, standard deviation, maximum, minimum and range (i.e., maximum – minimum).

3. Given a set of floating-point (double) numbers in array y[10,10], find the sum of all

   (a) the diagonal elements

   (b) the square of the numbers in the even rows (i.e., rows 0, 2, 4, 6, 8).

   (c) the square root of the numbers in the odd columns (i.e., columns 1, 3, 5, 7, 9).

4. Transpose the matrix x in question 3.

5. Given a set of floating-point numbers in matrices x[m,k] and y[k,n], find the product of x and y.

6. Generate 100 integer random numbers in [1000, 9999] in array rn[].

   (a) How many of these values fall in the range: 1000–2500, 2501–5000, 5001–7500 and 7501–9999?

   (b) How many of these are even numbers?

   (c) How many of these are divisible by 5?

   (d) How many of these are prime numbers?

7. Generate 100 unique integer random numbers in array x[]. Sort the numbers in ascending order of magnitude. Then, use a binary search to match a given number in the array. Display the position of the element in the array if a match is found; if not, display the message No match.

8. Enter a string and store it in an array. Then determine the position(s) of a specified character in the array. (For example, if the input string is "I love Malaysia", the positions of the character 'a' are 8, 10 and 14.)

9. What is a collection? Write a program to manipulate (add, insert, remove, reverse) a set of student objects using the collection ArrayList.

Chapter 8

Structures

Learning Outcomes:

After completing this chapter, you will be able to

- *Explain the purpose of structures.*
- *Declare structures.*
- *Declare arrays of structures.*
- *Declare nested structures.*
- *Write program to access structure elements.*

8.1 What Are Structures

Chapter 7 discussed arrays for storing and processing large amounts of *similar* data more compactly. By using a loop index (subscript), we could reference all or any element in an array. While arrays are convenient for many applications, they are not suitable when you want to store different data types.

For example, if you want to store student details such as name, mark and grade, you cannot use an array because their types are different: name is of type string, mark is of type int sand grade is of type char (assuming single character grade). This is where structures come in. Structures can be used to store and manipulate different types of data. Thus structures are useful for processing related data. We declare structures using the keyword struct.

8.2 Structure Declaration

A structure is a collection of *related* data items stored and referenced using a single name. These data types of these items are usually of different, each requiring different amounts of memory.

To use a structure, we first create a template using the keyword struct. The items (variables) in a structure are called structure elements or members. For example, to create a student record containing the fields id (identification number), name, age and gender we can declare as follows:

```
struct student
{
  public string id;
  public string name;
  public int age;
  public string gender;
}
```

The keyword struct tells the C# compiler that a structure template is being declared and student is a tag that identifies its data.

Accessing Structure Elements

A structure element can be accessed by using the structure variable name followed by the dot operator (.) and the element name. For example, the statement:

```
student.name = "Mariam";
```

assigns "Mariam" to the structure element name in thestructurestudent. The dot operator tells that name is an element of the structurestudent. The other elements are accessed in a similar way.

Program 8.1 declares the structure Simple using the keyword struct. Simple has four items: Name, Position, Exists, and LastValue of type string, int, bool and double respectively. The Main method declares the variables of type Simple using the statement Simple s. Notice that it does not use the keyword new. It is used like a value type such as string, int, double, etc.

Program 8.1

```
using System;
using System.Collections.Generic;
using System.Linq;
using System.Text;
using System.Threading.Tasks;

namespace Structure_Samples
{
    struct Simple
    {
        publicstring Name;
        publicint Position;
        publicbool Exists;
        publicdoubleLastValue;
    }

    public class structure
    {
        public static void Main(string[] args)
        {
            Simple s;
            s.Name = "Munir";
            s.Position = 1;
            s.Exists = false;
            s.LastValue = 5.5;
            Console.WriteLine("\nName: " + s.Name);
            Console.WriteLine("\nPosition:" + s.Position);
            Console.WriteLine("\nExist: " + s.Exists);
            Console.WriteLine("\nLast value: " + s.LastValue);
            Console.ReadLine();
        }
    }
}
```

Here is a sample run:

190

```
Name: Munir
Position:1
Exist: False
Last value: 5.5
```

Program 8.2 uses the tag `Books` with structure elements `title`, `author`, `subject`, and `book_id`. The `Main` methodthen declares the variables `Book1` and `Book2` of type `Books` and then accesses the elements.

Program 8.2

```
using System;
using System.Collections.Generic;
using System.Linq;
using System.Text;
using System.Threading.Tasks;

namespace Structure_Samples
{
    Struct Books
    {
        publicstring title;
        publicstring author;
        publicstring subject;
        publicintbook_id;
    }

    public class Structure
    {
        public static void Main(string[] args)
        {
            Books Book1;    // Declare Book1 object
            Books Book2;

            // book 1 info
            Book1.title = "C# Programming";
            Book1.author = "Sellappan";
            Book1.subject = "Principles of Programming";
            Book1.book_id = 6495407;

            // book 2 info
            Book2.title = "Telecom Billing";
            Book2.author = "Zara Ali";
            Book2.subject = "Telecom Billing Tutorial";
            Book2.book_id = 6495700;

            // print Book1 info
            Console.WriteLine("Book 1 title : {0}", Book1.title);
            Console.WriteLine("Book 1 author : {0}", Book1.author);
            Console.WriteLine("Book 1 subject : {0}", Book1.subject);
            Console.WriteLine("Book 1 book_id :{0}", Book1.book_id);

            // print Book2 info
            Console.WriteLine("\nBook 2 title : {0}", Book2.title);
            Console.WriteLine("Book 2 author : {0}", Book2.author);
            Console.WriteLine("Book 2 subject : {0}", Book2.subject);
```

191

```
        Console.WriteLine("Book 2 book_id : {0}", Book2.book_id);
        Console.ReadLine();
    }
  }
}
```

Here is the program output:

```
Book 1 title   : C# Programming
Book 1 author  : Sellappan
Book 1 subject : Principles of Programming
Book 1 book_id :6495407

Book 2 title   : Telecom Billing
Book 2 author  : Zara Ali
Book 2 subject : Telecom Billing Tutorial
Book 2 book_id : 6495700
```

Structure elements can also be passed to a method. Program 8.3 illustrates this.

Program 8.3

```csharp
using System;
using System.Collections.Generic;
using System.Linq;
using System.Text;
using System.Threading.Tasks;

namespace Structure_Samples
{
    public struct mySale
    {
        public string item;
        public string description;
        public int quantity;
        public double price;
        public double amount;
    }

    public class structure
    {
        public static void Main(string[] args)
        {
            mySale sale;
            sale.item = "Text book";
            sale.description = "Programming";
            sale.quantity = 7;
            sale.price = 65.50;
            sale.amount = sale.quantity * sale.price;
            showSale(sale);
            Console.ReadLine();
        }

        static public void showSale(mySale item_info)
        {
            Console.WriteLine("Item: {0}\nDescription: {1}\nQuantity: {2}\nPrice:
                {3}\nAmount: {4}", item_info.item, item_info.description,
                item_info.quantity, item_info.price, item_info.amount);
        }
    }
```

192

```
        }
}
```

Here is a sample run:

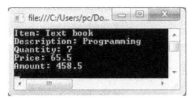

We can also create structure objects using the `new` operator. In this case, C# automatically creates an appropriate constructor for it.

Unlike classes, we can declare structures without using the `new` operator. In this case, there is no constructor call, which makes the allocation more efficient. However, the fields will remain unassigned and the object cannot be used until all of the fields are initialized. Program 8.4 illustrates this.

Program 8.4

```csharp
using System;
using System.Collections.Generic;
using System.Linq;
using System.Text;
using System.Threading.Tasks;
namespace Structure_Samples
{
    public struct Coordinates
    {
        public int x, y;

        public Coordinates(int p1, int p2)
        {
            x = p1;
            y = p2;
        }
    }

    public class Structure
    {
        public static void Main(string[] args)
        {
            // Initialize:
            Coordinates cord_1 = new Coordinates();
            Coordinates cord_2 = new Coordinates(25, 25);
            // Display results:
            Console.Write("Coordinates 1: ");
            Console.WriteLine("x = {0}, y = {1}", cord_1.x, cord_1.y);
            Console.Write("\nCoordinates 2: ");
            Console.WriteLine("x = {0}, y = {1}", cord_2.x, cord_2.y);
            Console.ReadLine();
        }
    }
}
```

Here is a sample run:

Program 8.5 demonstrates a feature that is unique to structures. It is similar to Program 8.4 except that it creates a Coordinates object without using the new operator. If you replace the word struct with the word class, the program will not compile.

Program 8.5

```
using System;
using System.Collections.Generic;
using System.Linq;
using System.Text;
using System.Threading.Tasks;

namespace Structure_Samples
{
    public struct Coordinates
    {
        public int x, y;

        public Coordinates(int p1, int p2)
        {
            x = p1;
            y = p2;
        }
    }

    public class Structure
    {
        public static void Main(string[] args)
        {
            Coordinates cord_1; // Declare an object
            cord_1.x = 20; // Initialize
            cord_1.y = 25;

            // Display results:
            Console.Write("Coordinates 1: ");
            Console.WriteLine("x = {0}, y = {1}", cord_1.x, cord_1.y);
            Console.ReadLine();
        }
    }
}
```

Here is a sample run:

8.3 Nested Structures

Structures can be nested, i.e., one structure can be declared within another structure. To illustrate the usefulness of nested structures, let's look at the two below structures:

```
struct student
{
    string id;
    string name;
    char gender;
    int age;
}

struct detail
{
    string id;
    string name;
    char gender;
    int age;
    string course;
}
```

Nesting one structure within another can save time when a program needs similar structures. So the above code (which is lengthy) can be rewritten as follows:

```
struct student
{
    string id;
    string name;
    char gender;
    int age;
}

struct detail
{
    student stud_1;      // Uses the above structure
    string course;
}
```

In the above code, the structure detail has two items: stud_1 (of type student structure) and course.

Program 8.6 illustrates the use of nested structures. It creates the structure person with two members: Name and dateBirth. The dateBirth is actually another structure consisting of day, month and year. With this, person has access to four variables. The Main method then creates an array of two persons and asks the user to enter their Name and dateBirth and display them.

Program 8.6

```
using System;
using System.Collections.Generic;
using System.Linq;
using System.Text;
using System.Threading.Tasks;
namespace Structure_Samples
{
    struct person
    {
        public string name;
        public datebirth date;
    }
```

195

```
struct dateBirth
{
    public int day;
    public int month;
    public int Year;
}

public class Structure
{
    public static void Main(string[] args)
    {
        string Name;
        int d ,m ,y;
        int n = 2;
        person[] p = new person[n];
        for (inti = 0; i< n; i++)
        {
            Console.Write("Enter name: ");
            Name = Console.ReadLine();
            p[i].Name = Name;
            Console.Write("Enter day: ");
            d = Convert.ToInt32(Console.ReadLine());
            p[i].Date.Day = d;
            Console.Write("Enter month: ");
            m = Convert.ToInt32(Console.ReadLine());
            p[i].Date.Month = m;
            Console.Write("Enter year: ");
            y = Convert.ToInt32(Console.ReadLine());
            p[i].Date.Year = y;
            Console.WriteLine("\nName: {0}\nDate of birth: {1}-{2}-{3}",
                p[i].Name, p[i].Date.Day, p[i].Date.Month, p[i].Date.Year);
            Console.ReadLine();
        }
    }
}
```

Here is a sample run:

Program 8.7 declares the structure position whose elements are themselves structures: north and south (of type country). The program prints the structure elements name and areacode contained in the structures north and south.

196

Program 8.7

```
using System;
using System.Collections.Generic;
using System.Linq;
using System.Text;
using System.Threading.Tasks;

namespace Structure_Samples
{
    struct country  // Declare structure type
    {
        public string name;
        public int areacode;
    }

    struct position //Declare structure type
    {
        public country north;  // Structure within structure
        public country south;  // Structure within structure
    }

    public class Structure
    {
        public static void Main(string[] args)
        {
            position[] poss=new position[2];
            poss[0].north.name = "Thailand";
            poss[0].north.areacode = 12;
            poss[1].south.name = "Singapore";
            poss[1].south.areacode = 02;

            Console.Write("COUNTRY UP NORTH\n");
            Console.WriteLine("Name: {0}\nArea code: {1}",
            poss[0].north.name, poss[0].north.areacode);
            Console.Write("\nCOUNTRY DOWN SOUTH\n");
            Console.WriteLine("Name: {0}\nArea code: {1}",
            poss[1].south.name, poss[1].south.areacode);
            Console.ReadLine();
        }
    }
}
```

Here is a sample run:

197

8.4 Arrays of Structures

C# lets you create arrays of structures. Program 9.8 illustrates how to do this.

Program 9.8

```
using System;
using System.Collections.Generic;
using System.Linq;
using System.Text;
using System.Threading.Tasks;

namespace Structure_Samples
{
    struct Student
    {
        string name;
        int age;
        int marks;

        public Student(string name, int age, int marks)
        {
            this.name = name;
            this.age = age;
            this.marks = marks;
        }

        public void display()
        {
            Console.WriteLine("{0}\t{1}\t{2}", name, age, marks);
        }
    }

    public class Structure
    {
        public static void Main(string[] args)
        {
            Student[] arr = new Student[3];
            arr[0] = new Student("Hamad", 10, 55);
            arr[1] = new Student("Munir", 20, 82);
            arr[2] = new Student("John", 30, 70);
            Console.Write("Name\tAge\tMark\n");
            foreach (Student element in arr)
            {
                element.display();
            }
            Console.ReadLine();
        }
    }
}
```

Here is a sample run:

198

Arrays of structures can also be declared and assigned values at the same time. Program 8.9 illustrates this.

Program 8.9

```
using System;
using System.Collections.Generic;
using System.Linq;
using System.Text;
using System.Threading.Tasks;

namespace Structure_Samples
{
    struct Student
    {
        string name;
        int age;
        int marks;

        public Student(string name, int age, int marks)
        {
            this.name = name;
            this.age = age;
            this.marks = marks;
        }

        public void display()
        {
            Console.WriteLine("{0}\t{1}\t{2}", name, age, marks);
        }
    }

    public class Structure
    {
        public static void Main(string[] args)
        {
            Student[] arr = {newStudent("Hamad", 10, 55),
            New Student("Munir", 20, 82),newStudent("John", 30, 70)};

            Console.Write("Name\tAge\tMark\n");

            foreach (Student element inarr)
            {
                element.display();
            }
            Console.ReadLine();
        }
    }
}
```

Here is a sample run:

199

8.5 Sample Programs

Program 8.10 declares the structure book consisting of three fields (title, author and cost). The program receives the book particulars from the keyboard and then displays the information in a specific format.

Program 8.10

```
using System;
using System.Collections.Generic;
using System.Linq;
using System.Text;
using System.Threading.Tasks;

namespace Structure_Samples
{
    struct book
    {
        public string title;
        public string author;
        public double cost;
    }

    public class Structure
    {
        public static void Main(string[] args)
        {
            book b;
            Console.Write("Enter book title: ");
            b.title = Console.ReadLine();
            Console.Write("Enter author name: ");
            b.author = Console.ReadLine();
            Console.Write("Enter cost: ");
            b.cost = Convert.ToInt32(Console.ReadLine());
            Console.WriteLine("\n{0} by {1}: ${2}", b.title, b.author, b.cost);
            Console.ReadLine();
        }
    }
}
```

Here is a sample run:

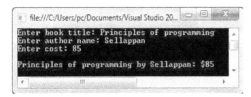

Program 8.11 illustrates how to display an increasing fractional number using structure.

Program 8.11

```
using System;
using System.Collections.Generic;
using System.Linq;
using System.Text;
using System.Threading.Tasks;
```

```
namespace Structure_Samples
{
    // Program to display an increasing fractional number
    struct Fraction
    {
        public int numerator;
        public int denominator;
    }

    public class Structure
    {
        public static void Main(string[] args)
        {
            int i, n = 10;
            Fraction[] frac=new Fraction[n];
            for (i = 0; i< n; i++)
            {
                frac[i].numerator = i+1;
                frac[i].denominator = n; //set the denominator to 10
                Console.WriteLine("{0}/{1}", frac[i].numerator,
                                             frac[i].denominator);
            }
            Console.ReadLine();
        }
    }
}
```

Here is a sample run:

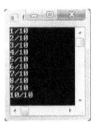

Program 8.12 illustrates the use of a public method to assign values to private variables in a structure and display the result.

Program 8.12

```
using System;
using System.Collections.Generic;
using System.Linq;
using System.Text;
using System.Threading.Tasks;

namespace Structure_Samples
{
    struct Books
    {
        private string title;
        private string author;
        private string subject;
        private int book_id;
```

```csharp
public void getValues(string t, string a, string s, int id)
{
    title = t;
    author = a;
    subject = s;
    book_id = id;
}

public void display()
{
    Console.WriteLine("\nTitle : {0}", title);
    Console.WriteLine("Author : {0}", author);
    Console.WriteLine("Subject : {0}", subject);
    Console.WriteLine("Book_id :{0}", book_id);
}
}

public class Structure
{
    public static void Main(string[] args)
    {
        Books Book1 = new Books();    /* Declare Book1 */
        Books Book2 = new Books();    /* Declare Book2 */

        /* book 1 info */
        Book1.getValues("C# Programming", "Sellappan",
                        "Principles of Programming", 6495407);

        /* book 2 info */
        Book2.getValues("Mobile Application Development",
                        "Munir", "Mobile Apps Tutorial", 6495700);

        /* print Book1 info */
        Book1.display();

        /* print Book2 info */
        Book2.display();
        Console.ReadLine();
    }
}
}
```

Here is a sample run:

```
file:///C:/Users/pc/Documents/Visual ...

Title : C# Programming
Author : Sellappan
Subject : Principles of Programming
Book_id :6495407

Title : Mobile Application Development
Author : Munir
Subject : Mobile Apps Tutorial
Book_id :6495700
```

202

Exercise

1. Write a program using structure to store club members' names, area codes and telephone numbers. Input values for these members and display them according to their area code.

2. Initialize the structure that has members' names and birthdays. Display the names of those who were born on a given date.

3. Declare a nested structure for the following student data:

   Student ID
   Name made up of first name, middle name, last name
   Date of birth made up of day, month and year
   An array of ten courses
   An array of ten grades

4. Given the following structure:

```
struct account
{
    long acc_no;
    string acc_type;
    string acc_name;
    double balance;
}
```

   Create an array of accounts, assign data for the members, and display the information with suitable headings.

Chapter 9

Exceptions

Learning Outcomes:

After completing this chapter, you will be able to

- *Explain what is an exception*
- *Explain the purpose of exception handling.*
- *Use exception classes.*
- *Write program to handle exceptions.*

9.1 What is an Exception

An exception is an error generated when the code behaves in an abnormal way such as when you divide a number by zero, when you access an array element with a subscript whose value exceeds the array size, or when you access a non-existent file.

An exception can cause a program to crash or run abnormally and produce wrong results. You can however write code to trap and catch the error and recover from it gracefully. The code you write to handle the exception is called an exception handler. C# provides several exception classes to handle all kinds of exceptions.

9.2 Exception Classes

The System.Exception class is the base type for of all exceptions. This class has several properties that all exceptions share:

- Message is a read-only property of type string that contains a human-readable description of the reason for the exception.

- InnerException is a read-only property of type Exception. If its value is non-null, it refers to the exception that caused the current exception. Otherwise, its value is null indicating that this exception was not caused by another exception.

- The value of these properties can be specified in calls to the instance constructor for System.Exception.

The table below gives a list of some common exception classes:

Exception Class	Description
System.OutOfMemoryException	This exception is thrown when an attempt to allocate memory fails.
System.StackOverflowException	Thrown when the memory allocated to a stack has been exhausted, for example, when there are too many method calls as in an unbounded recursion.
System.TypeInitializationException	Thrown when a static constructor throws an exception and

	no catch clauses exist to catch it.
System.NullReferenceException	Thrown when a null reference is used instead of a referenced object.
System.InvalidCastException	Thrown when an explicit conversion from a base type or interface to derive types fails at runtime.
System.ArrayTypeMismatchException	Thrown when a store into an array fails because the actual type of the stored element is incompatible with the actual type of the array.
System.IndexOutOfRangeException	Thrown when an attempt is made to index an array via an index whose value is less than zero or lies outside the bounds of the array.
System.MulticastNotSupportedException	Thrown when an attempt to combine two non-null delegates fails because the delegate type does not have a void return type.
System.ArithmeticException	Occurs during arithmetic operations.
System.DivideByZeroException	Occurs when an attempt is made to divide an integral value by zero.
System.OverflowException	Thrown when an arithmetic operation in a checked context overflow.

9.3 Exception Handling

C# provides several exception classes that you can use to write code to handle exceptions in a graceful manner so your programs don't crash. So it is always a good practice to write code to handle exceptions.

Exceptions can occur when a program runs and the compiler cannot detect and give adequate warning/error messages. An exception halts a program unless it is handled properly. Rather than let the program stop, it is better to write code to handle the exception.

There are four keywords for creating an exception handler – throw, try, catch and finally. Handling exceptions require two phases: signaling the exception condition to be thrown, and handling the thrown exception.

To signal the exception condition, use the throw statement with an instance of an exception class:

```
throw new newHandledException();
```

The try and catch blocks are used for handling the exception. It takes the form:

```
try
{
     // code to throw the exception
}
catch (exception_type exception_name)
{
     // code to handle the thrown exception
}
```

The code in the try block is first executed. If an exception is thrown, the rest of the code in the try block is skipped, and the program will catch the thrown exception by executing the catch block that matches the exception. You can have more than one catch block for each try statement as shown below:

```
try
{
     // statements causing exception
}
```

```
catch (exception_type exception_name_1)
{
      // error handling code
}
catch (exception_type exception_name_2)
{
      // error handling code
}
catch (exception_type exception_name_3)
{
      // error handling code
}
```

The try statement comes in three flavors:

- A try block followed by one or more catch blocks.
- A try block followed by a finally block.
- A try block followed by one or more catch blocks followed by a finally block.

The figure below shows the structure of the try-throw-catch blocks.

The catch block works in the same way as a method. There must be at least one catch statement for every try statement. The first catch statement that matches the parameter type of the exception object that was thrown is executed. For example, take the code below.

```
try
{
      SomeExceptionalMethod();
}
catch (OverflowException n)      // one type of exception object

{
      // code to handle the thrown exception
}
catch (OutOfMemoryException r) //another type of exception
{
      // code to handle thrown exception
}
```

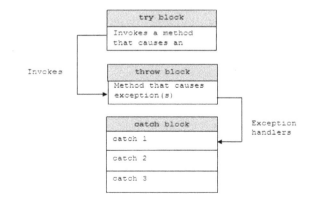

If `SomeExceptionalMethod()` causes an `OutOfMemeoryException` to be thrown, then the second catch block will be executed.

Program 9.1 catches an exception when a number is divided by zero.

Program 9.1

```
using System;
using System.Collections.Generic;
using System.Linq;
using System.Text;
using System.Threading.Tasks;
namespace Exception_Handling
{
    class ExceptionDemo
    {
        static void Main(string[] args)
        {
            int result, num=5;
            try
            {
                result = (num / 0);
            }
            catch (DivideByZeroException e)
            {
                Console.WriteLine("Error: attempt to divide by zero");
            }
            Console.ReadLine();
        }
    }
}
```

Here is the program output:

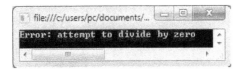

You can also use keyword finally with the try...catch statement. The code in the finally bock will *always* be executed. This is to ensure that the code is executed even when an exception occurs. You can add the finally block to the end of the catch block as the code below illustrates.

```
try
{
    // code to throw the exception
}

catch (exception_type exception_name)
{
    // code to handle the thrown exception
}

finally
{
    // code in this block will be executed
    // even when an exception has occurred
}
```

207

Program 9.2 illustrates the use of the `try...catch...finally` structure.

Program 9.2

```
using System;
using System.Collections.Generic;
using System.Linq;
using System.Text;
using System.Threading.Tasks;
namespace Exception_Handling
{
    class ExceptionDemo
    {
        static void Main(string[] args)
        {
            try
            {
                getException();
            }
            catch (Exception e)
            {
                Console.WriteLine("We got an exception");
            }
            finally
            {
                Console.WriteLine("End of the program");
            }
            Console.ReadLine();
        }

        public static void getException()
        {
            throw new Exception();
        }
    }
}
```

Here is the program output:

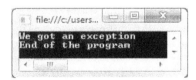

Program 9.3 catches the array out of bounds exception.

Program 9.3

```
using System;
using System.Collections.Generic;
using System.Linq;
using System.Text;
using System.Threading.Tasks;

namespace Exception_Handling
{
    class ExceptionDemo
```

208

```
    {
        static void Main(string[] args)
        {
            int[] x = { 0, 1, 2, 3, 4, 5, 6 };
            int i, n = 10;
            try
            {
                for (i = 0; i < n; i++)
                    Console.WriteLine(x[i]);
            }
            catch (Exception e)
            {
                Console.WriteLine(e.Message);
            }
            Console.ReadLine();
        }
    }
}
```

Here is the program output:

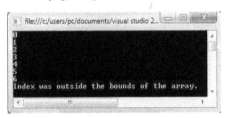

Program 9.4 throws an exception when dividing by zero. This is similar to Program 8.1 except that it uses a function and the finally block.

Program 9.4

```
using System;
using System.Collections.Generic;
using System.Linq;
using System.Text;
using System.Threading.Tasks;
namespace Exception_Handling
{
    class ExceptionDemo
    {
        static void Main(string[] args)
        {
            ExceptionDemo demo = new ExceptionDemo();
            demo.divide(25, 0);
            Console.ReadLine();
        }

        public void divide(int num1, int num2)
        {
            double answer=0;
            try
            {
                answer = num1 / num2;
            }
```

209

```csharp
            catch (DivideByZeroException e)
            {
                Console.WriteLine("Exception caught: attempt to
                                        divide by zero\n");
            }
            finally
            {
                Console.WriteLine("Answer: {0}", answer);
            }
        }
    }
}
```

Here is the program output:

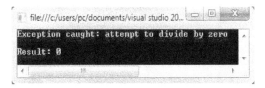

You can also define your own exception. This is called user-defined exception. User-defined exception classes are derived from the Exception class. Program 9.5 illustrates this.

Program 9.5

```csharp
using System;
using System.Collections.Generic;
using System.Linq;
using System.Text;
using System.Threading.Tasks;

namespace Exception_Handling
{
    class exceptionDemo
    {
        static void Main(string[] args)
        {
            Temperature temp = new Temperature();
            try
            {
                temp.showTemp();
            }
            catch (Temp_Is_Zero_Exception e)
            {
                Console.WriteLine("Exception: {0}", e.Message);
            }
            Console.ReadLine();
        }

    }
}

public class Temp_Is_Zero_Exception : Exception
{
    public Temp_Is_Zero_Exception(string message) : base(message)
    {
```

```
        }
}

public class Temperature
{
        int temperature = 0;
        public void showTemp()
        {
                if (temperature == 0)
                {
                        throw (new Temp_Is_Zero_Exception("Zero Temperature found"));
                }
                else
                {
                        Console.WriteLine("Temperature = {0}", temperature);
                }
        }
}
```

Here is the program output:

Exercise

1. What is an exception? Give some examples of exceptions.

2. For the exceptions identified in question 1, write code to catch them.

3. What is the difference between an exception and an error? Should you also write code to catch errors?

4. What is the purpose of finally in the `try...catch...finally` statement?

5. Assume your program requires data from a text file. What will happen to your program if it tries to read data from the file but the file is missing (e.g. accidentally deleted)?
(Text files are discussed in Chapter 10.)

6. Write an exception handler to deal with the problem in question 5.

7. List the classes for handling the following exceptions:

    (a) division by zero
    (b) console input errors
    (c) array out of bounds
    (d) comparing different data types
    (e) copying a large string to a smaller string

Chapter 10

Text Files

Learning Outcomes:

After completing this chapter, you will be able to

- *Work with text files.*
- *Explain the purpose of file streams.*
- *Use input/output classes.*
- *Read data from text files.*
- *Write data to text files.*

10.1 Input/Output

Data stored in the computer's RAM memory are volatile – they are lost when you switch off the computer. To store data permanently, you need secondary storage like hard disk or thumb/pen drive. You can also store more data on these devices than in the RAM memory.

Data stored on disk or thumb dive take the form of files. There are several types of files such database files, text files, binary files and index files. Here we are only concerned with ASCII or text files.

If a program requires lots of input data, it will be more convenient to store the data in a text file and then read the data from the file. Similarly, a program can also send output to a text file for later use. Thus text files can be used for both input and output.

You store data by writing to a text file and you read data by reading from the file. C# provides several classes to help you read and write to text files.

10.2 File Streams

File input/output involves file streams. A file is a collection of data stored in a disk with a specific name and a directory path. When a file is opened for reading or writing, it becomes a stream. A stream is an abstract representation of an input/output device that is a source or destination for data in your program. The input stream is used for reading data into computer memory from an external device. An output stream is used for writing data to an external device.

10.3 Classes for Input/Output

The `System.IO` namespace contains classes for reading data from and for writing data to text files. To use these classes you must include the namespace as shown below.

```
using System.IO;
```

The classes needed for file input/output are given below:

1. File – a utility class for moving, copying, and deleting files

   - `Copy()`   – copies a file to the specified location
   - `Create()`   – creates a file in the specified location
   - `Delete()`   – deletes a file
   - `Open()`   – returns a FileStream object to the specified path
   - `Move()`   – moves a specified file to a new location

2. Directory – a utility class for moving, copying, and deleting directories.

   - `CreateDirectory()` – creates a directory with the specified path
   - `Delete()`   – deletes the specified directory and all the files
   - `Move()`   – moves the specified directory to new location

3. Path – a utility class used to manipulate path names, e.g. `C:\LogFile.txt`

4. FileInfo – represents a physical file on disk, e.g.

   ```
   FileInfo newFile = new FileInfo("C:/Log.txt");
   ```

5. DirectoryInfo – represents a physical directory on disk.

6. `FileStream` – represents a file that can be read from or written to.

   ```
   FileStream newFile = new FileStream("Log.txt", FileMode.Open);
   ```

Other FileMode enumeration members are:

   - `Create`   – create a new file (if one already exists it is destroyed)
   - `CreateNew`   – create a new file (if one already exists, an exception will be thrown)
   - `OpenOrCreate` – open the file if it exists, otherwise create a new file

7. `StreamReader` – reads character data from a stream, can be created by using FileStream as a base.

8. `StreamWriter` – writes character data to a stream, can be created by using FileStream as a base.

The `System.IO` namespace contains classes for reading data from and for writing data to text files. To use these classes you must include the namespace as shown below.

Other input/output classes include:

Input/Output Classes	Description
BinaryReader	Reads primitive data from a binary stream
BinaryWriter	Writes primitive data in binary format.
BufferedStream	Temporary storage for a stream of bytes.
DriveInfo	Provides information for the drives.
MemoryStream	Is used for random access to streamed data stored in memory.
StringReader	Is used for reading from a string buffer.
StringWriter	Is used for writing into a string buffer.

10.4 Reading Data from Text Files

To read data from a text file, use the following steps:

1. Create the text file using Notepad and save is with .txt extension.

2. Create a new project and select C# Console Application.

3. Include the namespace as in the statement below:

    ```
    using System.IO;
    ```

4. Create a FileStream object.

    ```
    FileStream newFile = new FileStream("input.txt", FileMode.Open);
    ```

5. Create a StreamReader object.

    ```
    StreamReader sr = new StreamReader(newFile);
    ```

6. Build and run the project.

Program 10.1 illustrates reading data from a text file called input.txt

Program 10.1

```
using System;
using System.Collections.Generic;
using System.Linq;
using System.Text;
using System.Threading.Tasks;
using System.IO;

namespace Text_File_Sample
{
    class File
    {
        static void Main(string[] args)
        {
            string strLine;
            FileStream fs = new
                FileStream(@"C:\Users\pc\Desktop\input.txt", FileMode.Open);
            StreamReader sr = new StreamReader(fs);
            strLine = sr.ReadLine();
            while (strLine != null)
            {
                Console.WriteLine(strLine);
                strLine = sr.ReadLine();
            }
            sr.Close(); // close the file
            Console.ReadLine();
        }
    }
}
```

Text file input:

Here is a sample run:

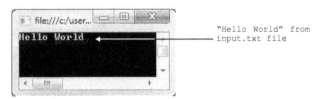

"Hello World" from input.txt file

Program 10.2 does the same thing as the previous example but using StreamReader.

Program 10.2

```
using System;
using System.Collections.Generic;
using System.Linq;
using System.Text;
using System.Threading.Tasks;
using System.IO;

namespace Text_File_Sample
{
    class File
    {
        static void Main(string[] args)
        {
            string strLine;
            StreamReader sr = new
                            StreamReader(@"C:\Users\pc\Desktop\input.txt");
            strLine = sr.ReadLine();
            while (strLine != null)
            {
                Console.WriteLine(strLine);
                strLine = sr.ReadLine();
            }
            sr.Close();   // close the file
            Console.ReadLine();
        }
    }
}
```

The output is same as above.

Program 10.3 reads data from the same text file as above but the file path is not specified. In this case, the program will throw an exception if there is a problem in reading the file.

215

Program 10.3

```csharp
using System;
using System.Collections.Generic;
using System.Linq;
using System.Text;
using System.Threading.Tasks;
using System.IO;

namespace Text_File_Sample
{
    // Reading data from text file with Exception Handling
    class File
    {
        static void Main(string[] args)
        {
            string strLine;
            try
            {
                FileStream newFile = new FileStream("input.txt", FileMode.Open);

                StreamReader sr = new StreamReader(newFile);
                strLine = sr.ReadLine();

                while (strLine != null)
                {
                    Console.WriteLine(strLine);
                    strLine = sr.ReadLine();
                }
                sr.Close();
            }
            catch (IOException e)
            {
                Console.WriteLine("IO exception has been thrown!");
                Console.ReadLine();
            }
        }
    }
}
```

Here is a sample run:

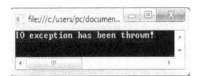

We would normally use commas to separate the different data in a file as shown below:

Peter, Wong, Hock, Bob

Program 10.3 opens the text file input.txt to read the data shown below.

Sellappan, Peter, Wong, Hock, Bob
Sam, Ken, Jason, Edmund, Munir

216

Program 10.3

```
using System;
using System.Collections.Generic;
using System.Linq;
using System.Text;
using System.Threading.Tasks;
using System.IO;

namespace Text_File_Sample
{
    // Reading data from comma-separated file
    class File
    {
        static void Main(string[] args)
        {
            string strLine;
            string[] strWordArray;
            try
            {
                FileStream fs = new
                    FileStream(@"C:\Users\pc\Desktop\input.txt", FileMode.Open);
                StreamReader sr = new StreamReader(fs);
                strLine = sr.ReadLine();

                while (strLine != null)
                {
                    // splits the comma-separated string into string array
                    strWordArray = strLine.Split(',');
                    foreach (string word in strWordArray)
                    {
                        // removes white space characters from
                        // the beginning and end of this instance
                        Console.WriteLine(word.Trim());
                    }
                    strLine = sr.ReadLine();
                }
                sr.Close();
            }
            catch (IOException e)
            {
                Console.WriteLine("IO exception has been thrown!");
                Console.WriteLine(e.ToString());
            }
            Console.ReadLine();
        }
    }
}
```

Text file input:

```
input.txt - Notepad
File  Edit  Format  View  Help
Sellappan,Peter, wong, Hock, Bob
Sam, Ken, Jason, Edmund, Munir
```

Here is a sample run:

file:///...

Sellappan
Peter
Wong
Hock
Bob
Sam
Ken
Jason
Edmund
Munir

Name list from
input.txt file

Program 10.4 does the same thing as Program 10.3 except that it uses only StreamReader to read the data.

Program 10.4

```
using System;
using System.Collections.Generic;
using System.Linq;
using System.Text;
using System.Threading.Tasks;
using System.IO;

namespace Text_File_Sample
{
    class File // Reading data from comma-separated file
    {
        static void Main(string[] args)
        {
            string strLine;
            string[] strWordArray;
            try
            {
                StreamReader sr = new
                StreamReader(@"C:\Users\pc\Desktop\input.txt");
                strLine = sr.ReadLine();

                while (strLine != null)
                {
                    strWordArray = strLine.Split(',');
                    foreach (string word in strWordArray)
                    {
                        Console.WriteLine(word.Trim());
                    }
                    strLine = sr.ReadLine();
                }
                sr.Close();
            }

            catch (IOException e)
            {
                Console.WriteLine("IO exception has been thrown!");
                Console.WriteLine(e.ToString());
            }
            Console.ReadLine();
        }
    }
}
```

218

Here is a sample run:

Program 10.5 illustrates reading a text file named Nigeria.txt. Note how the two keywords using and StreamReader were used together inside the program.

Program 10.5

```
using System;
using System.Collections.Generic;
using System.Linq;
using System.Text;
using System.Threading.Tasks;
using System.IO;

namespace Text_File_Sample
{
    class File
    {
        static void Main(string[] args)
        {
            string line;

            try
            {
                //Create instance of StreamReader to read from file.
                // The using statement also closes the StreamReader.
                using (StreamReader sr = new
                            StreamReader(@"C:\Users\pc\Desktop\Nigeria.txt"));

                // Read and display lines from the file until end of file
                while ((line = sr.ReadLine()) != null)
                {
                    Console.WriteLine(line);
                }
            }

            catch (Exception e)
            {
                // Let the user know what went wrong.
                Console.WriteLine("The file could not be read:");
                Console.WriteLine(e.Message);
            }
            Console.ReadLine();
        }
    }
}
```

Text file input:

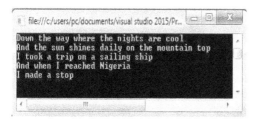

Here is a sample run:

Program 10.6 reads student name and mark from a text file named `data.txt` and computes the student grade (grade="Pass" if mark >= 40 otherwise grade="Fail").

Program 10.6

```
using System;
using System.Collections.Generic;
using System.Linq;
using System.Text;
using System.Threading.Tasks;
using System.IO;

namespace Text_File_Sample
{
    class Pro
    {
        static void Main(string[] args)
        {
            string[] input;
            string grade, name,list;
            int i = 0,mark;
            Console.Write("No\tName\tMark\tGrade\n");
            StreamReader sr = new StreamReader(@"C:\Users\pc\Desktop\data.txt");

            while ((list = sr.ReadLine()) != null)
            {
                i++;
                input = list.Split(',');
                name = input[0];
                mark = Convert.ToInt32(input[1]);
                if (mark < 40)
                    grade = "Fail";
                else
                    grade = "Pass";
```

```
                Console.WriteLine("{0}\t{1}\t{2}\t{3}",i, name, mark, grade);
            }
            Console.ReadLine();
        }
    }
}
```

Text file input:

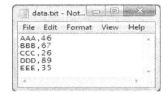

Here is a sample run:

Program 10.7 reads student names and marks from a text file named data.txt into a struct called details then computes the student grade.

Program 10.7

```
using System;
using System.Collections.Generic;
using System.Linq;
using System.Text;
using System.Threading.Tasks;
using System.IO;

namespace Text_File_Sample
    {
    //struct declaration
    struct details
    {
        public string name;
        public int mark;
    }

    class File
        {
            static void Main(string[] args)
            {
            string line, grade;
            int n = 5;
            string[] arr = new string[n];
```

221

```
            details d; //create an object of the struct

            Console.Write("Name\tMark\tGrade\n");
            using (StreamReader sr = new
                StreamReader(@"C:\Users\pc\Desktop\data.txt"))
                while ((line = sr.ReadLine()) != null)
                {
                    arr = line.Split(',');
                    //assigning value to struct
                    d.name = arr[0];
                    d.mark = Convert.ToInt32(arr[1]);
                    if (d.mark < 40)
                        grade = "Fail";
                    else
                        grade = "Pass";
                    Console.WriteLine("{0}\t{1}\t{2}", d.name, d.mark, grade);
                }
            Console.ReadLine();
            }
        }
    }
```

Text file input:

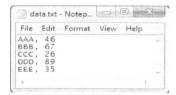

Here is a sample run:

Program 10.8 reads product name, price and quantity from a text file named lists.txt into a struct called Products and then computes the amount and the average.

Program 10.8

```
using System;
using System.Collections.Generic;
using System.Linq;
using System.Text;
using System.Threading.Tasks;
using System.IO;

namespace Text_File_Sample
{
```

222

```csharp
//struct declaration
struct Product
{
    public string pname;
    public double price;
    public int qty;
}

class File
{
    static void Main(string[] args)
    {
        string items;
        double amt,sum=0,avg;
        int n = 5,count=0;
        string[] arr = new string[n];
        Product p; // create an object of the struct

        Console.Write("Name\tPrice(RM)\tQuantity\tAmount(RM)\n");
        using (StreamReader sr = new
                       StreamReader(@"C:\Users\pc\Desktop\list.txt"));

        while ((items = sr.ReadLine()) != null)
        {
            count = count + 1;
            arr = items.Split(',');
            //assigning value to struct
            p.pname = arr[0].Trim('"');
            p.price = Convert.ToDouble(arr[1]);
            p.qty = Convert.ToInt32(arr[2]);
            //compute amount
            amt = p.price * p.qty;
            sum = sum + amt;
            Console.WriteLine("{0}\t{1}\t\t{2}\t\t{3}", p.pname,p.price,
                                                           p.qty,amt);
        }
        avg = sum / count;
        Console.WriteLine("\nAverage amount spent = RM{0}", avg);
        Console.ReadLine();
    }
}
```

Text file input:

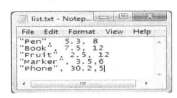

Here is a sample run:

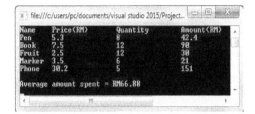

```
file:///c:/users/pc/documents/visual studio 2015/Project...
Name     Price(RM)        Quantity        Amount(RM)
Pen      5.3              8               42.4
Book     7.5              12              90
Fruit    2.5              12              30
Marker   3.5              6               21
Phone    30.2             5               151

Average amount spent = RM66.88
```

Program 10.9 creates a text file called countries to store n=15 country names and their capitals. Then it reads the file and stores the country names and their capitals in the arrays country and capital respectively. When the user enters a country name, the program displays a message "The capital of ... is ..." if there is a match or the message "The country name is not in the list." if there is no match.

Program 10.9

```
using System;
using System.Collections.Generic;
using System.Linq;
using System.Text;
using System.Threading.Tasks;
using System.IO;

namespace Text_File_Sample
{
    class File
    {
        static void Main(string[] args)
        {
            string[] countries;
            string ctry, search;
            int n = 15,i=0;
            string[] country = new string[n];
            string[] capital = new string[n];
            using (StreamReader sr = new
                StreamReader(@"C:\Users\pc\Desktop\countries.txt"))
            while ((ctry = sr.ReadLine()) != null)
            {
                countries = ctry.Split(',');
                country[i] = countries[0].Trim('"');
                capital[i] = countries[1].Trim('"');
                i = i + 1;
            }

            Console.Write("Enter country name: ");
            search = Console.ReadLine();
            for (i = 0; i < n; i++)
            {
                if (string.Equals(search, country[i]) )
                {
                    Console.WriteLine("The capital of {0} is {1}",
                                        search, capital[i]);
                    break;
                }

                else if (search != country[i] && i == n - 1)
                {
                    Console.WriteLine("The country name is not is the list");
```

224

```
        }
    }
        Console.ReadLine();
    }
  }
}
```

Text file input:

Here is a sample run:

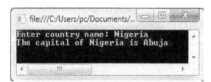

When there is no match the program output:

10.5 Writing Output to Text Files

To write output to a text file, use the following steps:

1. Create a new project and Select C# Console Application.

2. Create a `FileStream` object.

   ```
   FileStream newFile = new FileStream("out.txt", FileMode.CreateNew);
   ```

3. Create a `StreamWriter` object.

   ```
   StreamWriter sw = new StreamWriter(newFile);
   ```

4. Build and run the project.

Program 10.10 illustrates writing output to a text file. It writes the text `Hello World` to the text file `out.txt`.

Program 10.10

```
using System;
using System.Collections.Generic;
using System.Linq;
using System.Text;
using System.Threading.Tasks;
using System.IO;

namespace Text_File_Sample
{
    class File
    {
        static void Main(string[] args)
        {
            FileStream newFile = new
            FileStream(@"C:\Users\pc\Desktop\out.txt", FileMode.CreateNew);
            StreamWriter sw = new StreamWriter(newFile);
            sw.WriteLine("Hello World");
            sw.Close();  // close the file
            Console.ReadLine();
        }
    }
}
```

Here is the program output:

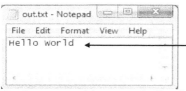

Search for **out.txt** file from the file location and open up the file. You should see the "**Hello World**" characters in the file.

Note that you can straight away put the file path and file name into the `StreamWriter` as illustrated in Program 10.11

Program 10.11

```
using System;
using System.Collections.Generic;
using System.Linq;
using System.Text;
using System.Threading.Tasks;
using System.IO;

namespace Text_File_Sample
{
    class File
    {
        static void Main(string[] args)
        {
```

226

```
            StreamWriter sw = new
            StreamWriter sw = new StreamWriter(@"C:\Users\pc\Desktop\out.txt");
            sw.WriteLine("Hello World");
            sw.Close();  // close the file
            Console.ReadLine();
        }
    }
}
```

The output will be the same as before.

Program 10.12 illustrates writing user input to a text file.

Program 10.12

```
using System;
using System.Collections.Generic;
using System.Linq;
using System.Text;
using System.Threading.Tasks;
using System.IO;
namespace Text_File_Sample
{
    // Writing user input to a text file
    class File
    {
        static void Main(string[] args)
        {
            string message;
            StreamWriter sw = new
                        StreamWriter(@"C:\Users\pc\Desktop\out.txt");
            Console.Write("Enter your message: ");
            message = Console.ReadLine();
            sw.WriteLine(message);
            sw.Close();  // close the file
            Console.ReadLine();
        }
    }
}
```

Here is a sample run:

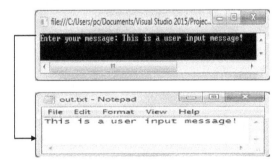

Program 10.13 illustrates writing user input to a text file using `struct`.

227

Program 10.13

```
using System;
using System.Collections.Generic;
using System.Linq;
using System.Text;
using System.Threading.Tasks;
using System.IO;

namespace Text_File_Sample
{
    struct output
    {
        public string message;
    }

    class File
    {
        static void Main(string[] args)
        {
            output stmt;
            StreamWriter sw = new StreamWriter(@"C:\Users\pc\Desktop\out.txt");
            Console.Write("Enter your message: ");
            stmt.message = Console.ReadLine();//assign message to struct
            sw.WriteLine(stmt.message); //write message to text file
            sw.Close();  // close the file
            Console.ReadLine();
        }
    }
}
```

Here is a sample run:

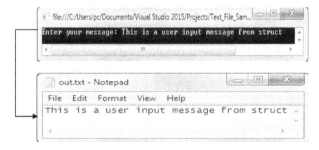

Program 10.14 illustrates writing to and reading from a text file using FileStream.

Program 10.14

```
using System;
using System.Collections.Generic;
using System.Linq;
using System.Text;
using System.Threading.Tasks;
using System.IO;

namespace Text_File_Sample
{
```

```
class File
{
    static void Main(string[] args)
    {
        int i, n = 20;
        FileStream F = new FileStream(@"C:\Users\pc\Desktop\text.txt",
                            FileMode.OpenOrCreate, FileAccess.ReadWrite);

        for (i = 1; i <= n; i++)
        {
            F.WriteByte((byte)i);
        }

        F.Position = 0;
        for (i = 1; i <= n; i++)
        {
            Console.Write(F.ReadByte() + " ");
        }
        F.Close();
        Console.ReadLine();
    }
}
```

Here is a sample run:

Program 10.15 illustrates writing text data into a file using the StreamWriter and reading same text using StreamReader.

Program 10.15

```
using System;
using System.Collections.Generic;
using System.Linq;
using System.Text;
using System.Threading.Tasks;
using System.IO;
namespace Text_File_Sample
{
    class File
    {
        static void Main(string[] args)
        {
            string[] names = new string[] {"Sellappan","Munir","Ali","Yip","Leon"};

            using (StreamWriter sw = new
                            StreamWriter(@"C:\Users\pc\Desktop\names.txt"));
            foreach (string s in names)
            {
                sw.WriteLine(s);//write each name into the file
            }

            // Read and show each line from the file.
            string line = "";
```

```
            using (StreamReader sr = new
                    StreamReader(@"C:\Users\pc\Desktop\names.txt"));

            while ((line = sr.ReadLine()) != null)
            {
                Console.WriteLine(line);
            }
            Console.ReadLine();
        }
    }
}
```

Here is a sample run:

Text File output:

Console output:

10.6 Sample Programs

Program 10.16 shows how to write data to and read data from the same file.

Program 10.16

```
using System;
using System.Collections.Generic;
using System.Linq;
using System.Text;
using System.Threading.Tasks;
using System.IO;

namespace Text_File_Sample
{
    // Writing to and reading data from the same text file
    class File
    {
        static void Main(string[] args)
        {
```

```csharp
        int choice;
        Console.Write("Enter your choice (1-read; 2-write): ");
        choice = Convert.ToInt32(Console.ReadLine());

        switch (choice)
        {
            case 1:
                read();
                break;
            case 2:
                write();
                break;
            default:
                Console.WriteLine("Invalid choice!");
                break;
        }
        Console.ReadLine();

    }

    static void write()
    {
        string message;
        FileStream newFile = new
            FileStream(@"C:\Users\pc\Desktop\data.txt", FileMode.Open);
        StreamWriter sw = new StreamWriter(newFile);

        Console.WriteLine("Enter your message: ");
        message = Console.ReadLine();

        sw.Write(message);
        sw.Close();
    }

    static void read()
    {
        string strLine;
        FileStream newFile = new
            FileStream(@"C:\Users\pc\Desktop\data.txt", FileMode.Open);
        StreamReader sr = new StreamReader(newFile);
        strLine = sr.ReadLine();
        while (strLine != null)
        {
            Console.WriteLine(strLine);
            strLine = sr.ReadLine();
        }
        sr.Close(); // close the file after reading the data
    }
  }
}
```

Here is a sample run:

Original text in
data.txt file

Run the application and choose 1 (read).

Run the application again and choose 2 (write).

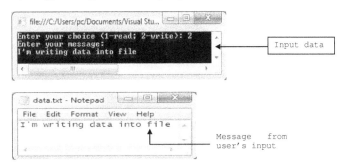

Program 10.17 illustrates the use of `DirectoryInfo` class to display the name and size of each file in the specified directory.

Program 10.17

```
using System;
using System.Collections.Generic;
using System.Linq;
using System.Text;
using System.Threading.Tasks;
using System.IO;
namespace Text_File_Sample
{
    class Test
    {
        static void Main(string[] args)
        {
            //creating a DirectoryInfo object
            DirectoryInfo mydir = new
                DirectoryInfo(@"C:\Users\pc\Desktop\Big Data\New folder");
            Console.Write("File Name\t\t\tSize\n");
            // getting the files in the directory, their names and size
            FileInfo[] f = mydir.GetFiles();
            foreach (FileInfo file in f)
            {
                Console.WriteLine("{0}\t\t{1}", file.Name, file.Length);
            }
            Console.ReadLine();
        }
    }
}
```

Here is a sample run:

Program 10.18 demonstrates the use of delegate. The delegate printString() can be used to reference a method that takes a string as input and returns nothing. We use this delegate to call two methods, the first prints the string to the console, and the second prints it to a file.

Program 10.18

```
using System;
using System.Collections.Generic;
using System.IO;
using System.Linq;
using System.Text;
using System.Threading.Tasks;

namespace Delegate_Example
{
    class PrintString
    {
        static FileStream fs;
        static StreamWriter sw;

        // delegate declaration
        public delegate void printString(string s);

        // this method prints to the console
        public static void WriteToScreen(string str)
        {
            Console.WriteLine("The String is: {0}", str);
        }

        //this method prints to a file
        public static void WriteToFile(string s)
        {
            fs = new FileStream(@"C:\Users\pc\Desktop\message.txt",
                                FileMode.Append, FileAccess.Write);
            sw = new StreamWriter(fs);
            sw.WriteLine(s);
            sw.Flush();
            sw.Close();
            fs.Close();
        }

        // this method takes the delegate as parameter and
           uses it to call the methods as required

        public static void sendString(printString ps)
        {
            ps("Hello World");
        }
        static void Main(string[] args)
        {
            printString ps1 = new printString(WriteToScreen);
```

233

```
           printString ps2 = new printString(WriteToFile);
           sendString(ps1);
           sendString(ps2);
           Console.ReadLine();
        }
    }
}
```

Here is the console output:

And here is the text file output:

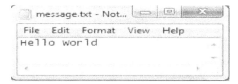

Exercise

1. What is the purpose of text file? List situations where a text file might be useful.

2. Write a program that will generate 50 integer random numbers between 500 and 900 and write the numbers to a text file (`random.txt`).

3. Read the data from the text file created in Question 2 and compute and display the average and standard deviation.

4. Write a program that will write the even numbers 2, 4, 6, …, 100 to a text file (`even.txt`) and then read and display the numbers (10 numbers to a row).

5. Create a text file using Notepad (under `Programs > Accessories`) that will store `ProductCode`, `ProductName`, `UnitPrice`. Then write a program that will request the user to enter a product code and quantity ordered and display the following information: `ProductCode`, `ProductName`, `UnitPrice`, `Quantity` and `Amount` (`Product * Quantity`). Format currencies to 2 decimal places.

Chapter 11

Accessing Databases

Learning Outcomes:

After completing this chapter, you will be able to

- *Explain database concepts.*
- *State the purpose of ADO.NET.*
- *Create Microsoft Access database.*
- *Use basic SQL commands.*
- *Write database applications.*
- *Use aggregate functions.*

11.1 Database Concepts

A database is a collection of related tables for one or more applications, where each table corresponds to some business entity such as customer, product, purchase, etc.

A table is a collection of rows and columns. The columns correspond to fields (attributes) while the rows correspond to records (tuples). It is not necessary to name the rows. The columns however must be named. A table can have many rows and columns. The columns are usually few in number (tens) while the rows usually number into hundreds or thousands.

All the columns in a table must have unique names, meaning, no two columns can have the same name. Similarly, the rows in the table must also be unique. The key value (which is unique) in each row guarantees this uniqueness.

The order of columns and rows in a table is not significant. That means, you can exchange rows or columns and it will not have no effect on the database.

A table has a key field (called **primary key**) consisting of one or a combination of fields (columns). The key value must be unique. This ensures that no two records (rows) in the table are identical.

The database system (MS Access) creates an index for the key field to speed up search operations and improve the access time. The index effectively sorts the table according to some key sequence - in ascending or descending order of key values. Sorting improves the performance of a database significantly.

Besides the primary key, a table may also have foreign keys. A foreign key is used to access another table where it is the primary key. For example, an inventory table may use a column to store the supplier code where the supplier code is the primary key in the supplier table.

11.2 What is ADO.NET

C# provides a set of classes to help programmers to access databases easily. These classes are collectively known as ADO.NET. ADO.NET comes with commands for reading, writing and updating records. It provides all the functionalities to access data from a database. The figure below shows the basic classes in ADO.NET.

Basic classes in ADO.NET

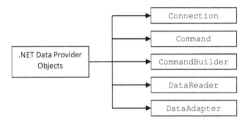

Class	Purpose
Connection	First object you need before you can use any other object.
Command	Gives commands such as query to a data source (e.g., SqlCommand for SQL Server and OleDBCommand for OLE DB).
CommandBuilder	Used to build SQL commands for data modification from objects based on a single-table query (e.g., SqlCommandBuilder for SQL Server and OleDBCommandBuilder for OLE DB).
DataReader	Used for reading data with maximum performance. It's a simple-to-use object (e.g., SqlDataReader for SQL Server; OleDBDataReader for OLE DB).
DataAdapter	Used to perform various operations specific to the data source including updating changed data and filling data sets (e.g., SqlDataAdapter for SQL Server; OleDBDataAdapter for OLE DB).

11.3 Creating Microsoft Access Database

You can create a relational database using Microsoft Access, SQL Server, MySQL or ORACLE, and access the database from C#. In this book, we will use the popular MS Access database.

As a simple illustration, let's create and access an inventory database with just one table. Let's call the database datInventory and the table tblInventory.

You can use the following steps to create the database:

1. Start Microsoft Access.

2. In the Microsoft Access window, select Blank Database.

236

3. In the File Name window, enter datInventory as file name and choose the destination to store the file (e.g., c:\datInventory.accdb). Then click Create.

4. In the datInventory:Database, Right-click on Table1:Table and choose Design View.

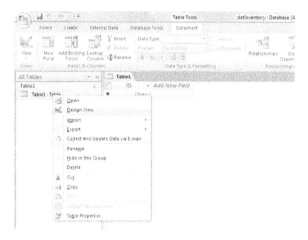

5. Enter `tblInventory` as the Table name and Click OK button.

6. Enter the fields and their data types as follows (make `Code` as primary key):

7. Save the database design.

8. In the datInventory:Database window, Double-click on the tblInventory icon and enter the
following data. Then save the table.

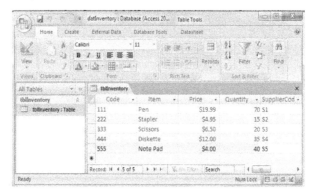

11.4 Basic SQL Commands

There are four basic SQL commands that are used for querying, updating, adding, and deleting rows in a
table.

Basic SQL Commands

SELECT command

The select command takes the form:

```
SELECT table_fields
FROM table_name
WHERE condition;
```

Here is an example.

```
SELECT *
FROM employee
```

(* is a shorthand for all fields)

UPDATE command

The update command takes the form:
```
UPDATE table_name
SET field_name = ?
WHERE (field_name = ?)
```

239

Here is an example.

```
UPDATE employee
SET emp_id = 112
WHERE (emp_name = 'AHMAD')
```

INSERT command

The `insert` command takes the form:

```
INSERT INTO table_name VALUES (?)
```

Here is an example.

```
INSERT INTO employee VALUES ('ALI', 552)
```

DELETE command

The `delete` command takes the form:

```
DELETE FROM table_name WHERE (field_name = ?)
```

Here is an example.

```
DELETE FROM employee WHERE (emp_id = 112)
```

Accessing Microsoft Access Database

In this section we will show how to access a Microsoft Access database from a Console application. We will use a simple bookshop database to illustrate the steps involved.

First, create an Access database. Before you do that, it would be a good idea to create a folder to store all your project files. You can do this, Right-Click on your `Desktop` or inside your `Document` > `New` > `Folder`.

Start Access and create the database. Let's call it `dbBookStore`. Follow the steps in the last section to create the database. Add the table below to the database and name it `tblBookStore`. The table has four records and eight fields.

ISBN	Title	Publisher	Author	Year	Price	Quantity	Category
999-99-9999-1	C++ Programming	Fong Hun	Dr James	2015	50.00	10	IT
999-99-9999-2	MS Access	Ang Tong	Dr ABC	2017	30.00	15	IT
999-99-9999-3	VB Programming	Ang Tong	Dr XYZ	2014	50.00	15	IT
999-99-9999-4	Networking	Fong Hun	Ms Cathie	2015	60.00	10	IT

To work with MS Access, you need to add the following namespace:

```
using System.Data.OleDb;
```

You also need a connection string. To do this, follow the steps below:

1. On your C# Console Application, Click on Server Explorer.

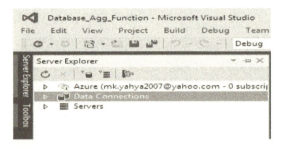

2. Click on Connect to Database

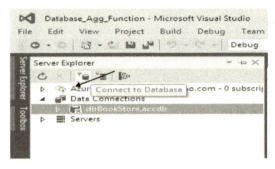

3. Click on Browse to select the database file.

4. Click the Advance button

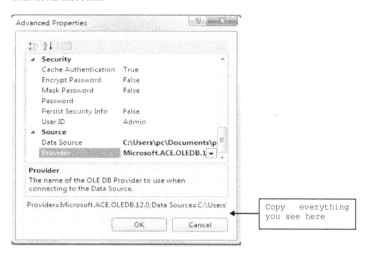

5. Close the two dialog boxes and Paste the connection string into OleDbConnection method as shown below:

```
OleDbConnection con = new
            OleDbConnection(@"Provider=Microsoft.ACE.OLEDB.12.0;
            Data Source=C:\Users\pc\Documents\product.accdb");
```

Note the use of '@' character in the connection string. This is to tell the compiler not to take '\' as an escape sequence.

Program 11.1 illustrates how to retrieve data from the dbBookStore database that we created earlier using several ADO.NET objects.

Program 11.1

```
using System;
using System.Collections.Generic;
using System.Linq;
using System.Text;
using System.Threading.Tasks;
using System.Data.OleDb;

namespace Database_Samples
{
    class OleDbProgram
    {
        static void Main(string[] args)
        {
            // Create a database connection
            OleDbConnection connection = new
                    OleDbConnection(@"Provider=Microsoft.ACE.OLEDB.12.0;
                    Data Source=C:\Users\pc\Documents\dbBookStore.accdb");

            // Create a command object and store the sql query
```

242

```csharp
OleDbCommand command = new OleDBCommand("Select * from
                tblBookStore", connection);
try
{
    // Open the connection
    connection.Open();

    // Create a datareader object to read the table
    OleDbDataReader reader = command.ExecuteReader();
    Console.WriteLine("This is the data returned from
                            tblBookStore\n");
    // Iterate through the database
    while (reader.Read())
    {
        Console.WriteLine("{0}\t{1}\t{2}",
            reader["ISBN"], reader["Title"], reader["Year"]);
    }
    Console.WriteLine();

    // Close the reader
    reader.Close()

    // Close the connection
    connection.Close();
}

// Usual exception handling
catch (OleDbException e)
{
    Console.WriteLine("Error:{0}", e.Errors[0].Message);
}
Console.ReadLine();
    }
}
```

Here is the program output:

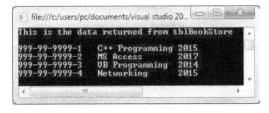

Program 11.2 illustrates how to insert data (records) into a database. The program will insert the following record into the table:

ISBN	Title	Publisher	Author	Year	Price	Quantity	Category
999-99-9999-5	C# Programming	ABC	Prof. Sellappan	2016	70.00	15	IT

243

Program 11.2

```
using System;
using System.Collections.Generic;
using System.Linq;
using System.Text;
using System.Threading.Tasks;
using System.Data.OleDb;

namespace Database_Samples
{
    class OleDbProgram
    {
        static void Main(string[] args)
        {
            // Create a database connection
            OleDbConnection connection = new
            OleDbConnection(@"Provider=Microsoft.ACE.OLEDB.12.0;Data
                Source=C:\Users\pc\Documents\dbBookStore.accdb");
            // Create a command object and store the sql query
            OleDbCommand command =new OleDbCommand("INSERT INTO
            tblBookStore VALUES ('999-99-9999-5', 'C# Programming', 'ABC',
            'Prof. Sellappan', 2016, 70, 15, 'IT')", connection);
            try
            {
                // Open the connection
                connection.Open();
                // Executes query and returns no. of affected rows
                int rows = command.ExecuteNonQuery();

                Console.WriteLine("Record inserted successfully.");
                Console.WriteLine("{0} row{1} affected.", rows,rows
                                            <= 1 ? "" : "s");

                // Close the connection
                connection.Close();
            }
            // Usual exception handling
            catch (OleDbException e)
            {
                Console.WriteLine("Error:{0}", e.Errors[0].Message);
            }
            Console.ReadLine();
        }
    }
}
```

Here is the program output:

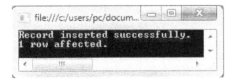

244

New record added

Program 11.3 illustrates how to delete data (record) from a database. The program will remove the following records from the database.

ISBN	Title	Publisher	Author	Year	Price	Quantity	Category
999-99-9999-5	C# Programming	ABC	Prof. Sellappan	2016	70.00	15	IT

Program 11.3

```
using System;
using System.Collections.Generic;
using System.Linq;
using System.Text;
using System.Threading.Tasks;
using System.Data.OleDb;

namespace Database_Samples
{
    class OleDbProgram
    {
        static void Main(string[] args)
        {
            // Create a database connection
            OleDbConnection connection = new
                OleDbConnection(@"Provider=Microsoft.ACE.OLEDB.12.0;
                Data Source=C:\Users\pc\Documents\dbBookStore.accdb");

            // Create a command object and store the sql query
            OleDbCommand command = new OleDbCommand("DELETE from
                tblBookStore where ISBN='999-99-9999-5'", connection);
            try
            {
                // Open the connection
                connection.Open();

                // Executes query and returns no.of affected rows
                int rows = command.ExecuteNonQuery();
                Console.WriteLine("Record deleted successfully.");
                Console.WriteLine("{0} row{1} affected.", rows, rows
                                    <= 1 ? "" : "s");
                // Close the connection
                connection.Close();
            }
```

```
            // Usual exception handling
            catch (OleDbException e)
            {
                Console.WriteLine("Error:{0}", e.Errors[0].Message);
            }
            Console.ReadLine();
        }
    }
}
```

Here is the program output:

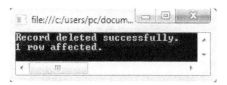

Program 11.4 illustrates how to update data (records) in a database. The program will update the Author field to the following record from "Dr James" and "Ms Cathie" to "Prof. Sellappan".

Target field

ISBN	Title	Publisher	Author	Year	Price	Quantity	Category
999-99-9999-1	C++ Programming	Fong Hun	Dr James	1999	50.00	10	IT

Program 11.4

```
using System;
using System.Collections.Generic;
using System.Linq;
using System.Text;
using System.Threading.Tasks;
using System.Data.OleDb;

namespace Database_Samples
{
    class OleDbSource
    {
```

246

```
static void Main(string[] args)
{
    // Create a database connection
    OleDbConnection connection = new
    OleDbConnection(@"Provider=Microsoft.ACE.OLEDB.12.0;
        Data Source=C:\Users\pc\Documents\dbBookStore.accdb");
    OleDbCommand command = new OleDbCommand("UPDATE tblBookStore
        SET Author = 'Prof. Sellappan' where Year = '2015'", connection);

    try
    {
        // Open the connection
        connection.Open();
        // Executes query and returns no. of affected rows
        int rows = command.ExecuteNonQuery();
        Console.WriteLine("Record updated successfully.");
        Console.WriteLine("{0} row{1} affected.", rows, rows
                                            <= 1 ? "" : "s");
        // Close the connection
        connection.Close();
    }
    // Usual exception handling
    catch (OleDbException e)
    {
        Console.WriteLine("Error:{0}", e.Errors[0].Message);
    }
    Console.ReadLine();
}
}
}
```

Here is the program output:

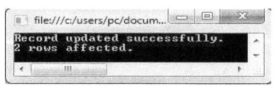

Updated

247

Program 11.5 creates a product database and adds a table called tblproduct as shown below. When a customer enters product code and quantity, it display the details of the customer's purchase including product code, product name, quantity purchased, unit price, total purchase value, date and time of purchase.

ProductCode	ProductName	Price ($)
AAA	Cheese	12.00
BBB	Milk	8.00
CCC	Bread	7.00
DDD	Ice cream	15.00
EEE	Butter	10.00
FFF	Chocolate	5.00
GGG	Yoghurt	12.00

Program 11.5

```
using System;
using System.Collections.Generic;
using System.Linq;
using System.Text;
using System.Threading.Tasks;
using System.Data.OleDb;

namespace Database_Samples
{
    class OleDbProgram
    {
        static void Main(string[] args)
        {
            string code,pcode,pname;
            int qty;
            double sum, price;
            Console.Write("Enter product code: ");
            code = Console.ReadLine();
            code.ToUpper();
            Console.Write("Enter quantity: ");
            qty = Convert.ToInt32(Console.ReadLine());
            OleDbConnection con = new
            OleDbConnection(@"Provider=Microsoft.ACE.OLEDB.12.0;
                Data Source=C:\Users\pc\Documents\product.accdb");

            OleDbCommand cmd = new OleDbCommand("select
                tblproduct.[ProductCode], tblproduct.[ProductName],
                tblproduct.[Price($)] from tblproduct
                WHERE(ProductCode=@aaa)", con);

            cmd.Parameters.AddWithValue("@aaa", code);

            con.Open();
            OleDbDataReader dr = cmd.ExecuteReader();
            while (dr.Read())
            {
                pcode = dr["ProductCode"].ToString();
                pname = dr["ProductName"].ToString();
                price = Convert.ToDouble(dr["Price($)"].ToString());
                sum = qty * price;
                Console.WriteLine();
                Console.WriteLine("\nProduct Code: {0}", pcode);
                Console.WriteLine("\nProduct Name: {0}", pname);
                Console.WriteLine("\nUnit Price: ${0}", price);
                Console.WriteLine("\nQuantity: {0}", qty);
                Console.WriteLine("\nTotal Purchase: ${0}", sum);
                Console.WriteLine("\nTime: {0}", DateTime.Now.ToString());
```

248

```
            }
            Console.ReadLine();
            con.Close();
        }
    }
}
```

Here is the program output:

11.5 Aggregate Functions

Access provides several aggregate functions to perform a variety of tasks such as calculating the average or total of a column. You can use functions to generate summary information. These functions are used in the SELECT statement, all of which take fields or expressions as arguments as shown below:

```
Aggregate_function (expression)
```

where

Aggregate_function is SUM, AVG, COUNT, MIN, MAX, STDEV, STDEVP, VAR or VARP.

expression identifies the field that contains the numeric data you want to evaluate.

Program 11.6 illustrates the use of an aggregate function COUNT to return the number of records in tblproduct table that was created in Program 11.5.

Program 11.6

```
using System;
using System.Collections.Generic;
using System.Linq;
using System.Text;
using System.Threading.Tasks;
using System.Data.OleDb;

namespace Database_Sample
{
    class OleDbProgram
    {
        static void Main(string[] args)
        {
            OleDbConnection con = new
```

249

```
             OleDbConnection(@"Provider=Microsoft.ACE.OLEDB.12.0;
       Data Source=C:\Users\pc\Documents\product.accdb");

             OleDbCommand cmd = new OleDbCommand("SELECT  Count(*)
                                    FROM tblproduct", con);
       con.Open();
             Console.WriteLine("The number of records inside our product
                  table is {0}",Convert.ToInt32(cmd.ExecuteScalar()));
       con.Close();
             Console.ReadLine();
        }
     }
}
```

Here is the program output:

Program 11.7 illustrates the use of aggregate functions MIN, MAX, SUM and AVG to return the minimum, maximum, total and average value of the product price from table tblproduct.

Program 11.7

```
using System;
using System.Collections.Generic;
using System.Linq;
using System.Text;
using System.Threading.Tasks;
using System.Data.OleDb;

namespace Database_Sample
{
    class OleDbProgram
    {
        static void Main(string[] args)
        {
            OleDbConnection con =
             NewOleDbConnection(@"Provider=Microsoft.ACE.OLEDB.12.0;
                  Data Source=C:\Users\pc\Documents\product.accdb");

             OleDbCommand cmdmin = new OleDbCommand("SELECT
                  Min(tblproduct.[Price($)]) FROM tblproduct", con);

             OleDbCommand cmdmax = new OleDbCommand("SELECT
                  Max(tblproduct.[Price($)]) FROM tblproduct", con);

             OleDbCommand cmdsum = new OleDbCommand("SELECT
                  Sum(tblproduct.[Price($)]) FROM tblproduct", con);

             OleDbCommand cmdavg = new OleDbCommand("SELECT
                  Avg(tblproduct.[Price($)]) FROM tblproduct", con);

            con.Open();
             Console.WriteLine("The minimum price = ${0}",
                       Convert.ToDouble(cmdmin.ExecuteScalar()));
```

250

```
Console.WriteLine("\nThe maximum price = ${0}",
            Convert.ToDouble(cmdmax.ExecuteScalar()));
Console.WriteLine("\nThe total price = ${0}",
            Convert.ToDouble(cmdsum.ExecuteScalar()));
Console.WriteLine("\nThe average price = ${0}",
            Convert.ToDouble(cmdavg.ExecuteScalar()));
con.Close();
Console.ReadLine();
        }
    }
}
```

Here is the program output:

Exercise

1. Create an employee database (datEmployee) using Access, then add the table tblEmployee with the fields:

```
EmpId       Text       5 characters
EmpName     Text       20 characters
Sex         Text       1 character (M, m, F, f)
DateBorn    Date
Dept        Text       10 characters
Salary      Currency   2 decimal places (between 0 and 10,000)
```

Enter data for seven records.

2. Use C# to display all the fields in the table.

3. Write code to display the first five fields of all the records in the table.

4. Develop a database system to keep personnel records for a company.

5. Develop a simple library information system that allows users to borrow and return books.

Chapter 12

Object-Oriented Programming

Learning Outcomes:

After completing this chapter, the student will be able to

- *Explain object oriented programming concepts.*
- *Explain classes, encapsulation and objects.*
- *Differentiate between static and instance members.*
- *Describe class inheritance.*
- *Explain polymorphism.*
- *State the purpose of constructors and destructors.*
- *Define abstract classes and interfaces*
- *Write code for object interaction.*

12.1 What is OOP

C# is an object-oriented programming language. It is based on object-oriented concepts like classes, objects, methods, inheritance, polymorphism, and method and operator overloading.

An object-based system consists of a collection of *interacting* objects. The objects (in each class) encapsulate the variables and methods they need. Variables store data the object details such as employee name, department and salary. Methods manipulate the values of these variables.

Accessing class members (variables and methods) take the form:

```
object_name.variable; // accessing an object's variable

object_name.method(argument list); // accessing an object's method
```

Note: The list of arguments in the method must be enclosed between a pair of parenthesis ( ) even if the list is empty.

By themselves the objects in a system do nothing. The objects must interact to perform useful business functions. The interaction between objects takes the form of passing (sending) messages with the required arguments (parameters). Message passing is similar to calling functions/methods.

12.2 Classes and Objects

A class declaration in C# takes the general form:

```
access_modifier class class_name
{
    // class members
}
```

where access_modifier can be `public` or `internal` (which is the default type). The `public` modifier tells that the class is available to all projects while the `internal` modifier tells that the class is available only to the current project.

If you want another class in the current project or another project to access a method or variable, you must specify the class as `public`. The declaration takes the form:

```
public class class_name
{
    // class members
}
```

A class may also be declared as abstract or sealed. An abstract class *cannot* be instantiated; it can only be inherited. A sealed class cannot be derived from.

The table below lists the various class access modifiers.

Modifier	Meaning
none or internal	Class accessible only from within the current project.
public	Class accessible from anywhere.
abstract or internal abstract	Class accessible only from within the current project, cannot be instantiated, only derived from.
public abstract	Class accessible from anywhere, cannot be instantiated, only derived from.
sealed or internal sealed	Class accessible only from within the current project, cannot be derived from, only instantiated.
public sealed	Class accessible from anywhere, cannot be derived from, only instantiated.

Defining Class Members

Class members – variables (fields/properties) and methods - can fall into the following categories as shown below.

Field   Provides access to an ordinary variable in an object.
Property   Provides access to a special variable which includes methods to store and retrieve values.
Method   Refers to a function exposed by an object.

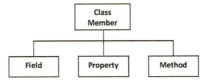

There are five levels of accessibility for class members:

Access modifier	Accessibility/Scope
public	Member is accessible from any class or project.
private	Member is accessible only from within the class.
internal	Member is accessible only from the code within the project where it is defined.
protected	Member is accessible only from within a class hierarchy.
protected internal	Member is accessible inside the assembly through objects and in derived classes outside the assembly through member functions.

253

Fields, methods and properties can be declared using the keyword static. A static member is owned by the class, not by a class instance. You use the keyword static when you don't need objects for a class.

By default, the scope of all members of a class is private. They can be accessed only from within the class. They cannot be accessed by members from other classes or projects.

In general, most data members will be private while most method members will be public.

Object declaration in C# takes the form:

```
class_name variable = new class_name();
```

The code below illustrates the structure of a class and its members (data and methods).

```
public class class_name
{
    // data members

    // method members
}
```

Program 12.1 illustrates class declaration and object instantiation.

Program 12.1

```
using System;
using System.Collections.Generic;
using System.Linq;
using System.Text;
using System.Threading.Tasks;

namespace O_O_Programming_Example
{
    class Employee // declaring a class
    {
        public string name = "AHMAD";
    }

    class MainClass
    {
        static void Main(string[] args)
        {
            Employee e = new Employee(); //creating a class object
            string n = e.name;   // accessing a class variable
            Console.WriteLine(n);
            Console.ReadLine();
        }
    }
}
```

Here is the program output:

Program 12.2 illustrates how private and public variables are declared and accessed.

Note: You cannot use the statement s = e.salary; to access salary because salary is private.

Program 12.2

```
using System;
using System.Collections.Generic;
using System.Linq;
using System.Text;
using System.Threading.Tasks;

namespace O_O_Programming_Example
{
    class Employee // declaring a class
    {
        public string name = "AHMAD";
        double salary = 900.00;  // private by default
        public double AccessSalary()
        {
            return salary;
        }
    }
    class MainClass
    {
        static void Main(string[] args)
        {
            Employee e = new Employee();
            // Accessing the public variable
            string n = e.name;
            // Accessing the private variable
            double s = e.AccessSalary();
            Console.WriteLine(n);
            Console.WriteLine(s);
            Console.ReadLine();
        }
    }
}
```

Here is the program output:

Program 12.3 gives another example of accessing the private fields of a class with public methods.

Program 12.3

```
using System;
using System.Collections.Generic;
using System.Linq;
using System.Text;
using System.Threading.Tasks;
```

```
namespace O_O_Programming_Example
{

    class Employee  // declaring a class
    {
        int id;
        double salary;
        public void assign_values(int id2, double salary2)
        {
            id = id2;
            salary = salary2;
        }

        public void display()
        {
            Console.WriteLine("id = " + id);
            Console.WriteLine("salary = " + salary);
        }
    }

    class MainClass
    {
        static void Main(string[] args)
        {
            Employee e = new Employee();
            e.assign_values(15542, 500.50);
            e.display();
            Console.ReadLine();
        }
    }
}
```

Here is the program output:

Program 12.4 shows a compiler error when the MainClass attempts to access the private members id and salary of the Employee class.

Program 12.4

```
using System;
using System.Collections.Generic;
using System.Linq;
using System.Text;
using System.Threading.Tasks;

namespace O_O_Programming_Example
{
    class Employee
    {
        int id;
        double salary;
```

```
        public void display()
        {
            Console.WriteLine("id = " + id);
            Console.WriteLine("salary = " + salary);
        }
    }

    class MainClass
    {
        static void Main(string[] args)
        {
            Employee e = new Employee();
            e.id = 15542;           // accessing private member
            e.salary = 500.50;      // accessing private member
            e.display();
            Console.ReadLine();
        }
    }
}
```

The Error List shows the errors when you compile and run the program.

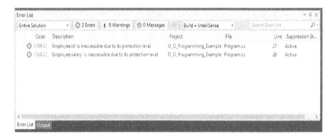

12.3 Static & Instance Class Members

A method may be declared static. A static method is attached to the class, not to any class instance. For static methods, you don't need a class instance to invoke it. A non-static method, however, will require a class instance.

Program 12.5 illustrates how a static method is declared and invoked. The program displays the same output as Program 12.3 but uses a class instance.

Program 12.5

```
using System;
using System.Collections.Generic;
using System.Linq;
using System.Text;
using System.Threading.Tasks;

namespace O_O_Programming_Example
{
    class Employee
    {
        public static void display(int id, double salary)
        {
```

```
                    Console.WriteLine("id = " + id);
                    Console.WriteLine("salary = " + salary);
            }
    }

    class MainClass
    {
        static void Main(string[] args)
        {
                //accessing a static method
                Employee.display(15542, 500.50);
                Console.ReadLine();
        }
    }
}
```

Here is the program output:

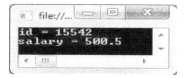

12.4 Class Inheritance

A class can inherit the variables (attributes) and methods of another class called the **base, parent** or **superclass**. The class that inherits is called the **derived, child** or **subclass**. The derived class automatically inherits the attributes and methods in the base class. That means it is not necessary to declare the variables and methods that have already been declared in the base class. Only additional variables and methods that are required need to be declared in the derived classes. Inheritance thus promotes software reuse.

The base class typically captures the *general* attributes and behaviours (operations) while the derived class captures *specific* attributes and behaviours. For example, the base class Person may include attributes such as name, address and id number while the derived classes, Employee and Student, may include attributes such as salary and job title, and course code and grade respectively.

Class inheritance can be hierarchical. It can take several levels. A derived class can become a base class for classes derived from it. For example, in the figure below, Person is the base class for Employee and Student, and Employee is the base class for Foreign Employee and Local Employee.

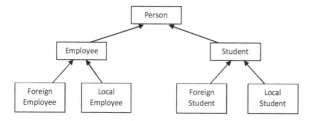

The code for the base class `Person` and the two derived classes (on the left) `Employee` and `Student` take the following form:

```
class Person
{
    // details
}

class Employee : Person  // inherits from Person
{
    // details
}

class Foreign_Employee : Employee  // inherits from Employee
{
    // details
}
```

A class in C# cannot inherit from multiple classes. This, however, does not apply to interfaces (which have the look of classes but have no implementation). Thus a class can inherit more than one interface. The class inheriting the interface must implement it.

Program 12.6 illustrates how class inheritance works. Note that `Main()` creates the `ChildClass` object CC. CC inherits the `Write()` method from the `BaseClass` and then executes it.

Program 12.6

```
using System;
using System.Collections.Generic;
using System.Linq;
using System.Text;
using System.Threading.Tasks;

namespace O_O_Programming_Example
{
    public class BaseClass
    {
        public BaseClass()
        {
            Console.WriteLine("Base Class Constructor executed");
        }

        public void Write()
        {
            Console.WriteLine("Write method in Base Class executed");

        }
    }

    public class ChildClass : BaseClass
    {
        public ChildClass()
        {
            Console.WriteLine("Child Class Constructor executed");
        }

        public static void Main(string[] args)
        {
            ChildClass CC = new ChildClass();
            CC.Write();
            Console.ReadLine();
```

259

```
        }
      }
    }
```

Here is the program output:

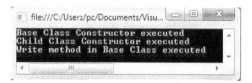

The output shows when the `ChildClass` object CC is created, it automatically calls the `BaseClass()` constructor.

Program 12.7 creates the class `Rectangle` from the base class `Shape` and then computes the area of a rectangle.

Program 12.7

```csharp
using System;
using System.Collections.Generic;
using System.Linq;
using System.Text;
using System.Threading.Tasks;

namespace O_O_Programming_Example
{
    class Shape
    {
        public void setWidth(int w)
        {
            width = w;
        }
        public void setHeight(int h)
        {
            height = h;
        }
        protected int width;
        protected int height;
    }

    class Rectangle : Shape  // Derived class
    {
        public int getArea()
        {
            return (width * height);
        }
    }

    class RectangleTester
    {
        static void Main(string[] args)
        {
            Rectangle Rect = new Rectangle();
            Rect.setWidth(5);
            Rect.setHeight(7);
```

```
            // Print the area of the object.
            Console.WriteLine("Area of the rectangle = {0}", Rect.getArea());
            Console.ReadLine();
        }
    }
}
```

Here is the program output:

Program 12.8 illustrates multi-level inheritance. Class B is derived from Class A. Class C is derived from Class B. So Class C will have access to all members of Class A and Class B. Thus Class C has access to A_Method(), B_Method() and C_Method().

Program 12.8

```
using System;
using System.Collections.Generic;
using System.Linq;
using System.Text;
using System.Threading.Tasks;

namespace O_O_Programming_Example
{
    public class A
    {
        public void A_Method()
        {
            Console.WriteLine("Class A Method Called");
        }
    }
    public class B : A
    {
        public void B_Method()
        {
            Console.WriteLine("Class B Method Called");
        }
    }
    public class C : B
    {
        public void C_Method()
        {
            Console.WriteLine("Class C Method Called");
        }

        public static void Main(string[] args)
        {
            C C1 = new C();
            C1.A_Method();
            C1.B_Method();
            C1.C_Method();
            Console.ReadLine();
        }
    }
```

261

```
        }
}
```

Here is the program output:

Program 12.9 illustrates one-level inheritance. It has three classes, each with its own variables and methods.

Program 12.9

```csharp
using System;
using System.Collections.Generic;
using System.Linq;
using System.Text;
using System.Threading.Tasks;

namespace O_O_Programming_Example
{
    class Person
    {
        string name;
        int age;
        public void get_info()
        {
            Console.Write("Enter name: ");
            name = Convert.ToString(Console.ReadLine());
            Console.Write("Enter age: ");
            age = Convert.ToInt32(Console.ReadLine());
        }

        public string display_info()
        {
            return ("\nName: " + name + "\nAge: " + age);
        }
    }

    class Employee : Person
    {
        double salary;

        public void get_salary()
        {
            Console.Write("Enter salary: ");
            salary = Convert.ToDouble(Console.ReadLine());
        }
        public string display_salary()
        {
            return ("\nSalary: " + salary);
        }
    }
```

```
class Student : Person
{
    int mark;

    public void get_mark()
    {
        Console.Write("Enter mark: ");
        mark = Convert.ToInt16(Console.ReadLine());
    }

    public string display_mark()
    {
        return ("\nMark: " + mark);
    }
}

class MainClass
{
    static void Main(string[] args)
    {
        int choice;
        string output = "";

        do
        {
            Console.Write("Enter choice (1-Person, 2-Employee,
                               3 - Student, 0 - Exit): ");
            choice = Convert.ToInt16(Console.ReadLine());

            switch (choice)
            {
                case 1:
                    Person p = new Person();
                    p.get_info();
                    output += p.display_info();
                    break;

                case 2:
                    Employee e = new Employee();
                    e.get_info();
                    e.get_salary();
                    output += e.display_info();
                    output += e.display_salary();
                    break;

                case 3:
                    Student s = new Student();
                    s.get_info();
                    s.get_mark();
                    output += s.display_info();
                    output += s.display_mark();
                    break;

                case 0:
                default:
                    break;
            }
        } while (choice > 0);

        Console.WriteLine(output);
        Console.ReadLine();
    }
}
```

}

Here is a sample run:

Polymorphism

Polymorphism means taking many forms. This concept is important in a class hierarchy where two or more derived classes have methods with the same name as the base class. Polymorphism allows objects from different classes to perform different operations even though they all have the same method name.

Program 12.10 illustrates polymorphism. Both `Superclass` and `Subclass` have the method `display()` but they are not the same - they do different things. To call the correct method, we prefix it with the correct class object (`superObj` or `subObj`).

Program 12.10

```
using System;
using System.Collections.Generic;
using System.Linq;
using System.Text;
using System.Threading.Tasks;

namespace O_O_Programming_Example
{
    class SuperClass
    {
        public int id = 2254;
        public string compName = "ABC SDN.BHD.";

        public void display()
        {
            Console.WriteLine("Method from Superclass");
            Console.WriteLine("Id: " + id);
        }
    }
```

264

```
class SubClass : SuperClass
{
    public new void display()
    {
        Console.WriteLine("Method from Subclass");
        Console.WriteLine("Company Name: " + compName);
    }
}

class MainClass
{
    static void Main(string[] args)
    {
        SuperClass superObj = new SuperClass();
        SubClass subObj = new SubClass();
        superObj.display();
        subObj.display();
        Console.ReadLine();
    }
}
}
```

Here is the program output:

Program 12.11 illustrates another way to call the correct display() method. Here, we cast the superObj to subObj and then call the display() method in the Subclass. You can also do the other way round. You can cast the subObj to superObj and then call the display() method in the Superclass.

Program 12.11

```
using System;
using System.Collections.Generic;
using System.Linq;
using System.Text;
using System.Threading.Tasks;
namespace O_O_Programming_Example
{
    class SuperClass
    {
        public int id = 2254;
        public string compName = "ABC SDN.BHD.";

        public void display()
        {
            Console.WriteLine("Method from Superclass");
            Console.WriteLine("Id: " + id);
        }
    }
```

265

```
class SubClass : SuperClass
{
    public new void display()
    {
        Console.WriteLine("Method from Subclass");
        Console.WriteLine("Company Name: " + compName);
    }
}

class MainClass
{
    static void Main(string[] args)
    {
        // Create a subclass object
        SubClass subObj = new SubClass();

        // Assign the subclass object to a superclass object
        SuperClass superObj = subObj;

        // Call method of superclass
        superObj.display();

        // Cast the superclass object to a subclass object
        SubClass nextObj = (SubClass)superObj;

        // Call method of subclass
        nextObj.display();
        Console.ReadLine();
    }
}
```

Here is the program output:

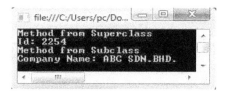

Program 12.12 illustrates a simpler way to call the correct method. First, we create a subclass object subObj. Then we use it to call the display() method in the Subclass. To call the display() method in the Superclass, we first cast subObj to superObj and then call the method.

Program 12.12

```
using System;
using System.Collections.Generic;
using System.Linq;
using System.Text;
using System.Threading.Tasks;

namespace O_O_Programming_Example
{
    class SuperClass
    {
        public int id = 2254;
```

266

```
        public string compName = "ABC SDN.BHD.";

        public void display()
        {
            Console.WriteLine("Method from Superclass");
            Console.WriteLine("Id: " + id);
        }
}

class SubClass : SuperClass
{
    public new void display()
    {
        Console.WriteLine("Method from Subclass");
        Console.WriteLine("Company Name: " + compName);
    }
}

class MainClass
{
    static void Main(string[] args)
    {
        SubClass subObj = new SubClass();

        // Call method of superclass by casting subclass object
        ((SuperClass)subObj).display();

        // Call method of subclass
        subObj.display();
        Console.ReadLine();
    }
}
}
```

Here is the program output:

Method Overloading

Method overloading refers to the *same* method name being used to do different tasks. To overload method, we use different number and/or parameter types. For example, you can overload display() by writing code for display(), display(int), display(double), display(string, int)

Program 12.13 illustrates method overloading. It calls display() twice – once with a string parameter and another with two integers. The number and type of parameters tell which method will be called.

Program 12.13

```
using System;
using System.Collections.Generic;
```

267

```
using System.Linq;
using System.Text;
using System.Threading.Tasks;

namespace O_O_Programming_Example
{
    class Program
    {
        public class Print
        {

            public void display(string name)
            {
                Console.WriteLine("Your name is {0}",name);
            }

            public void display(int age, int mark)
            {
                Console.WriteLine("Your age is {0} ", age);
                Console.WriteLine("Your mark is {0}", mark);
            }
        }

        static void Main(string[] args)
        {
            Print Pobj = new Print();
            Pobj.display("Munir");
            Pobj.display(30, 92);
            Console.ReadLine();
        }
    }
}
```

Here is the program output:

Program 12.14 further illustrates the use of method overloading.

Program 12.14

```
using System;
using System.Collections.Generic;
using System.Linq;
using System.Text;
using System.Threading.Tasks;

namespace O_O_Programming_Example
{
    class Program
    {
        public class Shape
        {
            // function overload with 1 parameter.
```

268

```
    public void Area(double r)
    {
        double area;
        area = Math.PI * r*r;

        Console.WriteLine("Area of a circle: {0}", area);
    }

    // function overload with 2 parameters.
    public void Area(double l, double b)
    {
        double areaRec;
        areaRec = l * b;
        Console.WriteLine("Area of a rectangle: {0}", areaRec);
    }

    // function overload with 3 parameters.
    public void Area(double a, double b, double c)
    {
        double result;
        result = (a * b * c) / 2;
        Console.WriteLine("Result: {0}", result);
    }
}

    static void Main(string[] args)
    {
        Shape s = new Shape();
        s.Area(4.2);
        s.Area(2.3, 3.5);
        s.Area(2.5, 3.8, 4.5);
        Console.ReadLine();
    }
}
}
```

Here is the program output:

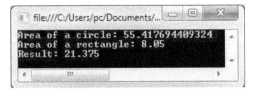

Program 12.15 illustrates how to change the functionality of a method without changing the signature (method overriding).

Program 12.15

```
using System;
using System.Collections.Generic;
using System.Linq;
using System.Text;
using System.Threading.Tasks;
```

```
namespace O_O_Programming_Example
{
    // Base class
    public class BaseClass
    {
        public virtual void Method1()
        {
            Console.WriteLine("Base Class Method");
        }
    }

    // Derived class
    public class DerivedClass : BaseClass
    {
        public override void Method1()
        {
            Console.WriteLine("Derived Class Method");
        }
    }

    // Using base and derived class
    public class Sample
    {
        static void Main(string[] args)
        {
            // calling the overriden method
            DerivedClass objDC = new DerivedClass();
            objDC.Method1();
            // calling the based class method
            BaseClass objBC = (BaseClass)objDC;
            objDC.Method1();
            Console.ReadLine();
        }
    }
}
```

Here is the program output:

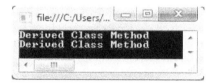

The this keyword

The keyword this refers to the current class instance. Static member functions do not have this reference. You can use this to access members from within constructors, instance methods and instance accessors.

Another use of this is to qualify members hidden by similar names as in below the code.

```
public Employee()
{
    name = "Mariam";
    alias = "Miriam";
}
```

270

```
    public Employee(string name, string alias)
    {
        this.name = name;
        this.alias = alias;
    }
```

Program 12.16(a) illustrates the use of this. Note that the method in the super class can be called from the subclass by casting the current instance of the subclass object (this) to the super class before calling the method.

Program 12.16(a)

```
using System;
using System.Collections.Generic;
using System.Linq;
using System.Text;
using System.Threading.Tasks;

namespace O_O_Programming_Example
{
    class SuperClass
    {
        public int id;
        public string compName;

        public void display()
        {
            Console.WriteLine("Method from Superclass");
            Console.WriteLine("Id: " + id);
        }
    }

    class SubClass : SuperClass
    {
        public SubClass(int id, string compName)
        {
            this.id = id;
            this.compName = compName;
        }
        public new void display()
        {
            // Call method of superclass by casting
            ((SuperClass)this).display();
            Console.WriteLine("Method from Subclass");
            Console.WriteLine("Company Name: " + compName);
        }
    }

    class MainClass
    {
        static void Main(string[] args)
        {
            SubClass subObj = new SubClass(2254, "ABC SDN.BHD.");
            subObj.display();
            Console.ReadLine();
        }
    }
}
```

Here is the program output:

Program 12.16(b) illustrates another way of calling a super class method from a subclass class using the keyword base.

Program 12.16(b)

```
using System;
using System.Collections.Generic;
using System.Linq;
using System.Text;
using System.Threading.Tasks;

namespace O_O_Programming_Example
{
    class SuperClass
    {
        public int id;
        public string compName;

        public void display()
        {
            Console.WriteLine("Method from Superclass");
            Console.WriteLine("Id: " + id);
        }
    }

    class SubClass : SuperClass
    {
        public SubClass(int id, string compName)
        {
            this.id = id;
            this.compName = compName;
        }
        public new void display()
        {
            base.display();//using base keyword
            Console.WriteLine("Method from Subclass");
            Console.WriteLine("Company Name: " + compName);
        }
    }

    class MainClass
    {
        static void Main(string[] args)
        {
            SubClass subObj = new SubClass(2254, "ABC SDN.BHD.");
            subObj.display();
            Console.ReadLine();
        }
    }
}
```

Here is the program output:

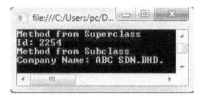

```
Method from Superclass
Id: 2254
Method from Subclass
Company Name: ABC SDN.BHD.
```

12.5 Constructors & Destructors

There are two special methods called **constructor** and **destructor** for each class object. The constructor has the same name as the class. The destructor also has the same name but is prefixed with a tilde (~). The constructor and destructor are automatically called when an object is created or deleted (or when it goes out of scope).

You use constructors to initialize variables. You can write your own constructor. C# also provides a default constructor for each object. It uses it to allocate memory for that object. You use destructor to perform close-up operations such as printing summaries.

The difference between normal methods and these special methods is this: constructors and destructors are automatically called when an object is created or deleted; normal methods must be called explicitly.

A class may have one or more constructors. In other words, constructors can be overloaded. The number and type of parameters will determine which constructor will be called at run time.

A constructor has the following characteristics:

1. A constructor has the same name as the class name.

2. A constructor does not return a value, and therefore it does not have a type modifier/specifier.

3. Arguments can be passed to a constructor.

4. A constructor is automatically called when an object is created.

Program 12.17 illustrates how a constructor works.

Program 12.17

```csharp
using System;
using System.Collections.Generic;
using System.Linq;
using System.Text;
using System.Threading.Tasks;

namespace O_O_Programming_Example
{
    class Employee
    {
        private string compName;

        // The default constructor, same name as the class
        public Employee()
```

273

```
        {
            compName = "ABC SDN. BHD.";
        }

        public void Print()
        {
            Console.WriteLine("Company Name: {0}", compName);
        }
    }

    class MainClass
    {
        static void Main(string[] args)
        {
            // Create objects using the default constructor
            Employee employee1 = new Employee();
            Employee employee2 = new Employee();

            Console.Write("Employee 1: ");
            employee1.Print();
            Console.Write("Employee 2: ");
            employee2.Print();
            Console.ReadLine();
        }
    }
}
```

Here is the program output:

Program 12.18 illustrates a class with two constructors, one with no argument and another with two arguments.

Program 12.18

```
using System;
using System.Collections.Generic;
using System.Linq;
using System.Text;
using System.Threading.Tasks;

namespace O_O_Programming_Example
{
    class Points
    {
        public int x, y;

        public Points()   // Default constructor
        {
            x = 0;
            y = 0;
        }
```

```csharp
        public Points(int x, int y)  // A constructor with two arguments
        {
            this.x = x;
            this.y = y;
        }


        // Override the ToString method:
        public override string ToString()
        {
            return (String.Format("({0},{1})", x, y));
        }
    }

    class MainClass
    {
        static void Main(string[] args)
        {
            // Create objects using the default constructor
            Points p1 = new Points();
            Points p2 = new Points(7, 2);
            // Display the results using the overriden ToString method:
            Console.WriteLine("Points #1 at {0}", p1);
            Console.WriteLine("Points #2 at {0}", p2);
            Console.ReadLine();
        }
    }
}
```

Here is the program output:

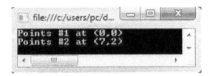

```
file:///c:/users/pc/d...
Points #1 at (0,0)
Points #2 at (7,2)
```

Program 12.19 has no constructor for the class Student. But C# provides a default constructor.

Program 12.19

```csharp
using System;
using System.Collections.Generic;
using System.Linq;
using System.Text;
using System.Threading.Tasks;
namespace O_O_Programming_Example
{
    public class Student
    {
        public int mark=67;
        public string name="Munir",grade="Pass";
    }

    class MainClass
    {
        static void Main(string[] args)
        {
            Student student = new Student();
```

275

```
            Console.WriteLine("Name: {0}\nMark: {1}\nGrade: {2}",
                        student.name, student.mark, student.grade);
            Console.ReadLine();
        }
    }
}
```

Here is the program output:

Program 12.20 illustrates the use of a default constructor. In this constructor every instance of the class will be initialized without any parameter values.

Program 12.20

```
using System;
using System.Collections.Generic;
using System.Linq;
using System.Text;
using System.Threading.Tasks;

namespace O_O_Programming_Example
{
    class DefaultCon
    {
        public string param1, param2;

        public DefaultCon()        // Default Constructor
        {
            param1 = "Default";
            param2 = "Constructor";
        }
    }

    class MainClass
    {
        static void Main(string[] args)
        {
            //Constructor is called automatically when an object is created
            DefaultCon dConst = new DefaultCon();
            Console.WriteLine("{0} {1}",dConst.param1, dConst.param2);
            Console.ReadLine();
        }
    }
}
```

Here is the program output:

Program 12.21 illustrates the use of parameterized constructors. In this constructor we can initialize each instance of the class to different values.

Program 12.21

```
using System;
using System.Collections.Generic;
using System.Linq;
using System.Text;
using System.Threading.Tasks;

namespace O_O_Programming_Example
{
    class DefaultCon
    {
        public string param1, param2;

        // Declaring Parameterized constructor with Parameters
        public DefaultCon(string word1, string word2)
        {
            param1 = word1;
            param2 = word2;
        }
    }

    class MainClass
    {
        static void Main(string[] args)
        {
            // Parameterized Constructor Called
            DefaultCon dConst = new DefaultCon("Parameterized","Constructor");
            Console.WriteLine("{0} {1}",dConst.param1, dConst.param2);
            Console.ReadLine();
        }
    }
}
```

Here is the program output:

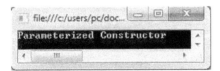

Program 12.22 illustrates how to overload constructors.

Program 12.22

```
using System;
using System.Collections.Generic;
using System.Linq;
```

277

```
using System.Text;
using System.Threading.Tasks;

namespace O_O_Programming_Example
{
    class DefaultCon
    {
        public string param1, param2;

        public DefaultCon()// Default Constructor
        {
            param1 = "Default";
            param2 = "Constructor";
        }

        // Declaring Parameterized constructor with Parameters
        public DefaultCon(string word1, string word2)
        {
            param1 = word1;
            param2 = word2;
        }
    }

    class MainClass
    {
        static void Main(string[] args)
        {
            // Default Constructor will Called
            DefaultCon dConst = new DefaultCon();

            // Parameterized Constructor will Called
            DefaultCon pConst = new DefaultCon ("Parameterized","Constructor");

            Console.WriteLine("{0} {1} called\n\n{2} {3} called",dConst.param1,
                                dConst.param2,pConst.param1,pConst.param2);
            Console.ReadLine();
        }
    }
}
```

Here is the program output:

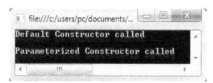

Program 12.23 also illustrates overloading constructors. it uses four constructors – one without parameters, two with one parameter (one of type int, another of type string), and one with two parameters.

Program 12.23

```
using System;
using System.Collections.Generic;
using System.Linq;
using System.Text;
using System.Threading.Tasks;
```

278

```
namespace O_O_Programming_Example
{
    class Employee
    {
        private int id;
        private string name;
        // The default constructor
        public Employee()
        {
            name = "N/A";
        }
        // Another constructor with one parameter of type int
        public Employee(int employeeId)
        {
            id = employeeId;
            name = "N/A";
        }

        // Another constructor with one parameter of type string
        public Employee(string employeeName)
        {

            name = employeeName;
        }

        // Another constructor with two parameters
        public Employee(string employeeName, int employeeId)
        {
            id = employeeId;
            name = employeeName;
        }
        public void Print()
        {
            Console.WriteLine("Name: {0}, Employee ID: {1} ", name, id);
        }
    }

    class MainClass
    {
        static void Main(string[] args)
        {
            // Create objects using the default constructor
            Employee employee1 = new Employee();
            // Create objects using constructor with int parameter
            Employee employee2 = new Employee(1135);
            // Create objects using constructor with string parameter
            Employee employee3 = new Employee("Ahmad");
            // Create objects using constructor with two parameters
            Employee employee4 = new Employee("Munir", 1145);

            // Display results
            Console.Write("Employee 1: ");
            employee1.Print();
            Console.Write("Employee 2: ");
            employee2.Print();
            Console.Write("Employee 3: ");
            employee3.Print();
            Console.Write("Employee 4: ");
            employee4.Print();
            Console.ReadLine();
        }
    }
}
```

Here is the program output:

```
file:///c:/users/pc/documents/visual studio 20...
Employee 1: Name: N/A, Employee ID: 0
Employee 2: Name: N/A, Employee ID: 1135
Employee 3: Name: Ahmad, Employee ID: 0
Employee 4: Name: Munir, Employee ID: 1145
```

Program 12.24 illustrates the use of copy constructor to initialize a new instance to the values of an existing instance.

Program 12.24

```csharp
using System;
using System.Collections.Generic;
using System.Linq;
using System.Text;
using System.Threading.Tasks;
namespace O_O_Programming_Example
{
    class ParaConstructor
    {
        public string param1, param2;

        public ParaConstructor(string word1, string word2)
        {
            param1 = word1;
            param2 = word2;
        }

        // Copy Constructor
        public ParaConstructor(ParaConstructor ParaObj)
        {
            param1 = ParaObj.param1;
            param2 = ParaObj.param2;
        }
    }
    class MainClass
    {
        static void Main(string[] args)
        {
            // Create instance of class ParaConstructor
            ParaConstructor PConst = new
                ParaConstructor("Copy","Constructor");

            //PConst details is copied to PConst1
            ParaConstructor PConst1 = new ParaConstructor(PConst);
            //Parameterized Constructor is Called
            ParaConstructor pConst = new
                ParaConstructor("Parameterized", "Constructor");
            Console.WriteLine("{0} {1} is called", PConst1.param1,
                                PConst1.param2);
            Console.ReadLine();
        }
    }
}
```

Here is the program output:

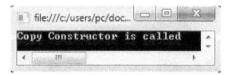

Program 12.25 illustrates the use of static constructor to initialize static fields of the class and write code that needs to be executed only once.

Program 12.25

```
using System;
using System.Collections.Generic;
using System.Linq;
using System.Text;
using System.Threading.Tasks;

namespace O_O_Programming_Example
{
    class StaticConstructor
    {
        public string param1, param2;
        static StaticConstructor()
        {
            Console.WriteLine("Static Constructor");
        }

        public StaticConstructor()
        {
            param1 = "Instance";
            param2 = "Constructor";
        }
    }
    class MainClass
    {
        static void Main(string[] args)
        {
            //Here Both Static and instance constructors are invoked
            // for first instance
            StaticConstructor StObj = new StaticConstructor();
            Console.WriteLine("{0} {1}", StObj.param1, StObj.param2);

            // Here only instance constructor will be invoked
            StaticConstructor StObj1 = new StaticConstructor();
            Console.WriteLine("{0} {1}", StObj1.param1, StObj1.param2);

            Console.ReadLine();
        }
    }
}
```

Here is the program output:

Program 12.26 illustrates the use of private constructor to restrict the class from being instantiated.

Program 12.26

```
using System;
using System.Collections.Generic;
using System.Linq;
using System.Text;
using System.Threading.Tasks;

namespace O_O_Programming_Example
{
    class PrivateConstructor
    {
        public string param1, param2;
        public PrivateConstructor(string word1, string word2)
        {
            param1 = word1;
            param2 = word2;
        }

        // Private Constructor Declaration
        private PrivateConstructor()
        {
            Console.WriteLine("Private Constructor with no prameters");
        }
    }
    class MainClass
    {
        static void Main(string[] args)
        {
            // Here we don't have chance to create instance for
               private constructor
            PrivateConstructor PrObj = new
                    PrivateConstructor("Private","Constructor");
            Console.WriteLine("Instance of {0} {1} cannot be
                    created", PrObj.param1, PrObj.param2);
            Console.ReadLine();
        }
    }
}
```

Here is the program output:

282

A **destructor** is a special method which is automatically called when an object is deleted or goes out of scope. The destructor performs close-up operations such as displaying totals and reclaiming memory allocated to the object.

The rules for destructors are as follows:

1. A destructor has the same name as the class name, but has a tilde (~) in front of it.

2. A destructor does not return a value; therefore it does not have a type modifier/specifier.

3. Unlike a constructor, you cannot pass arguments to a destructor.

4. A destructor is called automatically when an object is deleted or goes out of scope. So you don't have to explicitly call like other methods.

Program 12.27 illustrates how a destructor works. The program simply creates an object and then destroys it.

Program 12.27

```
using System;
using System.Collections.Generic;
using System.Linq;
using System.Text;
using System.Threading.Tasks;

namespace O_O_Programming_Example
{
    class Employee
    {
        public Employee()
        {
            Console.WriteLine("Calling Constructor.");
        }

        ~Employee()
        {
            Console.WriteLine("Calling Destructor.");
            Console.ReadLine();
        }
    }

    class MainClass
    {
        static void Main(string[] args)
        {
            Employee emp = new Employee();
            Console.ReadLine();
        }
    }
}
```

Here is the program output:

Program 12.28 illustrates destructors within a class hierarchy. It defines three classes and creates an object at the lowest subclass. Then it destroys the object by executing the destructors in the reverse order.

Program 12.28

```
using System;
using System.Collections.Generic;
using System.Linq;
using System.Text;
using System.Threading.Tasks;

namespace O_O_Programming_Example
{
    class First
    {
        ~First()
        {
            Console.WriteLine("First's destructor is called.");
            Console.ReadLine();
        }
    }
    class Second : First
    {
        ~Second()
        {
            Console.WriteLine("Second's destructor is called.");
            Console.ReadLine();
        }
    }
    class Third : Second
    {
        ~Third()
        {
            Console.WriteLine("Third's destructor is called.");
            Console.ReadLine();
        }
    }

    class TestDestructor
    {
        static void Main(string[] args)
        {
            Third t = new Third();
            Console.ReadLine();
        }
    }
}
```

Here is the program output:

284

Accessors

Properties combine aspects of both fields and methods. To the user of an object, a property appears to be a field. Accessing a property requires the same syntax. To the implementer of a class, a property is one or two code blocks, representing a get accessor and/or a set accessor.

The accessor of a property contains the executable statements associated with getting (reading or computing) or setting (writing) the property. The accessor declarations can contain a get accessor, a set accessor, or both. The declarations take the following forms:

```
set { accessor-body}

get { accessor-body}
```

where accessor-body is the block containing statements to be executed when the accessor is invoked.

The get Accessor

The body of the get accessor is similar to that of a method. It must return a value of the property type. The execution of the get accessor is equivalent to reading the value of the field. The following is a get accessor that returns the value of a private field name:

```
private string name;    // the name field
public string Name      // the Name property
{
    get
    {
        return name;
    }
}
```

When you reference the property, except as the target of an assignment, the get accessor is invoked to read the value of the property as illustrated below.

```
Employee e1 = new Employee();
...
Console.Write(e1.Name); //The get accessor is invoked here
```

Note that get accessor must terminate in a return or a throw statement, and control cannot flow off the accessor body.

The set Accessor

The set accessor is similar to a method that returns void. It uses an implicit parameter called value, whose type is the type of the property. In the illustration below, a set accessor is added to the Name property:

```
public string Name
{
```

285

```
        get
        {
            return name;
        }
        set
        {
            name = value;
        }
    }
```

When you assign a value to the property, the set accessor is invoked with an argument that provides the new value. For example:

```
e1.Name = "Munir";    // The set accessor is invoked here
```

It will be an error to use the implicit parameter name (value) for a local variable declaration in a set accessor.

The code block for the get accessor is executed when the property is read; the code block for the set accessor is executed when the property is assigned a new value. A property without a set accessor is considered read-only. A property without a get accessor is considered write-only. A property that has both accessors is read-write.

Unlike fields, properties are not classified as variables. Therefore, you cannot pass a property as a ref or out parameter.

Program 12.29 illustrates how to access a property in a base class that is hidden by another property with the same name in a derived class.

Program 12.29

```
using System;
using System.Collections.Generic;
using System.Linq;
using System.Text;
using System.Threading.Tasks;

namespace O_O_Programming_Example
{
    public class BaseClass
    {
        private string name;
        public string Name
        {
            get
            {
                return name;
            }
            set
            {
                name = value;
            }
        }
    }

    public class DerivedClass : BaseClass
    {
        private string name;
        public new string Name    //Notice the use of the new modifier
        {
            get
            {
```

```
                return name;
        }
        set
        {
            name = value;
        }
    }
}

public class MainClass
{
    static void Main(string[] args)
    {
        DerivedClass d1 = new DerivedClass();
        d1.Name = "Sellappan";  // Derived class property
        Console.WriteLine("Name in the derived class is: {0}", d1.Name);
        ((BaseClass)d1).Name = "Munir"; // Base class property
        Console.WriteLine("Name in the base class is: {0}",
            ((BaseClass)d1).Name);
        Console.ReadLine();
    }
}
}
```

Here is the program output:

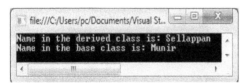

In Program 12.30 illustrates an instance, static, and read-only properties. It accepts the name of an employee from the keyboard, increments `NumberOfEmployees` by 1, and displays the Employee name and number.

Program 12.30

```
using System;
using System.Collections.Generic;
using System.Linq;
using System.Text;
using System.Threading.Tasks;

namespace O_O_Programming_Example
{
    public class Employee
    {
        public static int NumberOfEmployees;
        private static int counter;
        private string name;

        // A read-write instance property:
        public string Name
        {
            get { return name; }
            set { name = value; }
        }
```

287

```
// A read-only static property:
public static int Counter
{
    get { return counter; }
}

public Employee()  // A Constructor
{
    // Calculate the employee's number:
    counter = ++counter + NumberOfEmployees;
}
}

class TestEmployee
{
    static void Main(string[] args)
    {
        Employee.NumberOfEmployees = 123456;
        Employee e1 = new Employee();
        e1.Name = "Munir";
        Console.WriteLine("Employee number: {0}", Employee.Counter);
        Console.WriteLine("Employee name: {0}", e1.Name);
        Console.ReadLine();
    }
}
}
```

Here is the program output:

```
Employee number: 123457
Employee name: Munir
```

In Program 12.31, two classes, Cube and Square, implement an abstract class called Shape, and override its abstract Area property. Note the use of the override modifier on the properties. The program accepts the side as input and calculates the areas for the square and cube. It also accepts the area an input and calculates the corresponding side for the square and cube.

Program 12.31

```
using System;
using System.Collections.Generic;
using System.Linq;
using System.Text;
using System.Threading.Tasks;

namespace O_O_Programming_Example
{
    abstract class Shape
    {
        public abstract double Area
        {
            get;
            set;
        }
    }
```

288

```
class Square : Shape
{
    public double side;

    public Square(double s)  //constructor
    {
        side = s;
    }

    public override double Area
    {
        get
        {
            return side * side;
        }
        set
        {
            side = Math.Sqrt(value);
        }
    }
}

class Cube : Shape
{
    public double side;

    public Cube(double s)
    {
        side = s;
    }

    public override double Area
    {
        get
        {
            return 6 * side * side;
        }
        set
        {
            side = Math.Sqrt(value / 6);
        }
    }
}

class TestShapes
{
    static void Main(string[] args)
    {
        double side,area;

        // Input the side:
        Console.Write("Enter the side: ");
        side = double.Parse(Console.ReadLine());
        // Compute the areas:
        Square s = new Square(side);
        Cube c = new Cube(side);

        // Display the results:
        Console.WriteLine("Area of the square = {0}", s.Area);
        Console.WriteLine("Area of the cube = {0}", c.Area);
        Console.WriteLine();
```

289

```
// Input the area:
Console.Write("\nEnter the area: ");
area = double.Parse(Console.ReadLine());
s.Area = area; // Compute the sides:
c.Area = area;
// Display the results:
Console.WriteLine("Side of the square = {0}", s.side);
Console.WriteLine("Side of the cube = {0}", c.side);
Console.ReadLine();
        }
    }
}
```

Here is the program output:

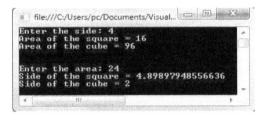

12.6 Abstract Classes

An **abstract class** cannot be instantiated. It can only be inherited. An abstract method has no implementation. It must be implemented by the class that inherits it.

Program 12.32 illustrates abstract class and abstract methods.

Program 12.32

```
using System;
using System.Collections.Generic;
using System.Linq;
using System.Text;
using System.Threading.Tasks;

namespace O_O_Programming_Example
{
    abstract class Account   // Abstract class
    {
        public string name;
        public int acct;

        public abstract void input();   // Abstract method
        public abstract void print();   // Abstract method
    }

    class Saving : Account
    {
        public override void input()
        {
            Console.WriteLine("Saving Account");
            Console.Write("Enter Name: ");
```

290

```
            name = Console.ReadLine();

            Console.Write("Enter Account Number: ");
            acct = Convert.ToInt32(Console.ReadLine());
        }

        public override void print()
        {
            Console.WriteLine("{0}\t\t{1}\t\t\tSaving", name, acct);
        }
    }

    class Current : Account
    {
        public override void input()
        {
            Console.WriteLine("\nCurrent Account");
            Console.Write("Enter Name: ");
            name = Console.ReadLine();
            Console.Write("Enter Account Number: ");
            acct = Convert.ToInt32(Console.ReadLine());
        }

        public override void print()
        {
            Console.WriteLine("{0}\t\t{1}\t\t\tCurrent", name, acct);
        }
    }

    class MainClass
    {
        static void Main(string[] args)
        {
            Saving sav = new Saving();
            Current cur = new Current();
            sav.input();
            cur.input();
            Console.WriteLine("\nName:\t\tAccountNumber:\t\tAccount Type:");
            sav.print();
            cur.print();
            Console.ReadLine();
        }
    }
}
```

Here is a sample run:

Program 12.33 illustrates how class `Square` provides implementation of `Area` that was derived from `ShapesClass`.

Program 12.33

```
using System;
using System.Collections.Generic;
using System.Linq;
using System.Text;
using System.Threading.Tasks;

namespace O_O_Programming_Example
{
    abstract class ShapesClass
    {
        abstract public int Area();
    }

    class Square : ShapesClass
    {
        int side = 0;
        public Square(int n)
        {
            side = n;
        }

        // Area method is required to avoid a compile-time error
        public override int Area()
        {
            return side * side;
        }

        static void Main(string[] args)
        {
            Square sq = new Square(12);
            Console.WriteLine("Area of the square = {0}", sq.Area());
            Console.ReadLine();
        }
    }
}
```

Here is the program output:

Program 12.34 illustrates how `DerivedClass` is derived from an abstract class `BaseClass`. The abstract class contains an abstract method, `AbstractMethod`, and two abstract properties, x and y.

Program 12.34

```
using System;
using System.Collections.Generic;
using System.Linq;
using System.Text;
using System.Threading.Tasks;
```

```
namespace O_O_Programming_Example
{
    abstract class BaseClass    // Abstract class
    {
        protected int _x = 100;
        protected int _y = 150;
        public abstract void AbstractMethod();    // Abstract method
        public abstract int x { get; }
        public abstract int y { get; }
    }

    class DerivedClass : BaseClass
    {
        public override void AbstractMethod()
        {
            _x++;
            _y++;
        }
        public override int x    // overriding property
        {
            get
            {
                return _x + 10;
            }
        }
        public override int y    // overriding property
        {
            get
            {
                return _y + 10;
            }
        }

        static void Main(string[] args)
        {
            DerivedClass o = new DerivedClass();
            o.AbstractMethod();
            Console.WriteLine("x = {0}, y = {1}", o.x, o.y);
            Console.ReadLine();
        }
    }
}
```

Here is the program output:

12.7 Interfaces

An **interface** is a collection of public methods and properties that are grouped together to provide certain functionality. It is defined in the same way as methods. However, it does not implement the methods. The class that inherits the interface must implement the methods. Interfaces cannot exist by themselves. Also, like abstract classes, they cannot be instantiated.

A class may only inherit from one base class. An interface, however, can inherit from more than one base interface. Also, more than one class can implement an interface.

The interface declaration takes the form:

```
public interface IMy
{
    // interface members
}
```

Note the following:

1. An interface is usually prefixed with I.

2. Access modifiers private and protected are not allowed in an interface. All interface members are inherently public.

3. No field members (using get/set) are allowed in an interface definition.

4. Keyword such as static, public, abstract and virtual is not allowed in an interface definition.

5. No type definition is allowed on members.

6. An interface has no code body.

The following code illustrates how interfaces are implemented.

```
public interface IMy
{
    void MyMethod()
}

public class MyClass : IMy
{
    public void MyMethod()
    {
        // code
    }
}
```

If a class inherits more than one interface, say IMy1 and IMy2, they are separated by commas as in the following code.

```
public class MyClass : IMy1, IMy2
{
    public void MyMethod1()  // for IMy1
    {
        // code
    }

    public void MyMethod2()  // for IMy2
    {
        // code
    }
}
```

Interface members may also be implemented in the base or derived classes as shown below.

```
public interface IMy
{
```

```
    void MyMethod1();
    void MyMethod2();
}

public class MyBase : IMy
{
    public void MyMethod1()   // for IMy
    {
        // code
    }
}

public class MyDerived : MyBase
{
    public void MyMethod2()   // for MyBase
    {
        // code
    }
}
```

You can override a method in a derived class by using virtual or override as the following code illustrates:

```
public interface IMy
{
    void MyMethod();
}

public class MyBase : IMy
{
    public virtual void MyMethod()
    {
        // code
    }
}

public class MyDerived : MyBase
{
    public override void MyMethod()
    {
        // code
    }
}
```

Interfaces are used to group together related methods and properties. Although you cannot instantiate interfaces, you can still create variables of those interfaces. You can then use them to access methods and properties exposed by them to objects that implement them.

For example, if we have an application with the base class Account and two derived classes Savings and Current. Let's say Account implements the method Open(). Now suppose instead of using Account, we define the interface IOpen which both Current and Saving implements. With this interface, we can now access this method using the code:

```
    Saving sav = new Saving();
    Current cur = new Current();
    IOpen Io;
    Io = sav;
    Io.Open();
    Io = cur;
    Io.Open();
```

Note: In the above code, the same interface Io is being used to access to sav and cur objects. `Io.Open()` can now call `Open()` in `Saving` or `Current` depending on the object being assigned to the interface variable.

We have seen abstract classes and interfaces. They appear to be quite similar. For example:

- Both can be inherited in a class.
- Both cannot be instantiated.
- Variables of both can be declared.

There are however some differences:

- A derived class can only inherit one abstract class whereas more than one interface can be inherited by a class.

- An abstract class may have virtual methods that are implemented in the class and which may be overridden in the derived class, and methods that are not implemented in the class but are implemented in the derived class, whereas all methods in an interface must be implemented in the derived classes.

- All interface methods are `public` whereas methods of an abstract class may also be `private`, `protected`, etc.

Which should you use and when? Abstract classes are primarily used as base classes for a family of objects that share common characteristics such as common purpose and structure. However, interfaces can be used even if they don't all share common characteristics.

Program 12.35 illustrates the implementation of an interface named ITransactions.

Program 12.35

```
using System;
using System.Collections.Generic;
using System.Linq;
using System.Text;
using System.Threading.Tasks;

namespace O_O_Programming_Example
{
    public interface ITransactions
    {
        // interface members
        void showTransaction();
        double getAmount();
    }

    public class Transaction : ITransactions
    {
        private string tCode;
        private string date;
        private double amount;

        public Transaction()
        {
            tCode = " ";
            date = " ";
            amount = 0.0;
        }
```

296

```
        public Transaction(string c, string d, double a)
        {
            tCode = c;
            date = d;
            amount = a;
        }

        public double getAmount()
        {
            return amount;
        }

        public void showTransaction()
        {
            Console.WriteLine("Transaction: {0}", tCode);
            Console.WriteLine("Date: {0}", date);
            Console.WriteLine("Amount: {0}\n", getAmount());
        }
    }
    class Program
    {
        static void Main(string[] args)
        {
            Transaction t1 = new Transaction("01", "5/11/2016",78900.00);
            Transaction t2 = new Transaction("02", "23/12/2016",451900.00);
            t1.showTransaction();
            t2.showTransaction();
            Console.ReadLine();
        }
    }
}
```

Here is the program output:

12.8 Object Interaction

In an object-oriented system, objects interact with one another in order to perform needed tasks. They do this by sending messages. Sending messages is similar to calling methods and passing arguments.

Program 12.36 illustrates object interaction. Main creates an Order object called ord. The ord object creates an Inventory object called inv and sends messages to retrieve the product price and product name.

Program 12.36

```
using System;
using System.Collections.Generic;
```

297

```csharp
using System.Linq;
using System.Text;
using System.Threading.Tasks;

namespace O_O_Programming_Example
{
    class Inventory
    {
        int[] prod_id = new int[5];
        double[] prod_price = new double[5];
        string[] prod_name = new string[5];

        public Inventory()
        {
            prod_id[0] = 1; prod_id[1] = 2;
            prod_id[2] = 3; prod_id[3] = 4;
            prod_price[0] = 1.0; prod_price[1] = 2.0;
            prod_price[2] = 3.0; prod_price[3] = 4.0;
            prod_name[0] = "AAA"; prod_name[1] = "BBB";
            prod_name[2] = "CCC"; prod_name[3] = "DDD";
        }

        public double get_price(int pid)
        {
            double price = 0.0;
            for (int i = 0; i < 4; i++)
                if (pid == prod_id[i])
                    price = prod_price[i];
            return price;
        }
        public string get_name(int pid)
        {
            string name = "";
            for (int i = 0; i < 4; i++)
                if (pid == prod_id[i])
                    name = prod_name[i];
            return name;
        }
    }

    class Order
    {
        int prod_id;
        string prod_name;
        int quantity;
        double price;
        double amount;

        public void get_data()
        {
            Console.Write("Enter product id (1, 2, 3, 4): ");
            prod_id = Convert.ToInt32(Console.ReadLine());

            while ((prod_id <= 0) || (prod_id > 4))
            {
                Console.WriteLine("Invalid Choice!");
                Console.Write("Enter product id (1, 2, 3, 4): ");
                prod_id = Convert.ToInt32(Console.ReadLine());
            }
            Console.Write("Enter quantity: ");
            quantity = Convert.ToInt32(Console.ReadLine());
        }
```

298

```
        public void get_info()
        {
            // create an inventory object
            Inventory inv = new Inventory();

            // send message to get product price and name
            price = inv.get_price(prod_id);
            prod_name = inv.get_name(prod_id);
        }

        public void compute()
        {
            amount = quantity * price;
        }

        public void gen_report()
        {
            Console.WriteLine("\nProduct id: {0}", prod_id);
            Console.WriteLine("Product name: {0}", prod_name);
            Console.WriteLine("Quantity: {0}", quantity);
            Console.WriteLine("Unit price: {0}", price);
            Console.WriteLine("Amount: {0}", amount);
        }
    }

    class MainClass
    {
        static void Main(string[] args)
        {
            Order ord = new Order();    // create order object
            ord.get_data();             // get data
            ord.get_info();
            ord.compute();
            ord.gen_report();
            Console.ReadLine();
        }
    }
}
```

Here is a sample run:

Exercise

1. Write a program to create and implement the class `student`, which will have the following attributes and methods:

   Attributes
   `StudId`   - string
   `StudName`   - string
   `Mark`   - integer

   Methods
   `GetData()`   - to get data from keyboard for StudId, StudName and Mark
   `ComputeGrade()`   - to compute the grade (A:80-100, B:60-79, C: 50-59, F: 0-49)
   `DisplayGrade()`   - to display StudId, StudName, Mark and Grade

2. Do Question 1 for 5 students. Also calculate and display the average.

3. Write a program to create and implement the class `employee`, which will have the following attributes and methods:

   Attributes
   `EmpId`   - string
   `EmpName`   - string
   `HoursWorked`   - double
   `Rate`   - static double (fixed at 25.00)

   Methods
   `GetData()`   - to get data from the keyboard for EmpId, EmpName and HoursWorked
   `ComputeSalary()`   - to compute the Salary (Salary = HoursWorked * Rate)
   `DisplayGrade()`   - to display EmpId, EmpName, HoursWorked and Salary.

4. Do Question 3 for 7 employees. The salary is now calculated as follows: For the first 40 hours worked, the rate is as given and for the remaining hours the rate is twice that amount.

5. Write a program to create three classes – `registration`, `course` and `student` – that will interact with one another such that the registration object will retrieve information from the Course and Student objects and display all the attributes. The attributes for the classes are as follows:

   Registration
   `StudId`   – string
   `CourseCode`   – string
   `StudName`   – string
   `CourseName`   – string

   Course
   `CourseCode`   – string
   `CourseName`   – string
   `Credits`   – integer

   Student
   `StudId`   – string
   `StudName`   – string
   `Email`   – string

6. Distinguish between static and instance methods. Write code to show the difference between the two.

7. Distinguish between static and instance variables. Write code to show the difference between the two.

8. What is (a) an abstract class (b) an abstract method? Write a program to illustrate these concepts.

9. Design a base class called box and two derived classes called textbox and listbox and implement code to display the messages "I am text box" and "I am list box" in the boxes respectively.

10. What is a (a) constructor (b) destructor? Why do you need them? Write code to illustrate these two methods.

11. What is polymorphism? What purpose does it serve? Write code to illustrate the concept of polymorphism.

12. What is an interface? In what way it is different from the abstract class? Write a program to illustrate the use of an interface.

References

1. Bradley Jones, *C# in 21 Days*, SAMS, 2002.

2. Charles Wright, *C# Tips and Techniques*, McGraw Hill, 2002.

3. Dan Clark *Beginning C# Object-Oriented Programming*, Apress, 2013.

4. Davis, *C# 2005 For Dummies*, John Wiley, 2005.

5. Deitel, et. al., *C# How To Program*, Pearson, 2005.

6. Drayton, Albahari and Neward, *C# in a Nutshell*, O'Reilly, 2002.

7. Grant Palmer, *C# Programmers' Reference*, WROX, 2002

8. Joe Mayo, *C# Unleashed*, SAMS, 2002.

9. Karli Watson, *Beginning C#*, Wrox Press, 2001.

10. Mark Michaelis & Eric Lippert *Essential C# 6.0*, Addison-Wesley Professional,2015.

11. Merrill, Drayton & *Albahari C# Essentials*, O'Reilly, 2002.

12. Michaelis & Spokas, *C# Developer's Headstart*, Osborne, 2002.

13. Pappas & Murray, *C# Essentials*, Prentice Hall, 2002.

14. Perkins, Jacob Vibe Hammer & Jon D. Reid *Beginning C# 6.0 Programming with Visual Studio 2015*, Wrox, 2015.

15. Schildt, *C# 2.0: The Complete Reference*, McGraw Hill, 2006.

16. Simon Robinson, *Professional C#*, WROX, 2001

17. Stanley Lippman, *C# Primer - A Practical Approach*, Addison Wesley, 2002.

18. Tutorialspoint *Learn C# Programming*, www.tutorialspoint.com, 2016.